PRAXIS
SCHOOL GUIDANCE AND COUNSELING 0420

By: Sharon Wynne, M.S.

XAMonline, INC.
Boston

To obtain permission(s) to use the material from this work for any purpose including workshops or seminars, please submit a written request to:

XAMonline, Inc.
25 First Street, Suite 106
Cambridge, MA 02141
Toll Free 1-800-509-4128
Email: info@xamonline.com
Web: www.xamonline.com
Fax: 1-617-583-5552

Library of Congress Cataloging-in-Publication Data

Wynne, Sharon A.
    PRAXIS School Guidance and Counseling 0420 / Sharon A. Wynne. 3rd ed
    ISBN 978-1-60787-067-8
    1. School Guidance and Counseling 0420
    2. Study Guides
    3. PRAXIS
    4. Teachers' Certification & Licensure
    5. Careers

Disclaimer:
The opinions expressed in this publication are the sole works of XAMonline and were created independently from the National Education Association, Educational Testing Service, or any State Department of Education, National Evaluation Systems or other testing affiliates.

Between the time of publication and printing, state specific standards as well as testing formats and Web site information may change and therefore would not be included in part or in whole within this product. Sample test questions are developed by XAMonline and reflect content similar to that on real tests; however, they are not former test questions. XAMonline assembles content that aligns with state standards but makes no claims nor guarantees teacher candidates a passing score. Numerical scores are determined by testing companies such as NES or ETS and then are compared with individual state standards. A passing score varies from state to state.

Printed in the United States of America   œ-1

PRAXIS School Guidance and Counseling 0420
ISBN: 978-1-60787-067-8

Table of Contents

COMPETENCY 4

DOMAIN II
CONSULTING

COMPETENCY 5

DOMAIN III
COORDINATING

COMPETENCY 6

SAMPLE TEST WITH RATIONALES

PRAXIS
SCHOOL GUIDANCE AND COUNSELING 0420

SECTION 1
ABOUT XAMONLINE

XAMonline—A Specialty Teacher Certification Company

Created in 1996, XAMonline was the first company to publish study guides for state-specific teacher certification examinations. Founder Sharon Wynne found it frustrating that materials were not available for teacher certification preparation and decided to create the first single, state-specific guide. XAMonline has grown into a company of over 1,800 contributors and writers and offers over 300 titles for the entire PRAXIS series and every state examination. No matter what state you plan on teaching in, XAMonline has a unique teacher certification study guide just for you.

XAMonline—Value and Innovation

We are committed to providing value and innovation. Our print-on-demand technology allows us to be the first in the market to reflect changes in test standards and user feedback as they occur. Our guides are written by experienced teachers who are experts in their fields. And our content reflects the highest standards of quality. Comprehensive practice tests with varied levels of rigor means that your study experience will closely match the actual in-test experience.

To date, XAMonline has helped nearly 600,000 teachers pass their certification or licensing exams. Our commitment to preparation exceeds simply providing the proper material for study—it extends to helping teachers **gain mastery** of the subject matter, giving them the **tools** to become the most effective classroom leaders possible, and ushering today's students toward a **successful future**.

SECTION 2
ABOUT THIS STUDY GUIDE

Purpose of This Guide

Is there a little voice inside of you saying, "Am I ready?" Our goal is to replace that little voice and remove all doubt with a new voice that says, "I AM READY. **Bring it on!**" by offering the highest quality of teacher certification study guides.

Organization of Content

You will see that while every test may start with overlapping general topics, each is very unique in the skills they wish to test. Only XAMonline presents custom content that analyzes deeper than a title, a subarea, or an objective. Only XAMonline presents content and sample test assessments along with **focus statements**, the deepest-level rationale and interpretation of the skills that are unique to the exam.

Title and field number of test

→Each exam has its own name and number. XAMonline's guides are written to give you the content you need to know for the specific exam you are taking. You can be confident when you buy our guide that it contains the information you need to study for the specific test you are taking.

Subareas

→These are the major content categories found on the exam. XAMonline's guides are written to cover all of the subareas found in the test frameworks developed for the exam.

Objectives

→These are standards that are unique to the exam and represent the main subcategories of the subareas/content categories. XAMonline's guides are written to address every specific objective required to pass the exam.

Focus statements

→These are examples and interpretations of the objectives. You find them in parenthesis directly following the objective. They provide detailed examples of the range, type, and level of content that appear on the test questions. **Only XAMonline's guides drill down to this level.**

How Do We Compare with Our Competitors?

XAMonline—drills down to the focus statement level.

CliffsNotes and REA—organized at the objective level

Kaplan—provides only links to content

MoMedia—content not specific to the state test

Each subarea is divided into manageable sections that cover the specific skill areas. Explanations are easy to understand and thorough. You'll find that every test answer contains a rejoinder so if you need a refresher or further review after taking the test, you'll know exactly to which section you must return.

How to Use This Book

Our informal polls show that most people begin studying up to eight weeks prior to the test date, so start early. Then ask yourself some questions: How much do you really know? Are you coming to the test straight from your teacher-education program or are you having to review subjects you haven't considered in ten years? Either way, take a **diagnostic or assessment test** first. Also, spend time on sample tests so that you become accustomed to the way the actual test will appear.

This guide comes with an online diagnostic test of 30 questions found online at *www.XAMonline.com*. It is a little boot camp to get you up for the task and reveal things about your compendium of knowledge in general. Although this guide is structured to follow the order of the test, you are not required to study in that order. By finding a time-management and study plan that fits your life you will be more effective. The results of your diagnostic or self-assessment test can be a guide for how to manage your time and point you toward an area that needs more attention.

After taking the diagnostic exam, fill out the **Personalized Study Plan** page at the beginning of each chapter. Review the competencies and skills covered in that chapter and check the boxes that apply to your study needs. If there are sections you already know you can skip, check the "skip it" box. Taking this step will give you a study plan for each chapter.

Week	Activity
8 weeks prior to test	Take a diagnostic test found at www.XAMonline.com
7 weeks prior to test	Build your Personalized Study Plan for each chapter. Check the "skip it" box for sections you feel you are already strong in. ✘ SKIP IT ☐
6-3 weeks prior to test	For each of these four weeks, choose a content area to study. You don't have to go in the order of the book. It may be that you start with the content that needs the most review. Alternately, you may want to ease yourself into plan by starting with the most familiar material.
2 weeks prior to test	Take the sample test, score it, and create a review plan for the final week before the test.
1 week prior to test	Following your plan (which will likely be aligned with the areas that need the most review) go back and study the sections that align with the questions you may have gotten wrong. Then go back and study the sections related to the questions you answered correctly. If need be, create flashcards and drill yourself on any area that you makes you anxious.

SECTION 3
ABOUT THE PRAXIS EXAMS

What Is PRAXIS?

PRAXIS II tests measure the knowledge of specific content areas in K-12 education. The test is a way of insuring that educators are prepared to not only teach in a particular subject area, but also have the necessary teaching skills to be effective. The Educational Testing Service administers the test in most states and has worked with the states to develop the material so that it is appropriate for state standards.

PRAXIS Points

1. The PRAXIS Series comprises more than 140 different tests in over 70 different subject areas.

2. Over 90% of the PRAXIS tests measure subject area knowledge.

3. The purpose of the test is to measure whether the teacher candidate possesses a sufficient level of knowledge and skills to perform job duties effectively and responsibly.

4. Your state sets the acceptable passing score.

5. Any candidate, whether from a traditional teaching-preparation path or an alternative route, can seek to enter the teaching profession by taking a PRAXIS test.

6. PRAXIS tests are updated regularly to ensure current content.

Often **your own state's requirements** determine whether or not you should take any particular test. The most reliable source of information regarding this is your state's Department of Education. This resource should have a complete list of testing centers and dates. Test dates vary by subject area and not all test dates necessarily include your particular test, so be sure to check carefully.

If you are in a teacher-education program, check with the Education Department or the Certification Officer for specific information for testing and testing timelines. The Certification Office should have most of the information you need.

If you choose an alternative route to certification you can either rely on our website at *www.XAMonline.com* or on the resources provided by an alternative certification program. Many states now have specific agencies devoted to alternative certification and there are some national organizations as well, for example:

National Association for Alternative Certification

http://www.alt-teachercert.org/index.asp

Interpreting Test Results

Contrary to what you may have heard, the results of a PRAXIS test are not based on time. More accurately, you will be scored on the raw number of points you earn in relation to the raw number of points available. Each question is worth one raw point. It is likely to your benefit to complete as many questions in the time allotted, but it will not necessarily work to your advantage if you hurry through the test.

Follow the guidelines provided by ETS for interpreting your score. The web site offers a sample test score sheet and clearly explains how the scores are scaled and what to expect if you have an essay portion on your test.

Scores are usually available by phone within a month of the test date and scores will be sent to your chosen institution(s) within six weeks. Additionally, ETS now makes online, downloadable reports available for 45 days from the reporting date. It is critical that you be aware of your own state's passing score. Your raw score may qualify you to teach in some states, but not all. ETS administers the test and assigns a score, but the states make their own interpretations and, in some cases, consider combined scores if you are testing in more than one area.

What's on the Test?

The Praxis School Guidance and Counseling 0420 exam lasts 2 hours and consists of 120 multiple-choice questions, including 40 based on a listening section. The breakdown of the questions is as follows:

Category	Approximate Number of Questions	Approximate Percentage of the Test
I: Counseling and Guidance	66	55%
II: Consulting	18	15%
III: Coordinating	18	15%
IV: Professional Issues	18	15%
V: Taped Portion	40	33%

Question Types

You're probably thinking, enough already, I want to study! Indulge us a little longer while we explain that there is actually more than one type of multiple-choice question. You can thank us later after you realize how well prepared you are for your exam.

1. **Complete the Statement.** The name says it all. In this question type you'll be asked to choose the correct completion of a given statement. For example:

> **The Dolch Basic Sight Words consist of a relatively short list of words that children should be able to:**
>
> A. Sound out
>
> B. Know the meaning of
>
> C. Recognize on sight
>
> D. Use in a sentence

The correct answer is C. In order to check your answer, test out the statement by adding the choices to the end of it.

2. **Which of the Following.** One way to test your answer choice for this type of question is to replace the phrase "which of the following" with your selection. Use this example:

> **Which of the following words is one of the twelve most frequently used in children's reading texts:**
>
> A. There
>
> B. This
>
> C. The
>
> D. An

Don't look! Test your answer. _____ is one of the twelve most frequently used in children's reading texts. Did you guess C? Then you guessed correctly.

3. Roman Numeral Choices. This question type is used when there is more than one possible correct answer. For example:

> **Which of the following two arguments accurately supports the use of cooperative learning as an effective method of instruction?**
> I.   Cooperative learning groups facilitate healthy competition between individuals in the group.
> II. Cooperative learning groups allow academic achievers to carry or cover for academic underachievers.
> III. Cooperative learning groups make each student in the group accountable for the success of the group.
> IV. Cooperative learning groups make it possible for students to reward other group members for achieving.
>
> A. I and II
> B. II and III
> C. I and III
> D. III and IV

Notice that the question states there are **two** possible answers. It's best to read all the possibilities first before looking at the answer choices. In this case, the correct answer is D.

4. Negative Questions. This type of question contains words such as "not," "least," and "except." Each correct answer will be the statement that does **not** fit the situation described in the question. Such as:

> **Multicultural education is not**
> A. An idea or concept
> B. A "tack-on" to the school curriculum
> C. An educational reform movement
> D. A process

Think to yourself that the statement could be anything but the correct answer. This question form is more open to interpretation than other types, so read carefully and don't forget that you're answering a negative statement.

5. **Questions that Include Graphs, Tables, or Reading Passages.** As always, read the question carefully. It likely asks for a very specific answer and not a broad interpretation of the visual. Here is a simple (though not statistically accurate) example of a graph question:

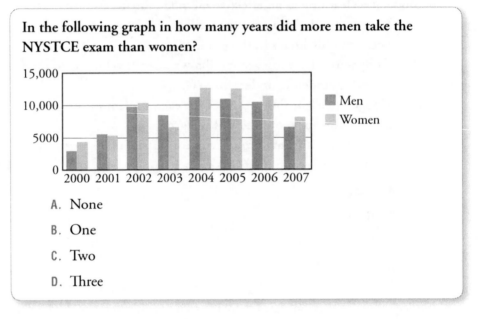

In the following graph in how many years did more men take the NYSTCE exam than women?

A. None

B. One

C. Two

D. Three

It may help you to simply circle the two years that answer the question. Make sure you've read the question thoroughly and once you've made your determination, double check your work. The correct answer is C.

SECTION 4
HELPFUL HINTS

Study Tips

1. **You are what you eat.** Certain foods aid the learning process by releasing natural memory enhancers called CCKs (cholecystokinin) composed of tryptophan, choline, and phenylalanine. All of these chemicals enhance the neurotransmitters associated with memory and certain foods release memory

enhancing chemicals. A light meal or snacks of one of the following foods fall into this category:

- Milk
- Rice
- Eggs
- Fish
- Nuts and seeds
- Oats
- Turkey

The better the connections, the more you comprehend!

2. See the forest for the trees. In other words, get the concept before you look at the details. One way to do this is to take notes as you read, paraphrasing or summarizing in your own words. Putting the concept in terms that are comfortable and familiar may increase retention.

3. Question authority. Ask why, why, why? Pull apart written material paragraph by paragraph and don't forget the captions under the illustrations. For example, if a heading reads *Stream Erosion* put it in the form of a question (Why do streams erode? What is stream erosion?) then find the answer within the material. If you train your mind to think in this manner you will learn more and prepare yourself for answering test questions.

4. Play mind games. Using your brain for reading or puzzles keeps it flexible. Even with a limited amount of time your brain can take in data (much like a computer) and store it for later use. In ten minutes you can: read two paragraphs (at least), quiz yourself with flash cards, or review notes. Even if you don't fully understand something on the first pass, your mind stores it for recall, which is why frequent reading or review increases chances of retention and comprehension.

5. Place yourself in exile and set the mood. Set aside a particular place and time to study that best suits your personal needs and biorhythms. If you're a night person, burn the midnight oil. If you're a morning person set yourself up with some coffee and get to it. Make your study time and place as free from distraction as possible and surround yourself with what you need, be it silence or music. Studies have shown that music can aid in concentration, absorption, and retrieval of information. Not all music, though. Classical music is said to work best

6. Get pointed in the right direction. Use arrows to point to important passages or pieces of information. It's easier to read than a page full of yellow highlights. Highlighting can be used sparingly, but add an arrow to the margin to call attention to it.

7. **The pen is mightier than the sword.** Learn to take great notes. A by-product of our modern culture is that we have grown accustomed to getting our information in short doses. We've subconsciously trained ourselves to assimilate information into neat little packages. Messy notes fragment the flow of information. Your notes can be much clearer with proper formatting. *The Cornell Method* is one such format. This method was popularized in *How to Study in College*, Ninth Edition, by Walter Pauk. You can benefit from the method without purchasing an additional book by simply looking up the method online. Below is a sample of how *The Cornell Method* can be adapted for use with this guide.

← 2½" → Cue Column	← 6" → Note Taking Column
	1. Record: During your reading, use the note-taking column to record important points.
	2. Questions: As soon as you finish a section, formulate questions based on the notes in the right-hand column. Writing questions helps to clarify meanings, reveal relationships, establish community, and strengthen memory. Also, the writing of questions sets the state for exam study later.
	3. Recite: Cover the note-taking column with a sheet of paper. Then, looking at the questions or cue-words in the question and cue column only, say aloud, in your own words, the answers to the questions, facts, or ideas indicated by the cue words.
	4. Reflect: Reflect on the material by asking yourself questions.
	5. Review: Spend at least ten minutes every week reviewing all your previous notes. Doing so helps you retain ideas and topics for the exam.
↑ 2" ↓	**Summary** After reading, use this space to summarize the notes from each page.

Adapted from How to Study in College, Ninth Edition, by Walter Pauk, ©2008 Wadsworth

8. **Check your budget.** You should at least review all the content material before your test, but allocate the most amount of time to the areas that need the most refreshing. It sounds obvious, but it's easy to forget. You can use the study rubric above to balance your study budget.

> The proctor will write the start time where it can be seen and then, later, provide the time remaining, typically fifteen minutes before the end of the test.

Testing Tips

1. **Get smart, play dumb.** Sometimes a question is just a question. No one is out to trick you, so don't assume that the test writer is looking for something other than what was asked. Stick to the question as written and don't overanalyze.

2. **Do a double take.** Read test questions and answer choices at least twice because it's easy to miss something, to transpose a word or some letters. If you have no idea what the correct answer is, skip it and come back later if there's time. If you're still clueless, it's okay to guess. Remember, you're scored on the number of questions you answer correctly and you're not penalized for wrong answers. The worst case scenario is that you miss a point from a good guess.

3. **Turn it on its ear.** The syntax of a question can often provide a clue, so make things interesting and turn the question into a statement to see if it changes the meaning or relates better (or worse) to the answer choices.

4. **Get out your magnifying glass.** Look for hidden clues in the questions because it's difficult to write a multiple-choice question without giving away part of the answer in the options presented. In most questions you can readily eliminate one or two potential answers, increasing your chances of answering correctly to 50/50, which will help out if you've skipped a question and gone back to it (see tip #2).

5. **Call it intuition.** Often your first instinct is correct. If you've been studying the content you've likely absorbed something and have subconsciously retained the knowledge. On questions you're not sure about trust your instincts because a first impression is usually correct.

6. **Graffiti.** Sometimes it's a good idea to mark your answers directly on the test booklet and go back to fill in the optical scan sheet later. You don't get extra points for perfectly blackened ovals. If you choose to manage your test this way, be sure not to mismark your answers when you transcribe to the scan sheet.

7. **Become a clock-watcher.** You have a set amount of time to answer the questions. Don't get bogged down laboring over a question you're not sure about when there are ten others you could answer more readily. If you choose to follow the advice of tip #6, be sure you leave time near the end to go back and fill in the scan sheet.

Do the Drill

No matter how prepared you feel it's sometimes a good idea to apply Murphy's Law. So the following tips might seem silly, mundane, or obvious, but we're including them anyway.

1. **Remember, you are what you eat, so bring a snack.** Choose from the list of energizing foods that appear earlier in the introduction.

2. **You're not too sexy for your test.** Wear comfortable clothes. You'll be distracted if your belt is too tight or if you're too cold or too hot.

3. **Lie to yourself.** Even if you think you're a prompt person, pretend you're not and leave plenty of time to get to the testing center. Map it out ahead of time and do a dry run if you have to. There's no need to add road rage to your list of anxieties.

4. **Bring sharp number 2 pencils.** It may seem impossible to forget this need from your school days, but you might. And make sure the erasers are intact, too.

5. **No ticket, no test.** Bring your admission ticket as well as **two** forms of identification, including one with a picture and signature. You will not be admitted to the test without these things.

6. **You can't take it with you.** Leave any study aids, dictionaries, notebooks, computers, and the like at home. Certain tests **do** allow a scientific or four-function calculator, so check ahead of time to see if your test does.

7. **Prepare for the desert.** Any time spent on a bathroom break **cannot** be made up later, so use your judgment on the amount you eat or drink.

8. **Quiet, Please!** Keeping your own time is a good idea, but not with a timepiece that has a loud ticker. If you use a watch, take it off and place it nearby but not so that it distracts you. And **silence your cell phone**.

To the best of our ability, we have compiled the content you need to know in this book and in the accompanying online resources. The rest is up to you. You can use the study and testing tips or you can follow your own methods. Either way, you can be confident that there aren't any missing pieces of information and there shouldn't be any surprises in the content on the test.

If you have questions about test fees, registration, electronic testing, or other content verification issues please visit *www.ets.org*.

Good luck!

Sharon Wynne
Founder, XAMonline

DOMAIN I
COUNSELING AND GUIDANCE

PERSONALIZED STUDY PLAN

KNOWN MATERIAL/ SKIP IT

COMPETENCY 1
HUMAN DEVELOPMENT AND LEARNING

There are many theories in the literature of human and personality development as well as in counseling and psychotherapy. The major theories explored in this section are psychoanalytic theory (created by Freud and developed by his followers), the related psychodynamic models of Erikson and Adler, and behaviorism. In subsequent sections, we address theories of cognitive development (*see Skill 1.3*) and other theories of counseling and behavior change such as existential, person-centered, Gestalt, cognitive-behavioral, reality, and solution-focused therapies (*see Skill 3.2*).

Psychoanalytic Theory

The basis of many theories of psychology and counseling is the psychoanalytic theory of Sigmund Freud. Others who embraced psychoanalytic theory were Otto Rank, Heinz Hartman, Ernest Jones, Anna Freud, Alfred Adler, Heinz Kohut, Erik Erikson, Carl Jung, Karen Horney, Harry Stack Sullivan, John Bowlby, Margaret Mahler, Jacques Lacan, and Nancy Chodorow. Many broadened Freud's original ideas into different schools; these are often collectively referred to as psychodynamic theory and therapy.

Freud viewed human behavior as primarily the manifestation of biological and instinctive drives, unconscious motivation, and irrational forces. He divided the personality into the following parts:

1. The id, which is blind, demanding, pleasure-seeking, and insistent; its function is to lessen tension and return the psyche to a sense of homoeostasis or status quo

2. The ego, which is the arbitrator between external reality and internal impulses and experiences

3. The superego, which represents moral training and whose goal is perfection and "doing the right thing"

He also explored the concept of the unconscious by using techniques of dream analysis, posthypnotic suggestion, and free association. Anxiety and various ego-defense mechanisms were other components of the personality.

PSYCHOANALYTIC THERAPY aims to reconstruct the personality instead of solving immediate problems, with a focus on the past in order to analyze aspects of the unconscious that affect present behavior. Goals for clients include insight into their unconscious psychodynamics, greater ability to understand the connection between their past and present behaviors, and more psychological awareness.

Stages of psychosexual development

According to psychoanalytic theory, there are five stages of psychosexual development:

1. Oral: The mouth is the source of satisfaction. If one's oral needs are not met, greediness and acquisitiveness may develop as well as the rejection of others' love, fear of intimate relationships, and mistrust of others.

2. Anal: Control of the feces is the source of satisfaction. Negative feelings, including rage, hatred, destructiveness, and hostility, are experienced if the need to control one's own bodily functions is not successfully resolved.

3. Phallic: The phallus (penis/clitoris) is the source of satisfaction. Penis envy and castration anxiety are associated with this stage of development. Resolution of sexual conflicts and sex-role identity is a critical task at this stage with the Electra and Oedipus complexes resulting from difficulties associated with this stage.

4. Latency: This stage has been thought to be a relatively calm period of inward and self-centered preoccupation. If not resolved adequately, narcissistic orientation can occur. The latency period usually occurs between the ages of 5 and 12.

5. Genital: This stage is signaled by physical maturity. Preoccupation with the sex organs is possible if this stage is not adequately resolved.

PSYCHOPATHOLOGY results from failing to meet one or more critical developmental tasks or becoming fixated at an early level of development. Neurotic personality development is regarded as an incomplete resolution of one of the stages of psychosexual development. Behavior is determined by unconscious forces, early experiences, and sexual and aggressive impetus.

> **PSYCHOANALYTIC THERAPY:** aims to reconstruct the personality instead of solving immediate problems, with a focus on the past in order to analyze aspects of the unconscious that affect present behavior

> **PSYCHOPATHOLOGY:** results from failing to meet one or more critical developmental tasks or becoming fixated at an early level of development

Psychoanalytic therapeutic techniques

Projection of the client's feelings upon the therapist is used to facilitate therapy; this is called **TRANSFERENCE**. To enhance this process, the therapist tries to remain a "blank slate."

Other techniques used in this therapy include:

- **Maintaining the analytic framework:** The therapist strives to adhere to strict relational rules, including nondisclosure on the part of the therapist/analyst, utilizing psychoanalytic techniques maintaining the contractual agreement for payment of fees, and having sessions regularly and consistently.

- **Free association:** This technique encourages the client to say whatever comes to mind in order to reveal the unconscious and give the therapist the opportunity to interpret the unconscious thoughts.

- **Interpretation:** This is the process of analyzing the material the client reveals from the unconscious via free association and dreams.

- **Dream analysis:** This process encourages clients to report and discuss their dreams. The client is then encouraged by the therapist to free associate about various parts of the dream and symbols contained in the dream. The analyst offers interpretations.

- **Analysis and interpretation of resistance:** This technique involves an analysis of the ways the client is resisting the process of change.

- **Analysis and interpretation of transference:** In this process, the therapist interprets and discusses the significance of the transference process and the therapist–client relationship.

> **TRANSFERENCE:** projection of the client's feelings upon the therapist

Psychodynamic theories

Subsequent developments in psychoanalytic theory that are considered "psychodynamic" are still grounded in key concepts from psychoanalytic theory. These include the role of the unconscious in conscious functioning, the relationship between childhood experiences and adult behavior, a developmental framework of personality, and some elements of the therapeutic process.

However, many of these offshoots are more likely to incorporate ideas about the role of external factors such as other people, the environment, and social norms in the development of personality as well as intervention. Psychodynamic theorists focus on the ego and its development, as well as the development of the self as an individual.

The goal of psychodynamic theories is to help the client become more aware of the unconscious, as well as to strengthen the ego system so that behavior is based upon reality. Psychodynamic theories include ego psychology, object relations, attachment theory, psychosocial theory, analytical psychology, and interpersonal therapy.

Object relations theory

Margaret Mahler was instrumental in developing the OBJECT RELATIONS THEORY of psychoanalysis. This theory focuses on predetermined stages of development in which the child focuses less and less on self and begins to see the world in relation to others. As development progresses, the child transitions through the following stages:

> **OBJECT RELATIONS THEORY:** focuses on predetermined stages of development in which the child focuses less and less on self and begins to see the world in relation to others

1. Normal infantile autism, when the infant responds to physical stress, does not see a unified self, and considers self and mother as one

2. Symbiotic relationship with the mother from 1–2 months of age, when the infant is dependent upon the mother and expects emotional congruence with the mother (mother also benefits from the relationship)

3. Separation from this symbiotic relationship, which occurs as the child gains cognitive awareness of being a separate person around 16–18 months of age

4. Individualized, a process that takes place from age 18 months to approximately age 3

5. Integration of self, or maturation, as a $3\frac{1}{2}$ to 4-year-old

If a trauma occurs during the separation–individuation phase, borderline and narcissistic personalities often develop; in other words, people who experience such a trauma often have difficulty regulating their sense of self and their relationships with others.

Interpersonal therapy

More recently, INTERPERSONAL THERAPY has emerged from psychoanalytic theories. This time-limited approach also incorporates concepts and structure from cognitive-behavioral therapy and other intervention approaches. It is commonly used with people experiencing depression.

> **INTERPERSONAL THERAPY:** an approach that incorporates concepts and structure from cognitive-behavioral therapy and other intervention approaches

Contributions and limitations of psychoanalytic theory

Contributions of psychoanalytic theory include:

- This theory is the basis for all subsequent psychological theories involved in the explanation of human behavior because it was the first theory.

- The approach provides a framework for exploring an individual's history and his or her relationship to the present by way of the unconscious.

- The concept of resolving resistance to the change process is a key aspect of the success of the therapeutic process.

- Many of the techniques of the therapy can be applied to other therapeutic models, including the development of interpersonal therapy.

Limitations of the theory include:

- For people utilizing traditional psychoanalytic therapy, a prolonged therapist training period is required. Furthermore, work with clients also tends to be long term.

- The importance of action to alleviate the problem is not recognized.

- The basic concepts of the theory are not verifiable by empirical research.

- The theory is based on neurotic rather than healthy personalities.

- The theory cannot be used in crisis counseling when immediate solutions are needed.

- Traditional psychoanalytic theory does not take into account social, cultural, and interpersonal variables, although some of the derivate schools of thought in psychodynamic theory do.

> *A structural overview of the various concepts and schools of thought in psychoanalytic and psychodynamic theory can be found at:*
>
> *www.en.wikipedia.org /wiki/psychoanalysis*

Key terms in psychoanalytic and psychodynamic therapy

- Abreaction: The emotional reliving of past painful experiences.

- Anxiety: The result of repressing threatening thoughts or feelings.

- Borderline Personality Disorder: The pathology that develops when an individual fails to adequately develop in the separation–individuation phase, characterized by instability, irritability, self-destruction, impulsive anger, and extreme mood shifts.

- Compensation: An ego-defense mechanism that helps develop positive traits to make up for individual limitations.

- Countertransference: A reaction toward the client by the therapist that can interfere with objectivity. It is generally related to the unmet and sometimes unconscious needs of the therapist.

- Denial: The distortion of reality in an attempt to avoid dealing with a particular situation.

- Displacement: The tendency to direct one's energy toward another person or object in order to reduce one's own anxiety.

- **Ego:** The part of the personality that mediates between the unconscious instincts and the environment.
- **Ego-Defense Mechanism:** The unconscious process that operates to protect the individual from threatening and anxiety-producing thoughts, feelings, and impulses. Examples include displacement, denial, repression, and rationalization.
- **Ego Psychology:** A theory of ego development reflecting different stages of life; formulated by Heinz Hartmann, Erik Erikson, and other theorists.
- **Electra Complex:** The unconscious sexual feelings of a daughter toward her father, coupled with hostility toward her mother.
- **Free Association:** The technique of permitting the client to say whatever comes to mind without censoring.
- **Fixation:** The process of getting stuck at a particular stage of psychosexual development.
- **Id:** The part of the personality that is ruled by the pleasure principle; the center of the instincts, which are largely unconscious.
- **Interpretation:** A technique of the therapist to explain a particular event or behavior.
- **Interjection:** An ego-defense mechanism in which the client takes on behavior learned from another.
- **Libido:** The energy of all life instincts, including sexual energy.
- **Narcissistic Personality Disorder:** A personality disorder characterized by extreme self-love, an exaggerated sense of self-importance, and an explosive attitude toward others; these attitudes usually hide a poor self-concept.
- **Object Relations:** The theory that describes the interactional system of self and other; this theory is strongly based in developmental concepts.
- **Oedipus Complex:** The unconscious sexual feelings of a son toward his mother, coupled with hostility toward his father.
- **Projection:** The tendency on the part of the client to attribute to others qualities that are unacceptable in his or her own personality.
- **Psychic Energy:** The drive that propels a person's behavior and psychological functioning.
- **Rationalization:** The method of explaining failures or negative occurrences.

- **Reaction Formation:** An ego-defense mechanism in which a client strives to hide a socially unacceptable thought or feeling with behavior that is considered appropriate.

- **Regression:** An ego-defense mechanism of reverting to a less mature stage of development.

- **Repression:** The unconscious act of pushing unacceptable or painful experiences into the unconscious.

- **Resistance:** The client's unwillingness to share feelings and thoughts, or to make changes, in order for the psychoanalytic process to be successful.

- **Sublimation:** The process of redirecting sexual and other biological energies into socially acceptable and creative avenues.

- **Superego:** The part of the personality that determines what is right and wrong and strives to "be good."

- **Symbiosis:** A relationship between two individuals that is advantageous or necessary to both; if an individual does not progress beyond this stage, borderline personality disorder can develop.

- **Transference:** The fostering of emotions originally experienced toward one individual upon another individual not connected with the original experience (usually the therapist).

- **Working Through:** The process of exploring unconscious material, ego defenses, transference, and resistance.

Erikson's Psychosocial Theory of Human Development

Erik Erikson built on Freud's work and developed what is referred to as **PSYCHOSOCIAL THEORY.** It focuses on developmental tasks in relation to self and others. The eight stages of life articulated in this theory are:

> **PSYCHOSOCIAL THEORY:** focuses on developmental tasks in relation to self and others

1. **Basic Trust vs. Basic Mistrust** (Birth to approximately 18 months of age): The infant's needs for nourishment and care are satisfied. The response to these needs must be consistent so that the infant develops a sense of trust and attachment to one or two adults. Mistrust results if the infant's needs are not met.

2. **Autonomy vs. Shame and Doubt** (18 to 30 months of age): The child develops an early sense of independence and a measure of some control over the environment. This independence is manifested by self-feeding, dressing, toileting, etc. In this stage the child needs reassurance and support from the adults around him or her. Overprotection should be avoided.

3. Initiative vs. Guilt ($2\frac{1}{2}$ to 5 years of age): The child develops an imagination and enjoys playacting adult roles. The child is also learning to perform adult roles and begins to realize restraints are necessary. A pervasive sense of guilt occurs if the child is not successful in initiating everyday activities and tasks.

4. Industry vs. Inferiority (Elementary and middle school years): The child becomes curious, with the need to explore and manipulate the environment around her or him. Competency is reached through accomplishments. The child becomes increasingly aware of interactions with others in the school and neighborhood. If a sense of adequacy is not acquired during this stage, feelings of inferiority occur.

5. Identity vs. Role Confusion (Adolescence): The child is striving for an identity and sense of self-worth. Adolescents seek to formulate their own values, beliefs, and lifestyle. They experiment with different lifestyles. If previous stages have not been resolved satisfactorily, the tasks may reoccur here as developmental problems. Resolving unfinished business is one of the major tasks of adolescence.

6. Intimacy vs. Isolation: This struggle occurs during young adulthood. The adult becomes willing to be open about self and to commit to a close personal relationship.

7. Generativity vs. Stagnation: Maturity is achieved. The task here is to establish and guide the next generation and come to terms with one's dreams and accomplishments.

8. Ego Integrity vs. Despair: This stage occurs during later life. The elderly may experience despair if ego integrity is not obtained. When successful, people have a sense of fulfillment about their lives.

Adlerian Theory

Alfred Adler was originally a follower of Freud. Subsequent Adlerians include Rudolf Dreikers and Harold Mosak. Rudolf Dreikers was instrumental in applying Adlerian principles to group work. Whereas Freud explored the psychosexual aspects of personality, Adler concentrated on the psychosocial aspects of human nature. He believed that people are in control of their lives, thus creating an individual lifestyle at an early age.

Adler called his approach individual psychology. In contrast to Freud, Adler felt that consciousness rather than unconsciousness was the core of personality theory. He did not believe in reliving childhood experiences, but rather in using early recollections as clues to understanding the lifestyle of the individual.

Adler emphasized the positive abilities of the individual as influenced by societal forces and the capacity of each individual to reach optimal development. His theory became the basis for the ensuing humanistic theories that abound today. The main goal of these theories is confronting basic mistakes and assumptions the client has made and attempting to redirect them. The focus is on examining the beliefs of the client as expressed by his or her behavior.

> Adler emphasized the positive abilities of the individual as influenced by societal forces and the capacity of each individual to reach optimal development.

Some key concepts in Adler's theory are:

- Childhood experiences themselves are not as crucial as the attitude toward those experiences

- All people have unique lifestyles, none of which are the same

- One's lifestyle is set by age 5 and is a reaction to perceived inferiority

- One's lifestyle is learned from early family interactions

- Behavior is motivated by social needs and has a goal-oriented direction

Contributions and limitations of Adlerian theory

Contributions of Adler's theory include:

- The theory was a major impetus for the development of other humanistic theories.

- The theory has influenced cognitive-behavioral theories, family therapies, and general mental health work. Currently, it is having an impact on emerging theories of culturally competent counseling.

Limitations of the theory include:

- An inability to validate the vaguely defined concepts with empirical data

- The oversimplification of complex human functioning

- It is based too heavily on a common sense perspective

Key terms in Adlerian theory

- Avoiding Traps: The therapist's efforts to avoid reinforcing clients' destructive behavior patterns

- Basic Mistakes: Self-defeating beliefs (such as an extreme need for security, unattainable goals, and doubting one's worth) that influence the formation of one's personality

- Catching Oneself: The client's process of becoming more aware of self-destructive behavior, irrational thoughts, and anticipating events before they happen
- Convictions: The results of life experiences
- Courage: The ability to take risks
- Encouragement: The process used in therapy to help clients reach realistic goals by using all their resources, recognizing their positive traits, and transforming negative traits into positive assets
- Family Constellations: "Pictures" of family dynamics and relationships
- Fictional Finalism: The ideal image one sees oneself becoming; one's ultimate goal
- Holism: The perception of one's personality as a whole
- Immediacy: Dealing with the present moment in the counseling process
- Individual Psychology: The uniqueness and unity of the individual
- Individuality: The way everyone develops his or her own style of striving for competence
- Inferiority Feelings: The negative feeling one has about oneself; these feelings can be both real and imagined
- Life Tasks: The life work of all humans to attain a satisfying lifestyle
- Lifestyle: The way in which one perceives life and upon which the personality is formed
- Motivational Modification: The therapist's interest in helping clients to want to change their negative lifestyle goals and challenging their basic negative concepts
- Paradoxical Intention: The technique characterized by helping the client invoke exaggerated debilitating thoughts and behaviors and accept and conquer his or her resistance, thus becoming more aware of his or her behavior and accepting responsibility for the consequences of that behavior
- Phenomenological Orientation: The technique the therapist uses that attempts to view the world from the client's point of view
- Priorities: A coping method used to obtain satisfaction in life; by pointing out a client's priorities, the therapist hopes to help the client realize the feelings invoked in others and the price the client pays by clinging to these negative priorities

- **Private Logic:** The central psychological framework of the client; the philosophy upon which one bases one's lifestyle, including basic mistakes and faulty assumptions that often do not conform to reality

- **Push-Button:** A technique that teaches the client that he or she can control his or her thoughts and feelings

- **Social Interest:** The attitude a client has regarding society; a sense of empathy and identification with the larger community

- **Spitting in the Client's Soup:** A technique that reduces the usefulness of a client's manipulative behavior; by pointing out the manipulation, the therapist effectively defeats the client's anticipated results of the manipulation

- **Striving for Superiority:** The desire to become competent and perfect; also known as the growth force

- **Task Setting and Commitment:** The technique taught to the client to formulate realistic, attainable goals that can be revised if necessary

Behaviorism

The behavioral theories of psychological development and therapy that developed in the 1950s and 1960s were a radical protest of the psychoanalytic theories that had held sway for many years. The key figures in behaviorism were Arnold Lazarus, Albert Bandura, Joseph Wolpe, and Alan Kazdin. They built on the work of learning theorists (*see Skill 1.3*). Contemporary BEHAVIOR THERAPY utilizes many concepts, research methods, and treatments to account for and change behavior. In contrast to the psychoanalytic theories, behavior therapies are focused on current behavior as well as methods to change self-destructive behaviors.

The main goal of behavior therapy is to eliminate negative learned behaviors or self-defeating behaviors by having the client learn new, more effective and positive ways of dealing with situations that create behavior problems. The client and the therapist work together to formulate goals. In this process, they detail specific methods to address the client's self-defeating behavior. The client must have a sense of ownership regarding the goals in order to make them work.

The job of the therapist in behavior therapy is to:

- Make the problem clear

- Verbalize the consequences of the behavior manifested by the client

- Serve as a role model for the client

BEHAVIOR THERAPY: a theory that is focused on current behavior as well as methods to change self-destructive behaviors

Behavior theory describes the principles of learned behavior.

- Help formulate alternative courses of action with possible consequences

- Advocate behavior change and provide reinforcement to the client when the behavior changes

There should be an objective assessment of the results of the therapy. The job of the client is to help the therapist explore the alternatives to the problematic behavior, be open to trying new strategies, and be willing to take the risk of trying these new strategies outside the therapeutic session.

Although the goals of the therapy are specific and concrete, and the problems are defined, the procedures and techniques of the therapy are contingent on the needs of each client. Therefore no set of specific techniques is used, although some methods are used more often than others. Some of these methods are relaxation, systematic desensitization, reinforcement, modeling, assertiveness training, multi-modal therapy, and self-management programs.

> *Therapy should focus on behavior change, not attitude change, and actions are expected to follow verbalization (in other words, practice in real life).*

Contributions and limitations of behaviorism

Contributions of behavior theory and therapy include:

- The techniques are based on empirical research. Any technique that is not effective empirically is discarded.

- Treatment is based on the assessment of individual needs.

- The therapy is effective in the short term, yielding results that can be widely applied.

- The approaches can be used with culturally diverse client populations because of the emphasis on teaching the client about the process and the structure of the therapy.

Limitations of behavior theory and therapy include:

- Success depends on the ability to control environmental factors.

- In institutional settings, there is a danger of imposing conformity at the expense of individual needs.

- The therapy does not address philosophical human problems such as values and identity issues.

- The therapist may sometimes direct a client toward the goals of the therapist instead of the goals of the client. This may occur, in particular, when the therapist does not agree with the client's value system.

- Past history is not an important factor in the therapy, therefore the assumption is that past experiences and childhood traumatic events do not play a role in present behaviors.

Key terms in behaviorism

- **Assertiveness Training:** Teaching skills and techniques for dealing with difficult situations in ways that are direct, firm, and clear. Assertiveness training often challenges beliefs that accompany a lack of assertiveness and employs the technique of rehearsal.

- **Basic ID:** An acronym for the seven major areas of personality functioning: behavior, affect, sensations, imagery, cognition, interpersonal and drugs/biology. (Lazarus, 1981).

- **Behavior Rehearsal:** A technique of trying out new behavioral approaches that can be used in real-life situations.

- **Coaching:** Providing clients with general principles of how to make effective behavioral changes.

- **Cognitive Restructuring:** The process of identifying and understanding the impact of negative behavior and thoughts, as well as learning to replace them with more realistic and appropriate actions and beliefs.

- **Contingency Contracting:** The specific delineation of behavior to be performed, changed, or discontinued, along with the rewards for the performance of these contractual items, the conditions under which these rewards are to be received, and the time limit involved.

- **Counterconditioning:** The process of retraining problem behaviors and introducing new behaviors.

- **Feedback:** The process of providing the client with verbal responses to behavior changes. The two parts of feedback are encouragement and praise for attempting the behavior change, and specific suggestions for making the behavior change work better.

- **Modeling:** The process of showing new ways to do something. The therapist can help the client do this by role-playing the type of behavior that is desired. Albert Bandura has done much of the work in this area.

- **Multimodal Therapy:** The process the therapist evokes in making an evaluation of the client's level of functioning at the beginning of the therapy and subsequently adjusting procedures and techniques to the goals of the client. The behavior change is a function of techniques, strategies, and modeling. Arnold Lazarus developed this type of therapy.

- **Negative Reinforcement:** When the removal of an aversive stimulus is likely to increase a problem behavior.

- **Operant Conditioning:** A concept from B. F. Skinner (a learning theorist) that says behaviors of an active organism are controlled and controllable, even without actual consequences each time.

- **Positive Reinforcement:** A conditioning technique in which an individual receives a desirable result for a positive behavior that subsequently increases the probability of that behavior reoccurring.

- **Progressive Relaxation:** A technique employed to increase the ability of the client to control his or her stress level by gradually having the client relax.

- **Reinforcement:** A specific response to a behavior that increases the probability of that behavior being repeated.

- **Self-Instructional Training/Management:** Strategies used to teach coping skills in problem situations such as anxiety, depression, and pain. Realistic goals are set and constantly evaluated. The consistent use of a particular strategy is essential, and support systems are important, as is the use of self-reinforcement in order to achieve success.

- **Self-Monitoring:** The process of observing one's behavior patterns and interactions in social situations.

- **Social Learning Theory:** A theory originated by Alfred Bandura, which holds that behavior is understood by taking into consideration the social conditions under which learning occurs as well as individual psychological factors.

- **Systematic Desensitization:** The process of teaching a client to become less sensitized to a particular stimulus, thereby reducing anxiety. The techniques consist of relaxation exercises combined with an imagined series of progressively more anxiety-producing situations. It was developed by Joseph Wolpe and is based on the principles of classical conditioning.

- **Technical Eclecticism:** The process of using different techniques from different therapies to achieve behavior change; the result is flexibility in the therapeutic process.

SKILL 1.2 Basic Milestones in Physical, Motor, and Language Development

The majority of changes in physical and motor growth and the development of language occur prior to age 5. The primary exception to this is the transition from preadolescence (approximately ages 9–12) into puberty. Hormonal shifts and ongoing physical growth become acute at preadolescence and bring children into adolescence and physical maturity.

Language development in elementary school proceeds primarily in terms of the development of vocabulary and increased sophistication in the use of words and concepts.

The key physical and motor developmental milestones for school-age children and adolescents are noted below.

Ages 6–8

- Growth slows but remains steady

- Body proportions change, with legs getting longer

- Body fat percentage decreases and more muscle develops, with an increase in overall strength

- Fine motor skills are enhanced, though muscle coordination is still uneven; this results in the ability to write in cursive in addition to the ability to print

- Permanent teeth come in, sometimes causing crowding if the mouth has not developed enough

Ages 9–12

- Significant body changes as puberty approaches: weight gain, pubic and body hair, increased sweating, oily skin, genital development

- May experience joint pain as a result of growth spurts

- Girls generally develop sooner; hips widen, breasts start to emerge, menstruation begins

- Boys enter preadolescence later and growth changes last longer

Ages 13–17

- Puberty is reached; the adolescent is physically mature

- Girls reach their adult height by age 17; boys continue to add height into their 20s

The following Web sites provide detailed information about developmental milestones and changes:

www.ces.ncsu.edu/depts /fcs/human.html

www.littleab.com/ABcare /development.html

www.education.com /reference/ontrack/

SKILL 1.3   Major Theories of Learning and Cognitive Development

For an interesting description of various theories and models related to learning, see:

www.learning-theories.com

Theories about learning are varied. Behaviorism (*see Skill 1.1*) describes much about how individuals learn, and many of the concepts of behaviorism are central to learning and cognitive development. The theorists in this area of study include the functionalists, the associationists, and the cognitive developmentalists.

The study of consciousness in the context of the environment, instead of as an isolated element, was the main contribution of functionalist theorists Edward Thorndike, B. F. Skinner, John G. Watson, and C. L. Hull to learning theory. They opposed the introspective techniques of psychoanalytic approaches because they did not explore the relationship with other elements in an individual's environment. The functionalists insisted that mental function be studied in relation to the world surrounding the individual. Many of the ideas in behaviorism developed from this work.

Associationist theorists Ivan Pavlov and William Estes believed that experience or recall of one object builds upon and causes the recall of other objects related to or associated with that object. This idea is based on the theories of Aristotle. The key concept is that living organisms' responses to environmental stimuli are governed by the sensory, response, and central nervous systems, which consist of innate circuitry and memories of past experiences. The response of organisms is therefore dependent upon associating past memories with present stimuli. This theory applied to learning explains how infants expand their sphere of knowledge.

Cognitive theorists Jean Piaget, Edward Tolman, Albert Bandura, and Donald Norman assign a prominent role to mental processes. The process of learning depends on information received and the processing of that information, which in turn depends on mental processes, past experiences or behaviors, and present environmental factors. The person, the environment, and behavior are interdependent. Faulty cognitive processes develop from inaccurate perceptions, overgeneralization, or incomplete or erroneous information.

Piaget

Jean Piaget focused on cognition from a developmental perspective. The child grows cognitively, socially, physically, and morally, gradually and at different rates. These four different types of growth and development have an impact on the learning process and the behavior patterns of the child.

In Piaget's view, development is defined as the adaptive, orderly changes experienced by the human organism from birth to death.

Four stages of cognitive development

Piaget studied how we organize knowledge at different times in our lives. He identified four stages of cognitive development:

1. Sensorimotor Stage: From birth to age 2. Development is based upon reflex; information is gained through the senses; the child begins to understand the concept of permanence and begins to develop problem-solving behavior through trial and error.

2. Preoperational Stage: From ages 2–7. The child starts to develop the ability to share experiences with others, uses symbols, and shows rudimentary logical mental operations. The child has yet to develop the concept of conservation or the ability to understand that certain properties of an object do not change even though their appearance has changed. The concept of CENTRATION is the child's logic at this stage. This is the ability to focus on only one aspect of the properties of an object and not being able to understand that an object can have multiple properties without inherently changing. REVERSIBILITY at this stage is the inability of the child to back up and rethink a problem. The child can only respond to perceived appearances.

3. Concrete Operational Stage: From ages 7–11. At this stage the child understands the concepts of conservation, centration, and reversibility; masters the operations of classification, the identification of characteristics and serialization; and is capable of inferences. The child can now respond to inferred reality or facts.

4. Formal Operational Stage: From age 11 to adulthood. At this stage the child develops and refines the capability of abstract thinking, can deal with hypothetical situations, and exercises higher-order thinking such as synthesis and evaluation.

One limitation of Piaget's theory is the fact that he did not consider the effect of culture and the social environment on children's development. Lev Vygotsky was one theorist who approached cognitive development from a more social standpoint. He suggested that cognitive development started with social interactions and moved inward.

Current Theories of Cognitive Development

Current theories of cognitive development focus on the concept that humans develop according to various information processing mechanisms that are specific to different areas of learning and growth. This is called DOMAIN SPECIFICITY. These theorists argue that information processing is grounded in evolutionary adaptation. A leading proponent of this approach in relation to language acquisition is Noam Chomsky.

CENTRATION: the ability to focus on only one aspect of the properties of an object and not being able to understand that an object can have multiple properties without inherently changing

REVERSIBILITY: the inability of the child to back up and rethink a problem

DOMAIN SPECIFICITY: the concept that humans develop according to various information processing mechanisms that are specific to different areas of learning and growth

SKILL
1.4 **Learning Styles and Individual Differences**

> *Exposure to varied learning approaches can be beneficial and enhance one's growth.*

Human learning is a complex behavior, and the way one learns is as individual and unique as each person. Learning styles refer to the preference a person may have for learning in a particular way; this does not suggest that students can only learn in one way.

Dunn and Dunn's Four Elements of Learning Styles

Research into learning styles has yielded eighteen different elements that contribute to various learning styles. In an attempt to classify this information, Dunn and Dunn isolated four different learning styles with varying components. These learning styles take into consideration the varied aspects of the way individuals learn. Further, Dunn and Dunn have developed a learning style inventory that assesses each of these elements.

There are four major aspects of learning styles and learning environments.

Environmental elements

There are four environmental elements that affect the way a student learns:

1. The element of sound varies with learning. Some children can block out sound completely when studying and learning; others require complete silence. Some need only relative quiet while others must have a familiar sound, such as music or television, to block out extraneous noises that interrupt their train of thought. Still others can concentrate with or without sound, in silence or with noise, or with any sound at all.

2. Light is also a factor in learning but not as critical as the element of sound. Some students need intensely bright lights in order to be comfortable reading or writing, and consequently become drowsy and lethargic in inadequate light. Some students prefer a subdued light to feel comfortable.

3. Tolerance to temperature varies greatly according to the individual. Concentration changes with the need for warmth or coolness, which can affect the degree of productivity of an individual.

4. The design of the study area is often critical to individual learning styles. Some students need an informal setting such as the floor or an easy chair. Others require a more formal setting such as a table or hard chair in order to concentrate adequately, and for others there is no need to take into account the design of the site where they study.

Emotional elements

The emotional elements involved in the way a student learns also have an impact on the quantity and quality of work produced.

The motivated student comes to the task with enthusiasm and excitement, asks questions, and goes beyond the requirements of the class to explore further related areas. The unmotivated student cannot take in too much at one time, needs short assignments, and requires the experience of success to continue to achieve. The unmotivated student will often respond to an individualized program of choices, teaming, or self-evaluation.

The trait of persistence is the ability to find the answer to a problem no matter how difficult. Persistent students will use resources or other students for help before asking the teacher for answers. They will not give up but will continue to work on a problem until it is solved. Other students—such as those with short attention spans—find it difficult to maintain interest in the subject, daydream, become irritated or disruptive, and do not continue to attempt to solve problems for any period of time. These students need to have rules and objectives set out clearly.

The emotionally mature student shows signs of responsibility for completing the task at hand without constant supervision. Students who have difficulty learning because of reading problems become easily discouraged and need different methods of receiving material. They may need taped instruction, games, small groups, or a structured multi-sensory learning packet. Their different learning styles do not conform to the expected norms.

The student who needs structure must have specific rules for completing an assignment. These include time limits, restriction of options, and a specific way of responding. Different students need different amounts of structure depending on their learning style and their ability to make decisions. The motivated, responsible, and persistent student needs little structure while the unmotivated student with learning problems needs the most structure to achieve success.

Sociological elements

The ability to learn varies with the student, depending on the atmosphere and the individuals involved in the teaching situation. Students can learn from different individuals at different times and in different settings. These settings include learning from peers, by themselves, in pairs or teams, with an adult or teacher, and in a mixed group. How students learn sociologically can be determined by allowing them to choose their own method of studying and completing assignments while the teacher monitors and checks on their progress.

> The emotional elements involved in the way a student learns also have an impact on the quantity and quality of work produced.

Physical elements

The senses of seeing, hearing, smelling, feeling, and touching are instrumental in the way many individuals learn. Those who learn visually can see images in their mind; those who learn through their auditory senses learn by listening to sounds; those who learn by the tactile approach must be able to touch and feel in order to understand; and those who learn through their kinesthetic senses need to have actual experiences with the shapes and forms of letters and words. Many students learn from a combination of some or all of these elements.

Other physical elements involved in the process of learning include taking food breaks, or intake; the optimum time of day or night; and the ability to move around at will. Making adjustments to the various elements that affect students' learning styles will produce the ideal atmosphere for learning.

Multiple Intelligences

Another theorist in learning styles is Howard Gardner, who has developed the idea of multiple intelligences. He posits that there are eight different kinds of intelligence and that each person is more or less inclined to demonstrate each of these. While this theory has engendered some debate in the field of education, it has opened up an important discussion about how schools can better respond to the diversity of students' learning styles.

In addition to the Dunn and Dunn learning styles inventory and Gardner's multiple intelligence test, there are other learning style and personality inventories that can help determine the style or combination of styles suited to individual students. These include the Schmeck, Ribich, and Ramanaiah Inventory of Learning Process for information processing preferences, the Myers-Briggs Type Indicator for personality preferences, and the Kolb Learning Style Inventory. The assessment of a student who is having problems learning might direct the teacher to useful methods for motivating and encouraging that student to succeed.

Gender Differences and Learning Styles

Recent research and educational practices have focused on differences in the ways girls and boys learn and function in the school environment. There is some indication that, as a group, boys tend to be more competitive and individualistic in their approach to learning, whereas girls are more inclined to work cooperatively with others, are more social, and are more interested in understanding ideas than assessing facts.

Perhaps the most important thing for school counselors to remember is that gender (or other aspects of social identity such as race and ethnicity, immigration

The senses of seeing, hearing, smelling, feeling, and touching are instrumental in the way many individuals learn.

A multiple intelligence survey is available to assess a student's approach to learning. For more information, see:

www.infed.org/thinkers/gardner.htm

Paying attention to each student's individual needs is the best approach to facilitating academic success.

status, or social class) is only one variable among a range of variables that contribute to the unique development and capabilities of a given individual. Furthermore, differences within a given group (such as girls or boys) are almost always greater than the differences between two such groups. In other words, there is great variation among any given group of students and a range of individual and social factors contribute to these differences.

SKILL 1.5	The Impact of Stress on School Performance and Students' Wellbeing

Students' academic performance and behavior is affected not only by the school environment but also by a range of external factors. Substance abuse, mental health, and other issues are addressed in this section. These circumstances, characteristics, and events can all be considered stressors on students.

Development as Stress

The normal challenges of developmental change can also function as stressors in a child's life. As children grow, experience hormonal shifts, increase their skill base, and gradually shift from a focus on family to peers and then to the larger world, they may experience the stress that often accompanies change. Some children seem to move easily from one stage to another; others feel each developmental shift acutely. Some experience generalized anxiety, revert to earlier levels of functioning for a short time, or become clingy and demanding. They may avoid opportunities to make new friends, develop skills, or participate in extracurricular activities.

It is important for counselors to have an awareness of the range of reactions to developmental change. These responses can be the primary factor underlying difficulties in peer relationships or academic performance.

Considering the role of development in each child's experience is crucial to addressing student needs and concerns effectively.

Impact of Stress on School Performance

Stressors can negatively affect academic achievement by making it difficult for the student to focus on learning. When a student is homeless, for example, it may be difficult for him or her to pay attention in class because of lack of sleep, worry about what is happening with a parent, or concerns about where dinner is coming from. Similarly, if a child is being abused at home, he or she may have difficulties with attention and focus.

Some stressors, such as medical conditions, may prevent a child from participating in school activities or may require home instruction. While accommodations need to be made for alternative programming, the inability to be "part of the group" still may impair peer relationships and affect skill development and motivation.

Stressors can also have a less direct impact. A challenging home life may make it hard for a student to complete homework assignments or study effectively. Chronic stress and traumatic events also contribute to a lack of self-confidence, poor motivation, inadequate social skills, depression, anxiety, and other mental health problems. These difficulties may interfere with a student's ability to participate effectively in the school environment. They can also disrupt the student's efforts to study and do homework.

Individuality and Resiliency

Individuals respond in different ways to the same or similar stressors, and the impact of such stressors needs to be assessed for each student. Mitigating factors include coping skills, personality traits, prior experience with stress and trauma, the degree of social isolation created by the stressful event(s), the quality of attachment to and presence of significant adults in the student's life, and the amount and kind of support the student receives in relation to the stressor.

Resiliency is the ability to thrive in spite of difficult circumstances. Helping students identify or find an important adult upon whom they can rely, teaching problem-solving and coping skills, and discussing ways to think about what life brings to us are all good strategies for helping students become more resilient. This, in turn, enhances their wellbeing as well as their capacity for academic and vocational achievement.

> Research suggests that several of the most important factors in building resiliency are the presence of a caring, competent adult in the child's life, an attitude of hope and interest in life, and good problem-solving skills.

SKILL 1.6 Child Abuse and Neglect

Governmental and nongovernmental sources report that between twelve and fifteen out of every thousand children are abused each year by immediate family members or people living in the home. This does not include abuse and violence perpetrated by others outside the home. Also, these numbers reflect only reported cases of abuse. Abuse or neglect may occur for years before it is discovered; in other cases, abuse continues unchecked. Many children are fearful about reporting abuse for a range of reasons, including the desire to protect one's caregivers and worry about the consequences of reporting.

Given the prevalence of abuse and neglect, it is important that counselors recognize potential signs of child abuse and neglect. When behavioral indicators are present, counselors should meet with students individually to gather more information about suspected abuse and to determine who in the child's family or network can be an ally.

The easiest type of abuse to detect is physical abuse. Unexplained bruises, bite marks, burns, fractures, and other physical indicators suggest that a child has been physically abused. In addition, the child may exhibit withdrawal and aggressive behavior, self-destructive behavior, self-injury (such as sticking a pencil into parts of the body or pinching), and avoidance of physical contact with others.

Child neglect is indicated by a need of medical care; reported lack of supervision; dirty, unkempt appearance; generally poor hygiene; and constantly being hungry. Common behavioral manifestations are falling asleep at inappropriate times, stealing food, frequent absences, expressions of hunger, and self-destructive behaviors.

For the child who has experienced sexual abuse, there may be some difficulty in sitting or walking, stained clothing, venereal disease, and pain or itching in the genital area. The behavioral manifestations vary. Overtly sexualized behavior in children under the age of twelve may be an indicator, as can attention problems at school, self-injury, depression, extremely volatile emotions, suicidal thoughts or gestures, and an inability to control one's behavior in children of all ages.

For the child who has experienced emotional abuse, the indicators are eating disorders, sleeping problems, loss of energy, and chronic complaints. The behavior manifestations include depression, low self-esteem, lack of self-confidence, poor peer relations, and suicidal thoughts or gestures.

> *When behavioral indicators are present, counselors should meet with students individually to gather more information about suspected abuse and to determine who in the child's family or network can be an ally.*

> **The Centers for Disease Control and Prevention have information about child abuse and neglect at:**
>
> *www.cdc.gov/ncipc/dvp /CMP/default.htm.*
>
> **Information about child sexual abuse is also available at:**
>
> *www.nlm.nih.gov /medlineplus /childsexualabuse.html*

SKILL 1.7 Substance Abuse and Addiction

Many students and families are affected by chemical addiction. School counselors need to have some basic information about drug and alcohol use and abuse. Many resources on addiction are available in the form of books and pamphlets as well as on the Internet; local treatment programs and rehabilitation centers are often willing to provide in-service training programs for guidance staff and can also provide free literature.

The job of the school counselor is to recognize the signs of addiction and substance abuse in students and, with the cooperation of the student's parents/

guardians, make referrals to the proper agency for treatment. Students may need residential care, or an outpatient or a partial hospital program may be adequate. It is the counselor's job to follow up with the treatment provider and facilitate the transition of the student back into the school setting, as needed.

Indicators of Substance Abuse

Some of the indicators of substance abuse in students are:

- An inability to perform at school and at home in spite of apparent cognitive capacity and the lack of other interfering factors

- Excessive sleepiness or irritability

- Mood swings or apparent personality changes

- Secretive behavior

- Sudden change in friends

- Use of substances in dangerous situations despite the possibility of physical harm, such as driving a motor vehicle or swimming

- Continued use that results in legal problems, such as prosecution for drunken driving, arrests for disturbing the peace, or possession of a controlled substance

- Inability to stop using the controlled substance in spite of social problems such as fights, conflict with family and peers, or poor school performance

Denial is not uncommon when confronting a student with a substance abuse problem. It may be effective for the school to require the student to attend alcohol and/or drug counseling before returning to school if there has been a breach of school rules and policies by the student. A referral to a professional in the drug abuse field for an evaluation is always an appropriate action when a counselor is concerned about the possibility of abuse or addiction.

Parental Substance Abuse

Some students are affected by their parent or guardian's use or abuse of drugs and alcohol; they may or may not be users themselves. Many of the indicators of addiction in the home are similar to other stress indicators, such as poor school performance, anxiety, avoidance of intimacy, depression, guilt, and over-responsibility.

For more information about students with substance-abusing parents, see:

www.kidshealth.org /teen/your_mind/families /coping_alcoholic.html

General online resources on substance abuse and addiction include:

www.drugabuse.gov /parent-teacher.html

www.niaaa.nih.gov/FAQs /General-English/default .htm

www.adolescent -substance-abuse.com /signs-drug-use.html

SKILL 1.8   Suicide, Self-Injury, Eating Disorders, and Interpersonal Violence

The problems of suicide, anorexia, bulimia, sexual assault, dating violence, and self-injury are serious, often long-term counseling problems beyond the scope of a school counselor's duties. They may require that the counselor communicate with a range of community agencies and personnel. The school counselor's primary tasks are identification, crisis counseling, parental notification, referral, support, and follow-up. It is essential that the counselor utilizes the school's protocol in these instances and report the information to school administration. It may also be appropriate for the school counselor to involve the student assistance team within the school setting.

Teen Suicide

The American Psychiatric Association notes on its Web page for teen suicide that although "…the teen suicide rate has declined by over 25 percent since the early 1990s, suicide is the third leading cause of death among young people ages 15 to 24."

The report also includes the following statistics about teen suicide:

- It is estimated that depression increases the risk of a first suicide attempt by at least fourteen-fold.

- Over half of all kids who suffer from depression will eventually attempt suicide at least once, and more than seven percent will die as a result.

- Four times as many men as women commit suicide, but young women attempt suicide three times more frequently than young men.

- Fifty-three percent of young people who commit suicide abuse substances.

- Firearms are used in a little more than half of all youth suicides.

One of the most common and effective methods school personnel have to recognize the suicidal student is reading the writings of that student. Often, an English teacher will come to the counselor with a sample of a student's writing that suggests thoughts and/or plans of suicide. Sometimes the counselor may learn that a student is thinking about suicide from comments made directly by the student or from friends of the student who are concerned.

When such information comes to the attention of the counselor, the counselor should meet with the student as soon as possible. If the counselor knows the student and the two have a rapport, it is appropriate to speak directly with the student, with the teacher's permission, about the material of concern. Even if the

The American Psychiatric Association notes on its Web page for teen suicide that although "…the teen suicide rate has declined by over 25 percent since the early 1990s, suicide is the third leading cause of death among young people ages 15 to 24."

One of the most common and effective methods school personnel have to recognize the suicidal student is reading the writings of that student.

counselor does not already have a relationship with the student, sometimes he or she must proceed without a prior connection and work at building rapport in the moment.

If confirmation of suicidal intent is received from the student (and in many cases, even if the student does not confirm suicidal intent), the counselor has a duty to inform the parent/guardian(s), the school administration, and the school nurse that the student is currently at risk. Plans for intervention should be made at the time of this discovery. It is critical not to delay until the next day or until after a weekend. Once the parent/guardian(s) and/or appropriate professionals are notified, the treatment is in the hands of those who have the skills and authority to deal with the problem.

Self-Injury

Self-injury is not uncommon in adolescents and sometimes occurs among middle school students as well. SELF-INJURY is direct harm to the body, such as cutting or burning; it is distinguished from a suicide attempt in that the intent behind the self-injury is not connected to a wish to die. Self-injury serves to release tension and helps the student manage emotional pain and distress. The counselor may learn about such behavior by direct observation (scars, wounds, bandages) or from the student engaging in self-injury or his or her friends. As with eating disorders, addressing this issue is a long-term problem and requires referral to appropriate mental health professionals. However, school counselors may be in the position of providing support to teens who self-injure as well as offering information and referral.

Eating Disorders

ANOREXIA NERVOSA, a disorder in which someone starves himself or herself or its variant, and BULIMIA, in which the person alternately binges on food and then purges by vomiting or using laxatives, are eating disorders that also arise particularly in adolescence. Again, the counselor may recognize the problem by direct observation and/or reports from the student's friends and peers. Addressing these problems with students can be difficult because the student often truly believes he or she is overweight or has normal eating patterns.

Eating disorders are often associated with depression and low self-esteem and, left unchecked, can lead to malnutrition, body-chemistry imbalance, cessation of the menstrual cycle, and other endocrine dysfunctions.

SELF-INJURY: direct harm to the body, such as cutting or burning; it is distinguished from a suicide attempt in that the intent behind the self-injury is not connected to a wish to die

For more information about self-injury, go to:

www.healingselfinjury.org/

ANOREXIA NERVOSA: a disorder in which someone starves himself or herself

BULIMIA: a disorder in which a person alternately binges on food and then purges by vomiting or using laxatives

For more information, warning signs, and resources for coping with eating disorders in teens, see:

www.kidshealth.org /parent/nutrition_fit /nutrition/eating_disorders .html

Intervening with Students

When a counselor learns that a student may have an eating disorder, is self-injuring, or is thought to be at risk for suicide, the counselor needs to meet with that student to explore the student's perceptions and concerns. It is also the professional responsibility of the counselor along with the school nurse and other medical school personnel to inform the parent/guardian(s). The parent/guardian(s) needs to be aware of the problem and may also need information, support, and encouragement in seeking help for their child from the appropriate medical or mental health professional. The school's student assistance team might also be useful in aiding with referral, support, and follow-up.

The issue of interpersonal physical or sexual violence is likely to be brought to school counselors along with the psychological issues noted above. It is not unusual for the friends of students who are being abused to come to a counselor or teacher. Reports of such situations require the same sensitivity and attention that other serious issues demand, including contact with parent/guardian(s) and appropriate referrals. These cases may also require the involvement of law enforcement personnel.

Interpersonal violence

One in three teenagers experience dating violence (www.acadv.org/dating .html), and a number of teens are also raped or sexually assaulted by either an acquaintance or a stranger.

COMPETENCY 2
DIVERSITY AND MULTICULTURALISM

SKILL 2.1 Special Needs, Individuals and Developmental Variations

Any given child's developmental path is never as tidy and consistent as theory and therefore does not always fit into ordered patterns. This is an important concept when considering theories, stages, and developmental milestones.

The differences in children and their rate of development are influenced by the experiences they have and the environment or culture in which they live. Basic differences in caregiver style and availability, the quality of nutrition, and the presence or lack of trauma and violence in the environment all affect children's development. Socioeconomic status, gender, language acquisition, basic cognitive

Stage theories and lists of developmental milestones need to be considered as markers to guide the observer, not absolute standards within which all children will neatly fit.

ability, and heredity are other factors that influence children's development, behavior, and perspective on the world, as do ethnicity and race.

School counselors and other professionals need to be aware of developmental theories and milestones. Such knowledge provides a background against which they are better able to determine if a child or adolescent is developmentally delayed or needs assistance in reaching his or her full potential. However, the uniqueness of each individual should also be perceived and valued when assessing a particular child's developmental status.

Special Populations

Although every student has special needs because he or she is an individual, there are some students who, by virtue of birth or life circumstance, belong to a group with specific needs. Again, as noted previously, not all children and adolescents who belong to a certain group will necessarily fit a description or profile of group characteristics, because each student is an individual. For example, a particular girl may express a learning style more commonly associated with boys.

However, for the purpose of alerting school counselors to issues their students may face, particular factors may be of concern to selected populations.

Migrant worker families

- Chronic disruption in living circumstances and education, resulting in significant gaps in learning

- Social isolation

- Inadequate nutrition and medical care

- Bias due to stereotyping

- Stress due to the problems noted above as well as economic hardship

Immigrant families and those for whom English is a second language

- Loss of homeland and extended family

- Difficulties with learning, socialization, and peer-group acceptance due to language limitations

- Bias due to stereotyping

- Post-traumatic stress due to precipitating events that prompted immigration and/or losses associated with relocation

Homeless families

- Multiple losses and traumas and related post-traumatic stress
- Disruption in living circumstances and education, resulting in significant gaps in learning
- Inadequate nutrition, sleep, and medical care
- Underlying anxiety due to chaotic and/or unpredictable environment
- Absenteeism for various reasons

Families displaced due to catastrophic events (such as hurricanes)

- Multiple losses and traumas and related post-traumatic stress
- Disruption in living circumstances and education
- Lack of social network and extended family support
- Sudden change in economic circumstances

Families living in poverty

- Chronic stress due to economic hardship and challenging life circumstances
- Inadequate resources for special events at school (field trips, testing, dances, sporting events, etc.)
- Inadequate nutrition and medical care
- Absenteeism due to the need to attend to pressing family matters

Gifted and talented students

- Boredom, which may lead to behavior problems
- Need for special services and/or creative programming
- Bias due to stereotyping

Learning support and special education students

- Increased need for appropriate attention and support from faculty and staff
- Specific accommodations during standardized testing situations
- Need for evaluation, special services, and/or creative programming
- Bias due to stereotyping

Emotional support students

- Presence of significant mental health issues

- Increased need for appropriate attention from faculty and staff, including consultation with other professionals, evaluation, referral, and follow-up

- Specific accommodations during standardized testing situations

- Need for special services and/or creative programming

- Bias due to stereotyping

Sensory-impaired students

- Specific accommodations for various classroom activities, as well as during standardized testing situations

- Increased need for consultation with other professionals and, at times, need for evaluation, referral, and follow-up

- Need for special services and/or creative programming

- Bias due to stereotyping

SKILL 2.2 Creating Positive School Environments

The school counselor can be instrumental in facilitating the positive school environment.

A fundamental task for all schools in addressing diversity issues is creating a positive environment within which all students are respected and can thrive. While the school counselor or the guidance department cannot achieve this goal alone, counselors need to be alert to the ways in which they can help establish positive school environments and can often be instrumental in effecting healthy changes.

Characteristics of Positive School Environments

Positive school environments share these qualities:

- Respect, integrity, cooperation, and care for one another are core values

- Adults strive to be caring, competent, and "in charge" without abusing their power and authority

- Clear and direct communication is valued, practiced, and taught

- Student success is measured not only by academic achievement but also by students' physical, mental, social, and emotional health

3 2

- Stereotyping and bias are avoided but diversity is acknowledged and valued

- There is an attitude of "we are all in this together" rather than an "us versus them" mentality, including a sense of partnership with parents/guardians and the community

- There are opportunities for students to get to know and work with students who are different from them

- Sexual harassment and other forms of harassment and bullying are not allowed

- Conflict resolution, problem-solving skills, and violence prevention programs are built into the curriculum

- Policies and procedures are proactive and preventive in nature, including but not limited to crisis management planning and the creation of a safe school climate

These qualities should exist across the entire school community. In positive school environments, the values and characteristics described above are present among the student population, the staff, the faculty, and the administration, as well as between the students and the adults in the school. Ideally, these qualities are also present at the school board level and in all interactions with parents/guardians and community members.

SKILL 2.3 Bullying, Stereotyping, and Prejudice

Bullying behavior often indicates a lack of respect for diversity. A number of factors lead to bullying behavior. Stereotypes and prejudice are major contributors, along with personal characteristics and life experiences of the bullying student. These may include poor social skills, distorted self-perceptions, problems with aggression and impulse control, and previous victimization experiences.

Increasingly, schools are finding they need to take action to address stereotyping, prejudice, and bullying among students.

Certain characteristics and personality traits of other individuals may serve as magnets for prejudice and stereotyping. Some of these characteristics are based on membership in a specific group such as gender, race, ethnicity, religion, physical ability, sexual orientation, and age. Stereotypes abound in our culture regarding these characteristics, and they are frequently brought into the school setting and used as the basis for teasing and bullying.

However, such stereotypes are not the only source of bias. Anything that makes a person different in the eyes of the perceiver—anything out of the "norm"—can trigger ridicule, ostracism, hate, and violence. Some of these perceptual biases are:

- Attractive versus unattractive people

- Thin versus obese individuals

- Effeminate males versus virile males

- Masculine females versus feminine females

- "In" group versus "out" group (i.e., "cool" versus "not cool")

The presence of difference, in and of itself, is not a problem in the larger world or the school setting. In fact, in a positive school environment, such differences are acknowledged and appreciated. The important issue, however, is the way individuals who are perceived as different are treated, and how that treatment affects the social and emotional wellbeing of the targeted individuals.

There is evidence to suggest that this type of stereotyping directly affects a student's self-esteem. Stereotyping and its effects can begin as early as the first time a child enters school and may continue throughout life.

As a result of excessive teasing or bullying, the targeted individual may:

- Believe there is something wrong with him or her and consider himself or herself a "loser"

- Develop emotional problems connected with the perceived inferiority

- Manifest a lack of motivation and desire to excel, with an attitude of "it doesn't matter what I do as I never do anything right"

- Display personality problems

- Begin to feel that life isn't worth living and contemplate suicide

- Begin to harbor thoughts of violence against the perpetrators of the perceived insult

- In extreme cases, carry out an act of violence against himself or herself or others

If not educated to accept differences among people, the perpetrator of the stereotyping, prejudice, or other bullying activities is likely to:

- Escalate the activity

- Enlist others to engage in the activity

- Become firm in their belief that the targeted individual is undesirable

- Feel superior to the targeted individual or groups and justify his or her actions

- Become resistant to changing attitudes and incorporate them into a way of life

- Resort to violence after justifying the violence in his or her mind

A good Web site for students as well as teachers and counselors on bullying prevention can be found at:

www.stopbullyingnow .hrsa.gov/index.asp

Programs to combat stereotyping, prejudice, and biases should be part of the school curriculum. Although the labeling of entire groups of people is irrational, the school must respond rationally and create programs to address these issues. Students can be taught to respect the rights of others through programs of cooperation and conflict resolution.

SKILL **Aggression, Violence, and Conflict Resolution**
2.4

School Violence

In 2005, the Centers for Disease Control and Prevention did a national survey of high school students' risk behaviors and reported the following information in relation to school violence:

- 13.6 percent reported being in a physical fight on school property in the twelve months preceding the survey

- 18.2 percent of male students and 8.8 percent of female students reported being in a physical fight on school property in the twelve months preceding the survey

- 29.8 percent of students reported having property stolen or deliberately damaged on school property

- 6.0 percent did not go to school on one or more days in the thirty days preceding the survey because they felt unsafe at school or on their way to or from school

- 6.5 percent reported carrying a weapon (gun, knife, or club) on school property on one or more days in the thirty days preceding the survey

- 7.9 percent reported being threatened or injured with a weapon on school property one or more times in the twelve months preceding the survey

We are all familiar with the school shootings that occur once in a while. However, the above data reflect the equally troubling and perhaps more relevant facts regarding everyday violence in schools. A major factor contributing to violence in schools is the acceptance of violence as a "normal" reaction to perceived injustices. Easy access to guns and other weapons and the effect of both drug abuse and the way the drug culture permeates the larger culture also may contribute to school violence.

In the school setting, administrators, teachers, counselors, and support staff have the responsibility to make the school a safe place for all students. Clear policies

To see the CDC survey, go to this site:

www.cdc.gov/ncipc/dvp /YV_DataSheet.pdf

Media depictions of violence may convey a perception that violent retaliation is "normal" and common.

that delineate safety and guide behavior are useful in working toward this goal. Policies should articulate appropriate behavior on school property and at school events with regard to the following topics, as well as others:

- Weapons
- Homicidal and/or suicidal intent
- Use of drugs and alcohol
- Self-harm

- Sexual harassment
- Bullying
- Violent threats

However, policies are not enough. Preventing violence and resolving conflicts in interpersonal relations are fundamentally related.

Conflict Resolution

Programs of violence prevention must be accompanied by programs of constructive conflict resolution so that students can learn methods of positive interactions with others, including those who are different. Not only do these programs help create a safe environment in the schools, but they also teach students the skills to resolve future conflicts in their careers, families, and communities as adults. A program of violence prevention and conflict resolution acknowledges that, while destructive and violent conflicts may be out of control in our society, we can strive to minimize them in any particular school, home, or other setting.

The conflict resolution program should:

- Create an atmosphere of cooperation

- Have a component of peer mediation training that teaches negotiation, mediation, and arbitration skills to students and teachers

- Include units in academic classes on methods of negotiation, mediation, and arbitration

Active violence-prevention programs include:

- The elimination of weapons in school by metal detectors, random locker searches, and appropriate personnel to monitor open school areas

- A law enforcement presence on property surrounding the school for monitoring and enforcement purposes

- Training programs for faculty and staff so they are better able to recognize and intervene before and during violent confrontations

- A system for identifying students who are or are at risk of becoming perpetrators of violence and referring them to behavior modification, anger management, or other appropriate programs

- The creation of a district task force to identify and address the causes of violence in the school district

- Effective policies addressing violent behavior and a program that assures student protection if students feel they are in danger

- Counseling and/or referral for students traumatized by violence

Bullying and violence prevention resources are available at:

www.cdc.gov/ncipc/dvp /YVP/YVP-data.htm

www.mentalhealth.samhsa .gov/15plus/aboutbullying .asp

www.safeyouth.org /scripts/topics/school.asp

COMPETENCY 3
COUNSELING APPROACHES AND TECHNIQUES

SKILL 3.1 The Scope of the School Counselor's Role

The number of guidance activities that the counselor provides for students can be quite extensive, depending on the expectations of school administrators, the specific job requirements in a particular school setting, and the interests and temperament of the counselor. Some guidance departments divide tasks such as coordinating all testing, serving as liaison with military and college recruiters, and being the contact person for the local vocational high school among counselors. In other districts, school counselors may function in all areas of guidance, even in more than one school and/or level (i.e., elementary, middle school or junior high, and high school).

Tasks of the School Counselor

The major tasks of the school counselor are to be a guide and an advisor for students and a conduit of information on various topics. The counselor's role often constitutes a kind of "connective tissue" among students, teachers, parents/guardians, and the administration. This is loosely referred to as "counseling."

The school counselor's role in personal counseling may vary significantly from one school district to the next. Some districts expect the school counselor to provide ongoing counseling in varied formats as well as crisis intervention and referral. Others limit the work of the counselor to very short-term work, focused primarily on the identification of problems with subsequent referral to community resources.

Each counselor needs to clarify the scope of his or her work with the head of the department and school administrators.

Except in specialized schools or alternative education programs, most counselors in a school setting are not in a position to provide in-depth mental health counseling. The demands on counselors are many, and the school environment cannot provide the kind of intervention and support some students require. Effective short-term counseling with referral for mental health evaluation by qualified personnel in the community often best meets the needs of students. Community agency clinicians or private practitioners in the area should provide ongoing therapy. Early identification of substance abuse and mental health concerns followed by collaboration with parent/guardian(s) and appropriate outside referrals can be key functions for school counselors.

Educational and career counseling generally fall within the purview of the school counselor's role. Other counseling tasks may involve short-term, target-specific psycho-educational groups such as anger management or interpersonal skill development, as well as crisis and/or grief counseling in the event of a death or other trauma in the school community.

Regardless of the extent of a counselor's work in counseling students, there is general agreement that school counselors should not be in the position of school disciplinarian. While there may be an occasion when the counselor must "write up" a student for a disciplinary problem, as would any faculty or staff member, disciplinary matters should routinely be handled by someone outside of the guidance department. Serving as a disciplinarian can undermine trust and interfere with counseling relationships.

Counselors need to be able to earn and maintain the trust of students; if students don't feel safe with counselors, they are unlikely to seek help from them or disclose sensitive information to them.

Individual Counseling

In many school settings, short-term individual counseling is the most common form of intervention. This modality can be utilized spontaneously as problems arise. Furthermore, it is not limited by the scheduling confines of group counseling. The counselor can tailor the interventions to the particular student's needs and make the most of each session. Drawing on varied techniques, the school counselor can respond to immediate situations as well as longer-term issues in individual counseling, helping the student effect change in his or her life.

Sometimes, a school counselor may engage in short-term (one to three sessions) counseling with a student, and then determine that the student needs a more intense level of intervention. At this point, a referral for therapy can be made to a community agency or private practitioner. The school counselor's role then shifts to one of follow-up and support. This role is important and should not be seen as less substantial but rather one of changed focus. The student may continue to rely on the counselor as a touchstone and source of information and reassurance, which often allows the outside therapy to be more productive than it might be otherwise.

Major Counseling Theories and Approaches

In Skill 1.1 we addressed several major human development theories that also include counseling approaches and techniques. The theories detailed below are intended to augment the information in Skill 1.1.

Cognitive-Behavioral Therapy

In cognitive-behavioral therapy, clients explore reasons for their behavior by understanding their thoughts. They are also encouraged to look at the ramifications of their behavior on themselves, others, and the environment in which they live and function.

One of the major approaches in the field of cognitive-behavioral therapy is rational emotive therapy (RET), also referred to as rational emotive behavior therapy (REBT). Albert Ellis developed rational-emotive therapy and is effectively the grandfather of all cognitive-behavioral therapies. He believed that the concepts of insight and awareness into childhood events do not result in the resolution of present emotional dysfunction. He also theorized that the connection between the past and the present was not explored fully in psychoanalytic theories.

The key concept in RET holds that even though emotional malfunction is rooted in childhood disturbances, individuals continue to reinforce their irrational and illogical thinking. Emotional problems are the result of irrational beliefs that need to be challenged in order for the individual to resolve the emotional reaction.

The A-B-C approach to personality is the basis of RET therapy: A = activating event, B = belief system, C = consequences. RET stresses action and practice in combating irrational and self-delusional ideas. The thinking and belief systems of the client are considered the basis for all personal problems. RET techniques include directed, time-limited, structured approaches for treating depression, anxiety, and phobic behavior. Further developments of cognitive-behavioral theory are Aaron Beck's cognitive theory and Donald Meichenbaum's cognitive-behavior modification theory.

Donald Meichenbaum developed a cognitive-behavioral theory that has three phases:

1. Conceptual: clients are instructed to monitor their own behavior in order to identify negative thoughts and feelings

> *The key concept in RET holds that even though emotional malfunction is rooted in childhood disturbances, individuals continue to reinforce their irrational and illogical thinking.*

> *Focusing on the client's inner speech is a technique used in cognitive-behavior modification theory.*

2. Rehearsal: clients create new internal systems by substituting positive thoughts and feelings

3. Application: clients apply more effective coping skills to real-life situations

Similarly, Aaron Beck emphasized the assumption that clients' conversations with themselves play a major role in their behavior. He theorized that the way people feel and behave is based on the way they view their experiences. The therapy is short-term, active, focused, and insightful. Beck's concept of automatic thoughts is the idea that certain events trigger emotional responses.

The goal of therapy is for clients to recognize and discard self-defeating thinking and correct erroneous beliefs. It has been applied particularly to the treatment of depression. The techniques used in all cognitive-behavioral therapies are derivative of the above theorists and are tailored to the needs of the client. Any method that works can be used, though there is a bias toward approaches with empirical validation.

> RET is directive, persuasive, and confrontational in contrast to cognitive therapy, which emphasizes dialogue to discover misconceptions.

- Cognitive techniques include disputing irrational beliefs, homework, humor, and the changing of language to a more positive approach.

- Emotive techniques include imagery, role-playing, and shame-attacking procedures.

- Behavioral techniques include operant conditioning, self-management, and modeling.

Contributions and limitations of cognitive-behavioral therapy

Contributions of cognitive-behavioral therapy include:

- Counseling tends to be brief and focused on outcome

- Practice and experimenting with new behaviors are emphasized

- The therapy stresses the client's ability to control his or her experience of the world

- It is easily used with clients who are action oriented and willing to accept responsibility for their difficulties

- The therapy can be effectively employed in crisis situations

Limitations of cognitive-behavioral therapy include:

- The underlying reasons for irrational beliefs are not explored, leaving the client open to incorporate additional different irrational beliefs into their belief system

- The dialogue aspect of the therapy does not lend itself to working with clients of low intelligence

- There is the danger of the therapist imposing his or her views on the client, with the potential for psychological harm

- Emotional issues are not explored, which may limit the effectiveness of the therapy in the long run

Key terms in cognitive-behavioral theory and therapy

- A-B-C Model: The construct stating that one's problems do not originate from events but from the beliefs one holds about those events; changing one's beliefs is the best way to change negative feelings.

- Arbitrary Inferences: The distorted view of making conclusions without the basis of supporting and relevant evidence; part of Aaron Beck's cognitive therapy.

- Automatic Thoughts: Ideas (usually outside one's awareness) triggered by a particular event that lead to emotional reactions.

- Cognitive Errors: Misconceptions and wrong assumptions on the part of the client.

- Cognitive Homework: The process used to help a client learn to cope with anxiety and challenge irrational thinking.

- Cognitive Restructuring: The process of replacing negative thoughts with positive thoughts and beliefs.

- Cognitive Therapy: A type of therapy focused on changing negative behavior by changing false thinking and beliefs.

- Collaborative Empiricism: A concept from Aaron Beck's cognitive therapy that views the client as capable of making objective interpretations of his or her behavior, with the collaboration of the therapist.

- Coping Skills Program: A set of procedures to help clients cope with stressful situations by changing their thinking.

- Disputational Method: A method taught to clients in RET to help clients challenge irrational beliefs.

- Distortion of Reality: Inaccurate thinking that causes the client to act irrationally, emotionally, and subjectively.

- Internal Dialogue/Inner Speech: The process used to recognize irrational thoughts.

- Irrational Belief: An unreasonable thought leading to emotional problems.

- Labeling and Mislabeling: The distorted view of basing one's identity on imperfections and mistakes made in the past.

- Musturbation: The word used by Albert Ellis to describe beliefs grounded in musts, shoulds, and oughts; a rigid and absolute way of thinking.

- Overgeneralization: The distorted process of forming rigid beliefs based on a single event and then applying them to subsequent events.

- Personalization: The tendency of individuals to relate events to themselves when there is no basis for this connection.

- Polarized Thinking: A cognitive error based on an all-or-nothing framework; there are no gray areas in polarized thinking.

- Rationality: A way of thinking that will help clients attain their goals.

- Role playing: The process of helping a client work through irrational beliefs by practicing new behaviors.

- Selective Abstraction: The distorted view of forming conclusions based on an isolated detail of an event.

- Self-Instructional Therapy: The concept that the self-talk an individual indulges in directly relates to the things he or she does in everyday life. The therapy consists of training the client to modify self-talk, a form of cognitive restructuring or cognitive-behavior modification developed by Donald Meichenbaum.

- Shame-Attacking Exercises: A technique of RET encouraging the individual to do things about which he or she feels shame without believing he or she is foolish or without becoming embarrassed.

- Stress-Inoculation Training: A cognitive-behavior modification technique aimed at giving the client the coping tools to restructure the thoughts that lead to stress and to rehearse the behavior changes in order to solve the emotional problems caused by stressful situations.

Existential Therapy

Existential therapy evolved as a reaction to the theories of psychoanalysis and behaviorism. Existential theory differs from the psychodynamic and behavior theories in its fundamental presumptions about the nature of human beings. Psychodynamic theories are based on a deterministic view of human nature; they see personal freedom controlled by irrational actions, past occurrences, and the unconscious. The behaviorists believe that freedom is restricted by societal forces.

Existentialists believe the early theorists did not take into account all aspects of human nature. By concentrating on external objective factors, the psychodynamic theorists and the behaviorists ignored the internal frame of reference and subjective experiences of the individual. Existentialists concern themselves with questions of freedom, responsibility, and choice and the meaning of reaching one's full potential.

This philosophical basis suggests that people must create their own meaning through their choices in a world that is fundamentally meaningless and lonely; the individual must explore what it means to be fully human. The assumption is that we are free and therefore responsible for our actions and the results of those actions and choices.

Some of the early European existentialists were Ludwig Binswanger, Karl Jaspers, Medard Boss, and Viktor Frankl. Contemporary figures are Rollo May and Irvin Yalom. Their work is based on the work of philosophers Dostoyevsky, Heidegger, Nietzsche, Sartre, and Buber.

Viktor Frankl expounded the theory of logotherapy, which literally means "healing through reason" (logic). In developing this approach, Frankl was influenced by the earlier European existentialists. Logotherapy is designed to help people find meaning in life through their experiences.

Irvin Yalom wrote *Existential Psychotherapy*, a central text in the field, in which he addresses the core issues that make up existential theory—isolation, meaninglessness, freedom, and death—in the context of the therapeutic relationship and process.

Rollo May is responsible for converting the European philosophy of existentialism into American theory and practice. He focuses on the subjective aspects of the therapy and believes that freedom and responsibility go hand in hand, with freedom requiring us to accept responsibility for who we become.

This theory requires an intellectual and philosophical approach on the part of the therapist. Existentialist-based therapy is relationship-oriented, experiential, and philosophical. It does not have a set regime of techniques but allows for incorporation of techniques from other therapies. The general approach is to focus on four major concerns of human existence: freedom, isolation, death, and meaninglessness.

The basic goals of existentialist therapy are to help clients become aware that they are free to make choices to improve their experience of daily life. Clients are encouraged to see past and future choices, to accept the responsibility of their choices, to recognize the factors that hinder their freedom to choose, and to experience an authentic existence.

> *For more information on existencial psychotherapy, see:*
> www.existentialpsychotherapy.net

> *The basic goals of existentialist therapy are to help clients become aware that they are free to make choices to improve their experience of daily life.*

Concepts of existential therapy

There are six concepts to which existential therapists ascribe:

1. **We are capable of self-awareness.** The expansion of this awareness, a basic goal of the therapy, is to increase our perception of the freedom to choose and to act on those choices.

2. **We are free beings and must accept the responsibility of that freedom** to decide our own fate. Although we did not choose to be in this world, how we live here and what we do with our lives are our own choices. Each choice we make creates who we are. Whatever the set of circumstances, it is our attitude that determines how we approach a situation and how we survive it.

3. **In preserving our uniqueness, we know who we are** through our relations and interactions with others. Our awareness of this individuality makes us better able to lead an authentic lifestyle.

4. **The meaning of our lives and existence is always in a state of fluidity** as we continue to create ourselves through our actions. These actions are the result of our own choices, and we are not victims of forces beyond our control.

5. **Anxiety is a normal state.** It is part of the human condition, an emotional recognition of one's vulnerability and the responsibility of choosing in an uncertain world without any guarantees. Anxiety is the result of a person's awareness of his or her aloneness. It is not a sickness, but rather a growth enhancer to motivate us to change conditions that have become intolerable.

6. **Awareness of death** is a human condition that gives meaning to living. Being aware of our ultimate death is the impetus for us to live our lives to the fullest. Life has meaning because it is not forever. The question is not how long we live, because we all will eventually die, but how we live that life, which creates meaning for our everyday existence.

The focus of existential therapy is:

- To confront the reality of being in the world alone and facing the anxiety of this isolation

- To understand one's subjective world

- To revise the assumptions arising from one's subjectivity

- To make choices that lead to the living of an authentic life

The approach is not based on curing sickness or solving immediate problems, but on utilizing the inherent knowledge of life experiences to live a fuller and more authentic existence.

Contributions and limitations of existential theory

Contributions of existential theory include:

- The client–therapist relationship is based on the humanity of the individual.

- The theory addresses the major concerns of healthy individuals as they go through their life cycles by concentrating on issues important to attaining life satisfaction.

- The model allows for the inclusion of many other modalities within the larger philosophical framework provided by existential theory. In other words, psychodynamic explorations and cognitive-behavioral techniques may be employed as part of the therapy.

Limitations of existential theory include:

- It lacks a systematic procedure.

- The concepts can be difficult to comprehend and require a particular orientation and effort on the part of the therapist.

- No scientific research has been done on the model.

- Lower-functioning clients, clients in crisis who need immediate direction, and nonverbal clients may not be able to benefit from a philosophical and intellectual approach to problem solving.

Key terms in existential theory

- Aloneness: A natural human condition from which we can derive strength to become free; when mastered, we will have the ability to stand beside others to lend them support in their own aloneness

- Anxiety: The experience we have when we realize we are not immortal, that we face constant choices in an uncertain world, and that we are fundamentally alone

- Authenticity: The ability to be true to our own ideas of a meaningful existence and to accept responsibility for the conditions of our lives, which are a result of the choices we have made

- Authorship: The concept that we create our own life situations, problems, and destinies

- Awareness: The freedom to choose and act on our choices
- "Bad Faith": The inauthenticity of not accepting the freedom to take responsibility for our own actions
- Existential Guilt: The result of the feelings we have when we permit others to shape our lives and make our choices
- Existential Neurosis: Feelings of despair resulting from a failure to make our own choices
- Existential Vacuum: A condition of emptiness and depression that results from a meaningless lifestyle
- Existentialism: A philosophical movement that stresses individual responsibility for creating one's own ways of behaving, thinking, and feeling
- Freedom: The ability to be responsible for our own destinies and accountable for our own actions
- Logotherapy: A branch of existential therapy developed by Viktor Frankl that challenges clients to search for meaning in life
- Meaninglessness: The fact that there is no inherent meaning in living, and it is up to us to create our own system of meaning
- Phenomenology: A method used in therapy to utilize subjective experiences as a therapeutic focus that is used in many existing theories
- Restricted Existence: The condition of functioning with a limited awareness of self and the inability to define the true nature of the problem
- "The Courage to Be": Our ability to live to our fullest capacity, rather than living within the constraints of what others expect; also, the ability to accept limitations and confront the feelings of emptiness that come when we are making new choices

Person-Centered Therapy

Rogers believed all people have a "formative tendency," or inner energy, which propels us toward fulfillment and self-actualization.

The founder of person-centered therapy is Carl Rogers. In the early 1940s, Rogers created the "nondirective counseling" approach. Later he was involved in advocating for the encounter group movement and was a pioneer in the humanistic approach to counseling. He was opposed to the therapist acting as the expert whose advice dictated what the client needed to do to be well. He felt that clients have the ability to become more fully functioning "self-actualized" people.

This theory rests on the assumption that individuals have internal resources to work toward wholeness and self-actualization if properly supported and encouraged. Person-centered therapists believe clients can move forward constructively on their own. The focus is on understanding the feelings and thoughts expressed by the client from the vantage point of the client's subjective world. The theory emphasizes the personality and attitude of the therapist/facilitator, rather than concentrating on techniques (although the skills of active listening and reflecting are most often used).

This approach is a "way of being rather than a way of doing." Positive attitudes and behaviors on the part of the therapist create a climate of growth that not only reaches, but surrounds, the client. This helps create an aura of "personal power"—or the awareness of one's own feelings, needs, and values—which is subsequently sensed by others and facilitates effective functioning.

The success of the therapy depends on the therapist maintaining this climate as the major tool for facilitating positive outcomes for the therapy. In this environment, the client begins to drop defensive attitudes and concentrates more on meaningful goals, leading to positive and appropriate actions. Eventually the client uses the learning acquired in the safe environment of the therapy and applies it to relationships outside the therapeutic setting. The focus is on experiencing and perceiving the immediate moment as an opportunity for change.

> *The therapist's role is to create an atmosphere of empathy, acceptance, warmth, and caring—an environment of unconditional positive regard.*

Characteristics of person-centered therapists

Three characteristics of the therapist lend themselves to creating the atmosphere needed for client self-actualization:

1. Genuineness is the goal of person-centered therapists: being aware of their feelings and attitudes, their shortcomings, and their humility. They do not hide behind a professional demeanor, but align themselves with the person being counseled.

2. Unconditional positive regard is a positive, nonjudgmental acceptance and caring attitude on the part of the therapist.

3. Empathic understanding is the ability to accurately sense the feelings and meanings of the client and to express these feeling and meanings so the client understands that the therapist is truly attuned to the client.

> *For more information, literature, and training options, contact the Association for the Development of the Person-Centered Approach at:*
>
> *www.adpca.org*

Contributions and limitations of person-centered therapy

The contributions of person-centered therapy include:

• The relevance of the therapist as a person breaks from more traditional forms of therapy and offers a more accessible model for some clients

• It is a relationship-centered therapy instead of a technique-centered therapy

- While the therapist assumes responsibility for creating an environment that is conducive to the client's success, the responsibility for the direction of the therapy lies with the client

- The theory concentrates on a person's need to account for his or her inner experiences and has relied on research to validate the concepts, practices, and approach

- The theory inherently respects individual differences and therefore is very amenable to culturally competent therapy

The major limitation of this approach is the personal limitations of the therapists themselves. Limitations may include:

> *The major limitation of this approach is the personal limitations of the therapists themselves.*

- There can be a lack of genuine empathy. The therapist may hold stereotypes about certain clients that make it difficult for the therapist to have positive regard, warmth, and acceptance for them.

- The inability of the therapist to practice appropriate self-disclosure can be a problem. A person-centered approach requires that the therapist have the capacity to self-disclose but also maintain boundaries. Finding this balance and being genuine requires a high degree of self-awareness and self-control on the part of the therapist.

- Temperamentally, a therapist may not be well suited to the person-centered approach. The therapist may not listen well or may make assumptions too readily. The therapist may also be anxious to solve problems rather than understanding the problem to be solved and having the capacity to allow the process of change to unfold.

- The therapist may lack the belief that the client can change behavior, thus creating an atmosphere conducive to failure.

- Person-centered therapy is not effective with people in crisis situations who are looking for immediate problem-solving strategies.

Key terms in person-centered therapy

- Accurate Empathic Understanding: The therapist's ability to sense the client's inner world (i.e., the client's subjective experience)

- Congruence: A state in which one's own experiences are accurately represented by one's self-concept; inner experience matches external expressions; also refers to the genuineness of the therapist

- Facilitato: The role the therapist takes in person-centered therapy

- Genuineness: A state of authenticity resulting from self-analysis and a willingness to accept the truth of one's identity

- Humanistic Psychology: A movement emphasizing freedom, choice, values, growth, self-actualization, spontaneity, creativity, play, humor, and psychological health

- Nondirective Counseling: A type of counseling that assumes the client is the one who knows what is best and should not be in a passive role; the therapist permits the client to lead the counseling

- Incongruence: The discrepancy between self-concept and ideal self-concept; usually results in anxiety, which can serve as a clue to the existence of a problem

- Internal Source of Evaluation: The process of looking to oneself for answers to problems

- Personal Power: The sense of strength that comes from knowing oneself and one's ability to mobilize energy; the therapist's ability to access his or her own personal power facilitates the client's development of personal power

- Self-Actualization: An inner growth force leading to the development of one's potential and the basis of clients being trusted to resolve their own problems in a therapeutic relationship

- Therapeutic Conditions: The necessary conditions of the therapeutic relationship, which allow the client to change, including therapist congruence, unconditional positive regard, and accurate empathic understanding

- Unconditional Positive Regard: The acceptance of the client's right to all of his or her feelings without conditions imposed by the therapist

Gestalt Therapy

Frederick Perls is considered the founder of Gestalt therapy. Erving and Miriam Polster were key figures in the development of Perls' concepts. The theory stresses the "here and now" and focuses on bringing together the parts of the personality that are not integrated into the whole person. It also focuses on the "what and how" of behavior as well as the role unfinished business from the past plays in preventing the individual from adequately functioning in the present. The most frequent cause of unfinished business is resentment. Other sources of unfinished business are avoidance, guilt, anger, grief, and other feelings that remain unresolved.

Five layers of neurosis

Perls's theory includes the following five layers of neurosis:

1. The phony layer: acting as others wish us to act, playing games

2. The phobic layer: avoiding the confrontation of who we really are

3. The impasse layer: the sense of deadness or foreboding doom

4. The implosive layer: fully experiencing our deadness

5. The explosive layer: releasing phony roles to experience a feeling of relief

Gestalt therapy is, in part, derived from existentialist therapy.

Gestalt therapy is, in part, derived from existentialist therapy. Some of the major concepts of the therapy are:

- Accepting responsibility for being in the here and now

- Becoming aware of the present moment (itself a therapeutic process)

- Facing issues of avoidance

- Dealing with impasses

- Dealing with unfinished business from the past

Clients are expected to be active in their own therapy, to do their own interpreting, and to grow through personal contact. Gestalt therapists emphasize the awareness of personal contact at our boundaries with the world via our senses. This awareness is necessary for growth and change. The client resists contact by a variety of methods such as introjection, projection, and retroflection.

The goals of the therapy are:

- To challenge the client to develop methods of self-support in order to replace the environmental support system presently in effect

- To become more aware of the "here and now" and the self

- To recognize the parts of the self that have been denied

- To assume ownership and responsibility for this denial

The focus is not on the techniques of the therapy, but on the therapist as a person in the role of helping the client make his or her own interpretations.

For more information about Gestalt theory and therapy, including access to key journals in the field, see:
www.gestalt.org

The techniques of the therapy are to intensify direct experience in the moment. Clients role-play and experiment with different scenarios to gain greater awareness of their inner conflicts and to intensify their experiences. In the role-playing aspects of the therapy, the therapist asks the client to play out all the roles experienced in a dream sequence, for example, in order for the client to better understand the dream. An empty chair may be placed in front of the client as a device to facilitate the expression of feelings.

Contributions and limitations of Gestalt theory

Contributions of Gestalt theory include:

- This approach can de-emphasize the intellectualization of the client's problems by focusing on the here-and-now experience of interpersonal contact

- It lends itself to brief therapy due to the intensity of the client's experiences

- It utilizes dreams and unfinished business from the past in order to understand current problems

- The theory can be applied to group counseling, school and classroom problems, and workshop settings as well as individual counseling sessions

Limitations of Gestalt theory include:

- It does not give much credence to cognitive factors, nor does it emphasize the importance of empathy and positive regard for the client

- It can become a technique-oriented theory with the potential for the therapist to misdirect the course of the therapy for the sake of the techniques

- The therapist can slip into autocracy, assuming the role of director rather than facilitator

- There is a lack of empirical research to validate the theory

Key terms in Gestalt therapy

- Aboutism: The tendency to speak about an incident in the past in contrast to speaking about the same incident in the present

- Avoidance: A technique used by clients to keep from facing unfinished business, feeling uncomfortable emotions, and having to make changes in their lives

- Awareness: The process of exploring one's thoughts, feelings, and actions

- Blaming Games: A technique used by clients to avoid taking responsibility for their growth, to avoid staying in the "now," and to prevent themselves from the pain of experiencing the "here and now"

- Boundary Disturbance/Resistance to Contact: A technique practiced by individuals who attempt to control their environment; it can have both negative and positive consequences

- **Confluence:** The blurring of awareness of the difference between oneself and the environment

- **Confrontation:** The act of becoming aware of differences between verbal and nonverbal expressions, feelings and actions, and thoughts and actions

- **Contact Boundary:** The interface, or point of contact, between an individual and the world around him or her, including other people

- **Deflection:** The process of distraction or inattention, which makes it difficult to sustain contact

- **Dichotomy/Polarity:** A split in which a person experiences opposing forces

- **Explosive Layer:** The mode of releasing the pretenses of phony roles in order to achieve a sense of relief and release

- **Here-and-Now Awareness:** The ability of the client to realize what he or she is experiencing in the present moment

- **Impasse:** The point at which the client is stuck in a stage of less than full maturation; it may be accompanied by feelings of deadness or impending doom and a wish to avoid threatening feelings

- **Implosive Level:** The mode in which one allows oneself to fully experience one's deadness or inauthenticity; it leads to the chance to make contact with one's genuine self

- **Introjection:** The acceptance of others' beliefs and standards without analyzing, assimilating, and internalizing them

- **Modes of Defense:** The five layers of neurotic avoidance: the phony, the phobic, the impasse, the implosive, and the explosive

- **Phobic Layer:** The mode of avoiding the emotional pain that comes with recognizing one's real self

- **Phony Layer:** The mode of reacting to others in stereotypical and inauthentic ways, or playing games

- **"Play the Projection":** A technique used to help clients see how they project things they do not want to recognize in themselves onto others

- **Projection:** Disowning parts of ourselves by blaming them on the environment

- **Resistance:** Defenses one develops that prevent full experience of the present

- Retroflection: Turning back to oneself what one would like to do or have done to others
- Unfinished Business: Unexpressed feelings (such as resentment, guilt, anger, and grief) from childhood that are presently preventing effective psychological functioning

Reality Therapy

William Glasser developed the concept of reality therapy in the 1950s and 1960s. Originally, the approach emphasized individual responsibility. In the 1980s, Glasser expanded this concept to a theory of control. Control theory emphasizes doing and thinking. It attempts to explain why and how people behave from the point of view of the subjective internal perception of their world. Glasser posits the purpose of behaving the way we do is to eliminate the discrepancy between what we presently have and what we want.

Control theory is also based on the assertion that we are in charge of our lives, we choose our forms of behavior, and that behavior is intended to increase self-esteem and a sense of belonging and to attain power and freedom. The therapy focuses on exploring ways to effectively manage our world so we can get what we want without hurting others in the process.

The purpose of reality therapy is to help clients achieve a satisfying, effective existence. The challenge in therapy is to examine how clients are presently functioning in order to improve that functioning. The therapy is short term and designed to help people develop a "success identity" by meeting the four psychological needs of belonging, power, freedom, and fun.

The therapist expresses concern, support, and warmth to the client. While the therapist is involved with the client in a positive way, he or she does not accept excuses for inappropriate behavior and continuously prods and pushes to help the client accept reality and responsibility for his or her actions. The client is expected to take responsibility for deciding what goals to pursue and committing to those goals, to make value judgments about his or her current behavior, to plan a specific course of action for future success, and to make a commitment to carry out those plans in everyday life.

The WDEP model

The WDEP MODEL is the procedure applied in the practice of reality therapy.

> Control theory emphasizes doing and thinking. It attempts to explain why and how people behave from the point of view of the subjective internal perception of their world.

> Reality therapy does not dwell on the past, the unconscious, or the role of insight or take into consideration the process of transference. Its goal is to help clients acquire skills to take control of their lives, better cope with life's demands, and solve present-day problems.

WDEP MODEL: the procedure applied in the practice of reality therapy

WDEP MODEL		
W	Wants	Through questioning by the therapist, clients are able to express their wants, needs, and perceptions of what is happening in everyday life
D	Doing	The therapist explores what clients are doing and what direction they are taking in their behavior to fulfill those wants and needs
E	Evaluation	The therapist encourages clients to evaluate their behavior patterns that help or do not help fulfill those needs and wants
P	Planning and Commitment	The therapist invites and encourages clients to plan for behavior change and commit to that change

Glasser originally used his therapy working with youthful offenders, but the theory of control has been successfully used in individual, marital, family, and group counseling; in alcohol and drug abuse clinics; and with students, teachers, and administrators.

Contribution and limitations of reality theory

Contributions of reality theory include:

- Clients are responsible for evaluating and changing their behavior.

- The client is the catalyst in making specific plans, forming contracts for action, and evaluating the success of these actions.

- The emphasis is upon accountability. No excuses for failure are accepted, but blame and punishment for not carrying out the stated changes are avoided. Instead, the focus is on what prevented the client from carrying out the plan of action and the readjustment to a more reasonable plan of action.

- There is a structure to evaluate the degree and nature of the changes affected.

- It is a short-term, clear, and easily understood therapy that is applicable to different situations and clients, some of whom may not usually be receptive to other therapy approaches.

Limitations of reality therapy include:

- Consideration is not given to feelings, the unconscious, or the past.

- The influence of the culture and environment of the client is not taken into consideration when looking for alternatives to the maladjusted behavior. The focus is on symptoms. The origin of the behavior is not taken into account.

- There is a lack of research on reality therapy to establish its effectiveness.

Key terms in reality therapy

- Autonomy: The acceptance of responsibility and taking control of the direction of one's life; a state of maturity

- Commitment: The ability on the part of the client to continue with a reasonable plan to effect the desired change

- Control Theory: A theory of why people act the way they do; the internal motivation to master one's own world

- Involvement: The role of the therapist with the client in reality therapy, a vital part of establishing a relationship with the client

- Paining Behaviors: The manifestation of pain symptoms, such as depression, to refocus the problem on the symptoms instead of the behavior

- Perceived World: One's subjective world

- Picture Album: The perceived reality of the client, formulated to meet his or her psychological needs

- Positive Addiction: The acts performed to gain psychological strength, such as physical activity and meditation

- Responsibility: The dependable manner in which we satisfy our needs without interfering with the rights of others

- Success Identity: The level of self-esteem needed to carry out the actions deemed necessary for attaining a more satisfying life experience; the end result is that the individual is able to give and receive love, has a sense of self-worth, and possesses the strength to create a satisfying life

- Total Behavior: The sum of all our activities that forms our personality and the person we have become

- Value Judgment: The evaluation of current behaviors to determine their value

- WDEP Model: The abbreviation for the components of reality therapy: the identification of **w**ants, the **d**irection of behavior, the **e**valuation of self, and the **p**lan for change

Solution-Focused Therapy

Solution-focused therapy was developed by de Shazer and Berg in recent years. The theory is based on work by various family therapists and the work of Milton Erickson. It is considered a brief therapy model, sometimes only comprising one session, which lends itself well to many guidance situations.

The core of solution-focused therapy lies not in the "why" but the "how." Theorists of this approach argue that the past cannot be changed, so therapy should focus on how the client can create a more satisfying future.

This model asserts that when clients come to counseling they have a picture of what they would like to be different about their lives and often have the answers to their problems. By providing a constructivist process, the counselor facilitates the process by helping the client define the problem, identify viable solutions, and plan to work toward the desired behavior or reality.

Guidelines

Walter and Peller identified the following guidelines for making therapeutic choices:

1. Don't bother with what works. Make a determination to do more of it. Success can only be maximized.

2. Build on small successes.

3. Experimentation is encouraged. Just because something was not solved in the past does not mean that what was tried is the only possible solution.

4. Change is about the "here and now." Make the most of the current session.

Effective goal setting is critical to the success of solution-focused therapy.

A major focus of the work involves the counselor asking a range of questions to help draw out possible solutions. The solution-focused counselor first asks about the goal the client is hoping to achieve and is not dissuaded or discouraged if the client replies, "I don't know." The counselor empathically reframes these initial questions in order to solicit a goal. Effective goal setting is critical to the success of solution-focused therapy.

The counselor facilitates the client's desire for change by asking what would be different if, after a night of sleep, the undesired behavior or situation had changed. The client is then engaged in the creative process of constructing a vision of positive behavioral difference or success. The counselor uses the vision as a framework upon which to define a solution.

Other questions are used to help the client identify desirable outcomes. The counselor's job is to reflect the answers in ways that help the client better understand his or her strengths and skills as well as the nature of the problem. By the end of the session, the counselor assigns the solution as homework to practice before the next session. The success of the applied solution can be reviewed in a following session, if there is one.

Contributions and limitations of solution-focused therapy

Contributions of solution-focused therapy include:

• Therapeutic work is accomplished in relatively few sessions.

- Counseling is focused on the reality of the client and is not dependent on the client's interpretation of past experience.

- Clients are empowered to make changes by how they envision themselves through magical thinking.

- The work is solution focused, not problem focused.

Limitations of solution-focused therapy include:

- Long-term and personality-based issues cannot be resolved by finding a solution.

- Problems are overgeneralized and oversimplified without in-depth consideration of the level of impact on the client's reality.

- More empirical research on the effectiveness of solution-focused therapy needs to be conducted.

Key terms in solution-focused therapy

- Coping Questions: A series of questions the counselor uses to help the client identify previously unrecognized coping skills and strengths

- Exception-Seeking Question: A way to help clients discover the times when the identified problem does not trouble them

- Miracle Question: A technique wherein the counselor encourages the client to imagine what it would be like if the problem he or she is facing were suddenly gone

- Scaling Questions: A tool where clients rate the problem according to varying degrees of severity in order to set goals and facilitate change

---

SKILL
3.3
Effective Communication Skills

Effective communication is essential to the school counselor's ability to do her or his job successfully. The need to listen and respond well cannot be overstated.

Equally important is the modeling that effective communication provides to students. Good role models are invaluable to students of all ages. When the school counselor shows students how to pay attention to others, express ideas and opinions, make suggestions, and ask questions clearly and respectfully, the counselor is teaching skills that students can use throughout their lives.

Good communication is not only important in order to meet the needs of the students, but also to enhance the functioning of the guidance department and the school's capacity to respond to student needs.

Elements of Effective Communication

The essential elements of effective communication are:

- Listening attentively without interrupting

- Responding in ways that ensure the speaker knows that she or he has been heard, including the expression of direct appreciation and validation of the speaker's views

- Articulating ideas, opinions, observations, and questions clearly and directly

- Seeking clarification rather than making assumptions about what the speaker is saying

- Maintaining an attitude of respect at all times, paying attention to things such as word usage, tone of voice, facial expressions, and other nonverbal behavior

- Working to manage one's emotional reactions so they don't interfere with good communication (e.g., not taking others' comments personally)

Listening skills

Listening is a highly subjective and selective activity. Listening is not just hearing words but also grasping the meaning the speaker wishes to impart. The meaning of the words spoken and how they are interpreted depends on the subjective world of both the speaker and the listener.

Some barriers to good listening include:

- Hearing what you want to hear, not what is actually said

- Not hearing what is said at all due to one's own need to speak; waiting for the speaker to finish so we can speak causes us to think about what we are going to say instead of listening to what is being said

- Biased listening: forming an opinion about the value of what is being said and therefore discounting the meaning of the words

- Allowing our emotions, either negative or positive, to interfere with our ability to listen

- Allowing both internal and external distractions to get in the way

Effective listening

Good listeners consistently and accurately understand the speaker's meaning by using their listening skills together with their thinking processes.

Effective listening not only involves tuning in to the words of the speaker, but also perceiving his or her tone of voice, nonverbal cues, and the emphasis given to the words.

Lyman Steil developed the SIER model, which includes four stages of listening:

1. *Sensing*, or attending to a stimulus

2. *Interpreting*, or assigning meaning to incoming information

3. *Evaluating* the message by forming a judgment about what is heard

4. *Responding* to the message

To be a good listener:

- Create a positive atmosphere by being alert and attentive and concentrating on the speaker.

- Make eye contact and maintain an expression of genuine interest.

- Allow the speaker to finish a thought before responding.

- Avoid critical judgments in your responses.

- Make an effort to remember what has been said.

- Avoid changing the subject unless there is a really good reason to do so. When you must change the subject, explain the reason to the speaker.

- Be as physically relaxed as possible because relaxed posture communicates that you have time to listen and are interested.

Responding skills

There are a number of ways that you can respond to a speaker to indicate that you have heard what he or she is trying to say. If you have listened well and thoughtfully to what the person is saying, your response will be appropriate, you will give good feedback, and the speaker will know that you have heard what was said.

To respond appropriately to a speaker:

- Clarify the meaning of what the speaker said by checking assumptions you have made while listening to be sure you understand the speaker.

- Continue to maintain eye contact as you give feedback.

- Keep anger and other emotions out of the interaction. Try to express your feelings in a non-threatening way.

- Help the speaker with problem solving by responding positively and asking good questions.

- Directly express your appreciation for the speaker's ideas, even if you disagree with them. You can address disagreements more effectively once you have thanked the speaker for sharing his or her ideas.

- Be physically alert and use appropriate body language.

These Web sites offer useful tips on listening and responding skills:

www.taft.cc.ca.us/lrc/class
/assignments/actlisten
.html

crs.uvm.edu/gopher/nerl
/personal/comm/e.html

www.psu.edu/dus/cfe
/actvlstn.htm.

- Reflect the speaker's feelings back to him or her.

- Summarize the speaker's major ideas and concepts for further clarification.

- Use verbal and nonverbal reinforcers (such as head nods) to let the speaker know his or her message has been received.

- Maintain a comfortable social distance.

- Give constructive feedback: feedback that is descriptive, not evaluative; offered, not imposed; and focused on behavior rather than on personal characteristics. Pay attention to the timing of feedback as well.

SKILL 3.4 Communicating Information to Students

The major task of the counselor in the school is communication: with the students, the parent/guardians, teachers, school administrators and support staff, other professionals, people in the community, and sometimes even members of the media. The primary client, however, is the student.

Keeping information confidential—within the limits of the need for parental notification and other school policies—is essential to building trust.

The ability to create rapport and meaningful relationships with students and others is the sign of an effective counselor. When the counselor has the trust of the student, the student is much more likely to listen to and act on the counselor's suggestions. Keeping information confidential—within the limits of the need for parental notification and other school policies—is essential to building trust.

If the counselor does not keep information confidential, trust is destroyed, and it is harder to help the student grow and mature. Trust is built up gradually. In order to facilitate trust, information given to the student must always be true, accurate, and timely. The counselor must be a visible presence in the school and be available to students. There are many ways to make contact with students, both formally and informally. When an atmosphere of accessibility is created, students will be much more inclined to contact the counselor in times of need and crisis.

Newsletters

Monthly newsletters to a student's home inform the student and the parent/guardian about counseling and guidance issues. Newsletters can contain deadline dates for national exams, dates of specific college visitations, notices of aptitude and school-generated exams, scholarship deadlines, workshops about financial aid, and other items of interest. If the principal or other school administrator sends out a monthly bulletin, a section of that newsletter could be set aside for guidance news.

Homeroom and Classroom Visitations

Visiting homerooms is an efficient way for counselors to get to know students. Students can also ask questions or be reminded of issues they may wish to discuss with the counselor. Visiting the classroom is also a means of disseminating information directly to students. For example, when it comes time to schedule the high school students for the following year, visiting the homeroom (or other classes such as social sciences) creates an opportunity to share the course schedule and other information efficiently.

> It is helpful for students to see counselors in various settings throughout the school so they don't associate the counselor only with problems or trouble.

Individual Interviews

Much of the real work of counseling occurs in the individual interviews the counselor holds with the student. These interviews should occur on a regular basis, although this may be challenging when the counselor's caseload is high.

At the high school level, freshmen and seniors should be scheduled as soon as possible within the first month of school. For freshmen, the interview is a chance to get acquainted and find out if there are any adjustment problems; for seniors, the discussion serves to inform them about post-secondary training and college application deadlines, tests needed for entrance to college, and other plans for post–high school activities. The initial interviews with freshmen can also help create the basis of trust needed to help students with future problems.

Dissemination of Forms

Each school has systematic ways to distribute necessary information to students. This information might include applications for national exams and local and state scholarships as well as other guidance-related material. Some schools utilize the homeroom setting; others send this information home with individual students or give it out in individual interviews.

> Quite often the counselor has access to a large group of students during a study-hall period or in the cafeteria. A study-hall situation may offer an ideal chance for answering questions about testing and other issues students wish to discuss.

Intercom Announcements

Announcements over the school intercom system are an excellent way to remind students of guidance and other activities that are occurring on a specific day. They are also a means of informing students of upcoming activities and deadline dates.

Informal Chance Meetings

It is important that the counselor get out of the office during the school day to meet students in areas they frequent during their time at school. The cafeteria, the hallways, and the student lounge are all places the counselor can meet students, ask how they are doing, remind them of specific issues, and make appointments for meetings.

SKILL 3.5 Merits and Limitations of Group Counseling

Both group and individual counseling require the counselor to have knowledge of the theoretical basis of counseling. All major counseling theories can be applied to both situations. During group counseling, the theories take on a more social nature. The theoretical method chosen depends on the orientation of the counselor, the needs of the client(s), and the goals of the counseling process.

Merits of Group Counseling

In a group situation, members have the ability, in a safe and non-threatening atmosphere, to test their attitudes and beliefs against those of the other members of the group. They can receive feedback and discover how others view them. The group setting can also be a support system for its members and can be particularly important when members have no other means of emotional support. Through group counseling, they can achieve some of the goals of becoming emotionally involved without the threat of rejection.

A counseling group is made up of various members of society and thus can be a representation of the client's outer world—the world outside the counseling room. Members can experiment with various styles of interaction with other people in a contained, managed environment. They can then transfer these techniques and behaviors into real-life situations. Members of the group can, as they process the observations of the group and their own reactions to others, get a better idea of who they want to become, as well as a better understanding of their own behavior.

A counseling group is made up of various members of society and thus can be a representation of the client's outer world—the world outside the counseling room.

For the counselor, the advantages of groups include the ability to reach more clients, to become familiar with different populations of the school community, and to become more aware of current trends in youth culture.

An excellent resource on all aspects of group counseling is:

The Theory and Practice of Group Psychotherapy *by Yalom and Leszcz (2005)*

Limitations of Group Counseling

There may be a tendency to view group counseling as a quick, easy solution when, in fact, the counselor may find that the workload required for preparation increases in proportion to the number of members in the group. Often, individual members need different theoretical approaches as well as extended follow-up.

For more information about group counseling, see:

www.agpa.org/guidelines /factorsandmechanisms .html

Some people function poorly in a group situation. For one reason or another they cannot accept the group's perceptions and fall further into a psychological "funk." Some may find the group setting threatening in spite of the counselor's efforts to create a safe environment.

The personalities or acute life circumstances of some individuals may prevent them from making changes in their lives. They might use the group to justify their present status and therefore might not gain from the group's insights.

Group Dynamics

Understanding group dynamics is based on knowledge of the psychological and social forces inherent within groups. These forces operate in all human interactions. Over the last fifty years, the concept of group dynamics has become more developed, and there are a number of different definitions of group dynamics.

Different Concepts of Group Dynamics

One definition states that group dynamics is a political ideology built on the concept of the organization and management of the group. It emphasizes democratic leadership, equality of membership in decision making, and the benefits of group interaction to both society in general and to the individual group members specifically. Critics of this definition say the emphasis on the group is a method of operating rather than a way of understanding the goals and purpose of the group.

A second definition is derived from the techniques used in group processes. Some of these techniques include role-playing, observation and feedback from group members, the decision-making process, and the concept of "buzz sessions." This type of group process was developed at the National Training Laboratories (www. ntl.org), among other places.

A third definition encompasses the entire field of research and application concerning the nature of groups, the history of their development, and their interrelations with individuals, other groups, and established institutions. This is the most accepted definition of group dynamics at this time, with a focus on human behavior and relationships.

Application of Group Dynamics

School counselors have many opportunities to utilize knowledge of group dynamics. In the classroom setting, in group counseling, and in understanding the dynamics of peer groups, counselors can draw on ideas about how groups affect individual students' behavior.

Always being mindful of the power of groups to affect individuals can be an asset in many school counselor functions.

Groups naturally progress through several stages of development. Different models describe different developmental pathways, although they often show the following pattern:

- Meeting and coming together

- A struggle for power and acknowledgement of differences

- Overcoming the differences to allow intimacy and to work together

- A process of individuals differentiating from the group

- Members moving on and ending or leaving the group

All groups tend to develop patterns of communication and role distinction. These patterns tend to be emotionally charged with regard to conflict. These patterns may or may not be healthy, but awareness of them is commonly a part of the group process.

Attending to the power dynamics operating within the group, including the overt or stated leader as well as the informal or unstated leader, is important and informative. Different group members may exhibit power in different arenas at different points in time.

SKILL 3.7 Similarities and Differences of Career Development Theories

Classification of Career Development Theories

There are five different classifications or methods of approach into which most major career counseling theories fall:

1. The trait-factor theories assume there is a direct relationship between an individual's interests and abilities and vocational choices. When interests and abilities are matched, the individual has found his or her future vocation. Interest inventories, aptitude tests, and the general field of vocational testing have been generated from this theory.

2. The societal circumstances of career choice theory contends that circumstances of society beyond the control of the individual are the contributing factors in career choice. In this theory, the only control the individual has is learning to cope with his or her social environment.

3. Developmental (or self-concept) theories hold that as an individual grows older, self-concept changes along with the view of the reality of

his or her vocational choice. The satisfaction derived from the chosen career is based on the individual's self-concept and the relation of that self-concept to the vocational choice.

4. The personality and vocational choice theories are based on the concept that people with similar personalities choose the same types of vocations. The needs of like personalities are the same, and therefore like personalities will select the same vocations to satisfy those needs. The research done in this area has studied individuals who are already in a specific field as the norm group; their personalities are compared to those wishing to enter the field.

5. Environmental behavioral theories incorporate elements of the societal circumstances and personality theories into a classification system that observes the relationship between the interaction of individuals in the environment and their behavior.

Key Concepts of Career Development Theories

Most theorists in career development borrow from each other in formulating their theories. Some of the key concepts of the most enduring theories are discussed below.

Bordin, Nachmann, and Segal developed a framework for vocational development using psychoanalytic theory as their base. Using the occupations of accounting, social work, and plumbing, they attempted to generalize a system that might be used to classify occupations into areas of psychoanalytic dimensions.

Ginzberg, Ginzberg, Axelrad, and Herma developed a theory that vocational choice is divided into three stages:

1. The fantasy period is characterized by the lack of reality of the child in vocational choice. Any idea of vocational choice is based on the child's imaginings and interests.

2. The tentative period is characterized by a shift from the child's interests as the child becomes aware that he or she has more capacities in one area than another. The child then begins to consider these abilities when thinking about vocational choice.

3. As children become older they begin to consider the value or satisfaction they get from some activities more than from others, and in the final stage, they begin to incorporate all of these subdivisions into the transition period and move into the realistic period. This period leads to the exploration stage, when all the elements of the transition period are incorporated,

with the added insight of what is feasible for the individual. These results come together in the crystallization stage, which finally leads to the stage of specification, when the individual chooses a specific occupation. The theory is based on the general concepts of developmental psychology.

Holland's theory of vocational personalities and work environments is based on the individual's adjustment to six occupational environments and the interaction of those environments with the personality of the individual.

These six occupational environments/personality types are described as follows.

Realistic individuals deal better with things than with ideas or people, are oriented toward the present, and value tangible things such as money, power, and status. They avoid dealing with subjectivity and intellectualism and lack social skills. They are persistent, mature, and simple. These people are in engineering, technical fields, skilled trades, and agriculture.

The investigative person thinks, organizes, understands, and copes with problems intellectually. Investigative people think of themselves as intellectuals and scholars and tend to avoid interpersonal relationships. Their achievement is in academic and scientific areas. They hold less conventional attitudes and are found in occupations related to math and science.

The social personality seeks satisfaction in therapeutic situations and is skilled in close interpersonal relations. Social people are sensitive to the needs of others. They are involved in teaching, understanding others, helping others by using their verbal and social skills for behavioral changes, and are optimistic, scholarly, and verbally oriented. They are found in the helping occupations.

The conventional personality values rules and regulations, has a great deal of self-control, is neat and organized, and needs structure and order. Conventional people think of themselves as conforming and orderly. They identify with power and status but do not necessarily aspire to obtain those things for themselves. They follow orders well. They are found in accounting, business, and clerical vocations.

Enterprising individuals are skilled verbally but use these skills for manipulation and domination and aspire to obtain power and status. They are aggressive, self-confident, verbal, and social. Political, leadership, and power roles are important to them, and they aspire to obtain these roles. They are found in sales and supervisory and leadership positions.

Finally, the artistic personality relates to others through artistic expression, dislikes structure, and relies on feelings and imagination. Artistic people think of themselves as intuitive, introspective, nonconforming, and independent. They value artistic qualities and are not interested in politics. They relate through the use of their artistic abilities. They are found in the arts, music, literature, and other creative occupations.

Roe developed the concept that every individual inherits certain ways of expending his or her energy. This, combined with childhood experiences, results in a style that manifests itself in vocational choices. She draws on the needs theory of Maslow as well. The concept of genetic disposition, needs theory, and the influence of childhood experiences and innate style combine to form the basis of vocational choice.

Super's theory of vocational behavior is based on the development of a vocational self-concept. This theory emerges from developmental psychology and behavior theory in relation to self-concept. Super proposes that people express their self-concepts by entering occupations they perceive as allowing self-expression. Individuals behave in ways that enhance their self-concept; different behaviors occur as a result of one's present stage of life development. As an individual matures, the self-concept becomes stable, but external conditions contribute to the way that self-concept is expressed vocationally.

Super explored the developmental life stages of the individual in reference to vocational behavior. These stages are similar to Ginzberg's classifications. They include crystallization, specification, implementation, stabilization, and, finally, consolidation. The adolescent is in the explorer stage, in search of a career direction; the young adult seeks job training; and the mature adult finds a vocation and secures a position.

Tiedman and his colleagues saw career development as a result of the developing self. The components of his theory include situational, societal, and biological factors. The decision-making process involves anticipation, implementation, and adjustment. This sequence is characterized by an initial level of disorganized thinking about vocations, followed by clearer thinking, and, finally, evaluation of the advantages, disadvantages, and values of each vocation. Teidman believes the career decision-making process evolves from the relationship between work and non-work activities.

Similarities Among Career Development Theories

There are many similarities among the career development theories:

- Most of the theories are constructive; they describe the nature of the relationship between the person and vocational choice.

- The theories are generally descriptive rather than explanatory.

For more information on Maslow's Hierarchy of Needs, see:
http://webspace.ship.edu/cgboer/maslow.html

- There is a great similarity in their explanations.

- The research has not been experimental. Rather, these theories sort by group and predict vocational choice based on characteristics of each group.

- Most of the theories have roots in personality theory.

- The theories are generally simple and uncomplicated.

Differences Among Career Development Theories

There are also differences among the theories:

- Each of the theories states a particular set of objectives the individual is trying to accomplish through vocational choice

- Some theories have sufficient empirical data to support them and others have little empirical support

- There is a difference in when the most significant experiences for career development occur and what the critical sources of influence are

- The role of aptitudes is given various degrees of influence on career choice by the different theorists

- The role of family influence on career choice is treated with varying degrees of importance

Generally, the similarities among the theories are greater than the differences. They emphasize the same types of critical periods in career development and have their roots in personality theory. The differences lie in the choice of emphasis, the research methods appropriate for use in each theory, and the degree to which the relationships between various events occur.

SKILL 3.8 Decision Making and Career Development

Theories of Decision Making

H. B. Gelatt, in 1962, advocated "a totally rational approach to making decisions." Since then, he has changed his view of decision making to one that includes flexiblity, keeping an open mind, and using one's intuition. His definition of decision making is "the process of arranging and rearranging information into a course of action."

The three parts of Gelatt's decision-making process are:

1. Obtain the information that forms the basis for making the decision. All information is biased by the fact that it is always changing and by the intentions of the sender of the information.

2. Arrange and rearrange this information by being flexible and having knowledge of your individual needs.

3. Make a choice. Try to be rational, but if the decision seems irrational, have a good reason for making that decision.

> The decision making process is used in all stages of career development. Although it is a continuous process, there are critical points that occur in the selection of an entry-level job, a change of job, or a change in educational plans.

Tiedman and O'Hara have noted that career choices are made by decision-making processes that are subjective and depend on the comprehension and control of the person making the decision. Their model tries to make the individual aware of all factors involved in making the decision so the individual can make choices based on knowledge of himself or herself and all the external factors involved.

They describe a decision-making process that is divided into two phases: the anticipation phase and the accommodation phase. Each phase has several steps.

Anticipation phase

The anticipation phase of the decision-making process has four steps:

1. In the exploration stage, the individual investigates all educational, occupational, and personal alternatives. He or she identifies interests and capabilities and considers the relationships among them and the alternatives suggested. The counselor provides support and teaching experiences related to the method of exploration and provides career information.

2. In the crystallization stage, the individual organizes, evaluates, synthesizes, and orders the personal information and the alternatives from the exploration stage. Ideas about possible career choices are formed and stabilized. The counselor helps with the organization, evaluation, and synthesis of the information. Free discussion of issues and options continues to take place.

3. In the choice stage, the individual makes a choice based on the information gained in the crystallization stage, with the consequences of the choice as part of the process.

4. In the clarification stage, the individual forms and carries out a plan to implement the choice. The counselor continues to supply information, support, and feedback about the implementation of the choice.

Accommodation phase
The accommodation phase has three steps:

1. In the induction stage, usually during the first months of the implementation of the choice, individuals come to understand the reality of the choice they have made. They begin to learn what is expected and required of them.

2. In the reformation stage, individuals work out the realities of the choices they have made, become more comfortable with those choices, and begin to rely less on the support and advice of the counselor.

3. In the integration stage, individuals integrate their identities with those in the chosen setting and experience a sense of equilibrium.

Counselors should provide the information and resources to help individuals use that information so an intelligent choice can be made. The counselor should also help individuals improve upon and perhaps learn different decision-making strategies. Ultimately, once the necessary tools and resources are obtained, the decision is the responsibility of the individual.

> *Because decision making is a product of one's personality and values, it is important for the individual to have experiences that contribute to his or her emotional maturity, self-concept, and values.*

SKILL 3.9 Student Appraisal Data Relevant to Career Development

Career development is a continuing process. It involves the evaluation of assessment results throughout the life span of an individual. Reflecting this concept, career counseling has grown from a trait-factor, counselor-dominated process to a developmental, client-centered process. This approach views assessment as a tool to increase self-awareness at every major transition period of the individual.

> *For more information and resources from NOICC, go to:*
>
> *www.ed.gov/pubs /TeachersGuide/noicc .html*

Career Development Objectives
The role of assessment in career development counseling has been recognized as important by the National Occupational Information Coordinating Committee (NOICC), a federal interagency program, by establishing national guidelines for student and adult career development competencies.

At the elementary school level, a career development objective might be increased self-awareness in relation to the world of work. This might entail the identification of personal interests, abilities, strengths, and weaknesses as well as learning to value the benefits of education. Students could describe school activities that might help them be successful in a job and identify academic skills needed in specific occupations of interest to the student.

At the middle school level, a career development objective might be to measure student preferences in different areas and their influence on the student's positive self-concept. This might involve the student's describing his or her likes and dislikes and understanding the benefits of education in terms of career opportunities. The student should learn about his or her strengths and weaknesses in school subjects, the requirements and skills needed for present and future occupations, the importance of academic and occupational skills in the working world, and the relationship of aptitudes and abilities to occupational groups.

At the high school level, it is important for the student to understand the relationship between educational success and work requirements, the role a positive self-concept plays in the world of work, and how individual characteristics relate to achieving life goals. At this level the student should be able to describe the relationship between academic and vocational skills and their own personal interests, ability, and skills as well as how they can apply their own skills to present and future occupational needs.

Vernon Zunker, with influence from other theorists, has established a model for the use of assessment results in developmental career counseling. He describes four major steps: analyzing needs, establishing the purpose of testing, determining the instruments to be used, and utilizing the results in decision making for training and education.

Assessment Results in Career Counseling

There are four steps for using assessment results in career counseling:

1. Analyze needs: A needs analysis should be conducted using biographical data, interviews, and educational and work records. The cooperation and participation of the individual in establishing his or her needs is important for the success of the results. To assist the counselor in identifying needs, a counseling relationship must be established to help the student articulate his or her needs. The acceptance and adoption of the student's views will enhance the relationship and help in exploring his or her views in relation to realistic career goals. The lifestyle needs of the individual should be part of the needs assessment in order to relate the world of work to the student's

values, recreational requirements, financial needs, family responsibilities, and societal obligations. The specific needs of the individual for assessment should then be examined. A decision should be made regarding the need for an assessment instrument.

2. Establish the purpose of testing: After the needs analysis is completed, the counselor and student should determine the purpose of testing. Testing can be used for diagnosis, prediction, and comparison of individuals with a normed group. Testing does not always meet all needs that have been identified. The purpose of testing can be specific, as in predicting success in an education or training program, or more general, as in establishing an overall direction for career exploration. The counselor should explain the purpose of each test to be administered as well as the desired results in relation to the stated needs.

3. Determine the instruments to be used: Tests to be used for career assessment should measure ability, achievement, career maturity, interests, personality, and values. Achievement tests measure academic strengths and weaknesses. Career maturity inventories measure vocational development in reference to self-awareness, planning, and decision-making abilities. Interest tests compare the individual's interests with reference groups. Personality and value inventories reflect traits that influence behavior. Any of the test results can stimulate interaction between the counselor and the student about the relationship between work satisfaction and the actual work.

> *Any of the test results can stimulate interaction between the counselor and the student about the relationship between work satisfaction and the actual work.*

4. Utilize the results: The counselor and the student use the results of the assessments to discuss the unique individual characteristics of the student and their relation to career exploration. The test results are also used to help students view themselves as whole people. Individual traits and characteristics are used to determine plans for the present and to look toward the future.

SKILL 3.10 Strategies for Developing Employability Skills

Attitude and Motivation

When students succeed in their studies, they are eager to continue their education. They are also more likely to understand the relationship between the acquisition of education and their future lifestyles. When students do not succeed, it is difficult for them to see the value of education and how it relates to their future. When basic survival is demanding the student's attention and the student does poorly in school, the tendency to drop out of school or to engage in illicit profit-able activities, such as crime and drug dealing, has a fatal attraction.

Counselors can help students facing these challenges to marshal resources to cope with life, as well as help them learn to defer present wants and needs (and peer pressure) in order to receive enhanced rewards at a later date. These students may need specific support with academic achievement such as tutoring or special classes.

Exposure to role models who have escaped from poverty and/or crime is impor-tant for some students. Persuading such role models to mentor unmotivated students and providing satisfying educational opportunities in the school may help students explore their potential more fully. Innovative programs can be found by using the resources of the community and the school and enlisting the coop-eration of parents. Grant monies may also be available to implement programs for unmotivated students in some settings.

Another method of motivating students to acquire employable skills is to engage community businesses in making a commitment to employ students who adequately prepare themselves for entrance into the job market of the sponsoring business or industry. Apprenticeships, internships, and supervised employment while still in school, as a requirement for graduation in a particular area, will encourage students to acquire the skills needed to go from high school graduation to a job that is waiting for them.

> *Throughout a student's high school career, the opportunity to relate subject matter to career and job opportunities should be included in the curriculum of each subject. Job fairs and other types of exposure to job requirements should be presented to students at every opportunity.*

When students have incentives they are more likely to work at acquiring the math, English, science, and technical skills that employers require. They will also work at studying other subject areas in which they are not as interested in order to obtain the requirements needed for graduation. When they are working in satisfying positions, they have a concrete opportunity to see the need for future education; they may also be able to get their tuition paid for by their employer.

Skill Development

Helping students develop skills in various arenas can also be central to school and subsequent career success. Three important skill areas are delineated here: decision making, studying, and job seeking.

Developing students' decision-making skills

The school counselor's role is to help students understand the decision-making process, not to make decisions for students. This need is particularly acute for adolescents who are facing many life choices. Supporting students actively as they approach decisions and teaching decision-making skills can help the student

> *An example of the need for good decision-making skills is the case of a senior who has received multiple offers from colleges and is uncertain about which offer to accept.*

minimize the chance that the impact of any one decision causes irreversible harm to the student's present or future.

Elementary and middle school counselors may not face the same demands as high school counselors regarding student decision making. However, helping students with decisions regarding school projects, elective courses, and extracurricular activities, for example, can facilitate better decision making at the high school level and prepare students for employment and post-secondary education.

Decision-making steps

The process of decision making can be broken down into the following steps:

1. Define the problem clearly

2. Formulate goals of ideal, acceptable, and unacceptable outcomes

3. Delineate all possible options, including the option of making no decision at all

4. Explore the barriers to all options

5. Explore the consequences of eliminating one or more options

6. Narrow the options down to manageable choices

7. Make an informed decision based on the manageable choices

Describing these steps to students and helping them with the practical application of these skills can be extremely helpful. Decision making is best learned incrementally. Therefore, developmentally appropriate opportunities to make decisions at all educational levels results in adolescents who are more competent at making good choices.

Developing students' study skills

Actively teaching study skills to students can be effective in enhancing cognitive development. Efficient ways of studying have been researched by psychologists and others; this research has yielded methods of studying that help students retain information and learn in a more organized manner.

Some students naturally study well, and others need help with focus and organization.

The following suggestions are the result of this research:

- Make a schedule and stick to it. Study at a certain time each day.

- Find a place that is comfortable, that suits your individual learning style, and that is consistently available and convenient.

- Have all the materials you need in one place before starting work so study will not be interrupted.

- Study every day in order to develop the habit of knowing how to study when it is really needed.

- Keep an accurate and comprehensible notebook in case you need to refer to it.

- Keep a careful record of assignments. Use a calendar to record the due dates of all projects.

- Use shortcut devices for retaining information such as flash cards, self-tests, or "cover cards," which succinctly detail the material to be retained. Repeat the material orally.

- Take good notes that list the main points of the material.

- After learning the material, continue to study to "over-learn." This helps you retain the material for a longer period of time.

- Review frequently after learning the material for the first time.

Developing students' job-seeking skills

Helping students develop the skills they need to seek and secure a job is also critical, particularly at the high school level. While some of these skills may be taught directly by the school counselor, collaborative efforts with teachers in English, the social sciences, and other disciplines may be most productive. These teachers can incorporate skill development opportunities into the curriculum, with input from the guidance department.

Some of the areas that may be included are:

- Résumé writing

- Filling out job applications

- How to read the want ads

- How to search online for jobs

- Interviewing skills, including how to dress, how to prepare, and appropriate follow-up after the interview

SKILL 3.11 Exploring Education and Career Options

There are many methods of exploring the careers and the educational options open to students. They include computer-generated career inventories, career and educational search materials, and detailed information about specific careers and training requirements. The role of the counselor is to help students gather data so they make intelligent, informed, and realistic choices. This entails providing information in a timely fashion at the appropriate developmental stages and following through with support to help them explore their possibilities.

Computer-Generated Career Inventories and Search Procedures

Computer-assisted advising can be useful to students, counselors, and others involved in helping students with educational and career decisions. CHOICES, of Ottawa, Ontario (Canada) is a commercial system available to help students explore and research different vocational and career choices.

Other career exploration programs include Discover, Career Information Systems (CIS), Coordinate Occupational Information Network (COIN), Guidance Information System (GIS), and Systems of Interactive Guidance and Information (SIGI).

These programs can give students the ability to hone in on the occupations suited to their personalities and fitting their academic achievements and interests. It is the counselor's responsibility to become familiar with various networks and programs and to teach the student how to access the material. It is also the counselor's responsibility to help the student sift through the data and further explore selected occupations through other means.

Career Days

Community resources are always available to aid the counselor in presenting real-life career situations. Organizing career-day programs is a time-consuming activity, but it offers many opportunities for both the student and the counselor. The counselor makes valuable contacts in the community for future jobs for the students, for creating business relationships to help students, and for enhancing the image of the school.

Community business institutions are eager to influence young people to enter their professions in order to create a pool of future applicants. The students gather a wealth of occupational information and can hone in on the areas that interest them most. Students can also make their own contacts and make arrangements with businesspeople for further contact. The counselor should be sure to have a representative from each career cluster in order to draw students of varying abilities and interests.

SHADOWING: the process of spending an extended period of time with a particular person in a field that interests the student as a possible future career

Job Shadowing

SHADOWING is the process of spending an extended period of time with a particular person in a field that interests the student as a possible future career. The student does not have to be fully committed to pursuing this career, but should have narrowed down his or her choices to a few specific careers in order to make the best use of everyone's time. The student should be given a set of rules to follow when choosing to participate and a form to fill out to evaluate the experience.

The community businessperson should also fill out a form before students engage in job shadowing. Questions such as what the business expects to get from the experience, how much time they are willing to spend with the student, and what their general practices are should be included in the questionnaire. The businessperson should also fill out an evaluation after the student has completed the shadowing experience. A bad experience on the part of the community businessperson might mean that this businessperson will not participate in the program the following year, and the counselor needs to know how the process went from the businessperson's perspective.

School-to-Work Programs

One of the best ways to help students develop employability skills is to have them participate in a supervised job experience. Incorporating this activity into the vocational curriculum and awarding high school credit to a student for successful completion would motivate students to participate.

Many students do not understand the importance of appearance and personal hygiene in obtaining and maintaining a job. These are basics that often have to be taught. In addition, many students have an attitude problem that may carry over from school. Students need to understand that negative attitudes are not tolerated in employment situations.

The instructional component of the school-to-work program should contain extensive material for the employer to evaluate the student's attitude, work habits, personal hygiene, and attendance, as well as his or her knowledge of the job and ability and willingness to learn and to be taught. Weekly work evaluation sheets completed by the employee and the employer show both what the student has learned and done well and those areas that need improvement. Many school-to-work programs provide these evaluation instruments.

Such programs convey essential information about effective functioning in the world of work to students. This information includes the necessity of getting to the job on time, avoiding absences for all reasons other than illness, and calling the employer if in the case of illness.

Educational and Vocational Training Opportunities

There are many opportunities for students to obtain work training and education other than pursuing a bachelor's degree. Often these other paths lead to higher-paying positions in areas that are wide open for employment due to a lack of trained personnel. Some of these options include:

- **Vocational education:** Often offered by public or regional vocational centers in daytime, evening, and weekend classes. These classes range from basic entry-level programs to advanced classes to help students develop a

For more information on vocational education, see:

www.directoryofschools .com/North-American -Trade-Schools/Home.htm

variety of skills in fields such as computers, electricity, and plumbing. If a student is of high school age, the program is usually part of the high school curriculum. If the individual is an adult, the cost is usually low or there is an opportunity to obtain financial aid.

- **Community colleges, junior colleges, and vocational/technical colleges:** Most of these schools admit students who might not have the qualifications to enter a four-year institution. This gives the student who is a late bloomer or has not done well in high school a second chance. Classes are scheduled so that individuals who hold full-time jobs can attend. The cost is usually reasonable and financial aid is available. The completion of these programs can lead to an associate's degree, a certificate, a job promotion, or a new career.

- **Private career/proprietary schools:** These for-profit schools offer training in specific skill areas. They are usually more expensive than a public institution, but they have placement facilities. Financial aid is usually available. They are accredited by state and/or national groups.

- **Apprenticeship programs:** These are usually administered through a labor-union industrial council. Forty to fifty occupations are represented, and include both classroom instruction and on-the-job training. Apprenticeship programs range from two to six years. Contacts for apprenticeship programs can usually be made through the state employment office.

- **On-the-job training:** These programs are similar to apprenticeship programs but are of shorter duration and are usually part of a job orientation program for new employees.

- **The Job Training Partnership Act (JTPA):** This is an adult training or retraining program funded by the government and run by a local private industry council (PIC) in localities where there is a need for employment training.

- **Health-related training:** This type of training is usually available at hospitals or hospital-related institutions where there is an opportunity for clinical or field study as part of the formal instruction.

- **Military service:** The military services offer training and continued training in fields that can be used after the individual leaves the service.

A guide to choosing a private career school is Getting Skilled, Getting Ahead by James R. Myers and Elizabeth Warner Scott.

The Reserve Officers' Training Corps (ROTC) program offers students the opportunity to receive up to a full scholarship for four years of study in exchange for an extended time in the military.

SKILL **Application of Counseling Theories and Techniques to a Specific**
3.12 **Situation**

Although a number of students need counseling for emotional issues or have serious issues in their personal life, these problems usually come to the attention of school personnel when the child runs into trouble academically or displays disruptive classroom behavior. Once a student meets with the counselor, problems of a personal nature may be revealed. Addressing these problems within the context of the goal of success in school is part of the counselor's role.

CASE STUDY

In the following case study, a student has been referred to the counselor because of poor performance. We will see what happens in the counseling situation to better understand what is going on with the student and how resolution was achieved.

In October, Donna, a fifteen-year-old ninth grader, was referred to the school counselor because she was failing her first-year algebra course. The teacher did not feel she was capable of doing the work and was suggesting that she drop the course and go into a general math class instead. This would fulfill her math requirement for high school graduation, and she would not be behind one year in math. Donna objected to the move. Her parents wanted her to go to college and general math did not meet the requirements for college entrance. Donna had done well in middle school, earning grades of 80s and 85s in eighth-grade math. Her test scores on diagnostic math tests in May of the previous year, when she was in eighth grade, indicated she performed at a grade level of 9.3.

Donna's mother was contacted by telephone and told of the teacher's concern. The mother felt Donna could do the work, but that she was lazy and did not apply herself. When discussing with Donna her feelings about why she was failing, the counselor found that Donna did not complete her homework assignments; she said that when she ran into problems, she had no way of solving them. When told she could come in after school for additional help from the teacher, Donna said that the days the teacher had designated for extra help were days on which she had soccer practice.

In discussing a plan for Donna to be successful on the next unit exam in three weeks, it emerged that Donna participated in many extracurricular activities. She took dance lessons, participated in multiple sports, and volunteered two nights a week at the local nursing home, reading to elderly patients. She had soccer games on the weekends, and her family visited an ailing grandparent on Sundays. Donna had an older sister in her freshman year in college at a school out of town. Her father owned his own business and was active in local politics, and her mother was a teacher.

It was obvious to the counselor that Donna was juggling too many activities and did not have a block of time to devote to her studies. Although she was not failing any of her other courses, her grades were not high enough for entrance into the college her sister attended, which her parents wanted her to attend. The problem, as the counselor saw it, was that Donna not only wanted to please her parents by participating in all her

Continued on next page

---

extracurricular activities, but her self-esteem and self-confidence were derived from these activities. She enjoyed them and did not want to give them up. She continued to think that she could pass the course simply by passing the final exam in June, which was a school policy.

The counselor decided to use reality therapy with Donna. Donna had a study hall one period a day. She and the counselor decided to use this time for counseling and learning study techniques in the counselor's office. Donna liked this idea because she realized she was not getting any studying done in the study hall because of the disruptive behavior of some of the other students. It was decided that Donna and the counselor would talk for twenty minutes and Donna would do her math work for another twenty minutes. Because Donna did not have the time to see the teacher after school, a student from the honor society would come into the guidance office for twenty minutes every other day to help her study the math. Donna was pleased with this arrangement because the immediate problem of math was being addressed.

In the twenty minutes of counseling time, the counselor focused on Donna's lifestyle. Donna had a need to keep busy every minute, the inability to say no to many of the projects her parents suggested she do after school, and feelings of guilt about her own need to sometimes just do nothing. It was difficult for Donna to accept the fact that she was not able to juggle all these activities and do well in all of them. She also struggled with the reality that she needed to be able to prioritize and think through what she felt was important in her life, rather than relying on her parents to make these decisions for her. As she began to understand and do better in her algebra class, she continued to feel she could still participate in all her activities.

After Thanksgiving, the honor society tutor could no longer help Donna because she needed the time to fill out her own college applications. During the time between Thanksgiving break and winter break, Donna's grades in algebra dropped to failing. Donna began to realize that even though she could do the math work, as evidenced by her ability to raise her grades when she had the tutor, she could not do it and still maintain her present lifestyle. She needed the discipline to sit down and concentrate. She appealed to the counselor for help in resolving this problem. The counselor began to see a shift in Donna's attitude as Donna acknowledged that she needed to change her behavior patterns.

A plan was drawn up for Donna to make time for studying. She decided she would not try out for softball in the spring and would use that time to study and bring her overall grades up. Donna was concerned about telling her parents that she was not going to play softball. A meeting was arranged to present her decision to her parents. At the meeting Donna's parents were surprised and hurt that she had not confided in them. They felt she had been the one who chose to be constantly busy. They did not realize that she felt that her parents demanded the high activity level. The family redefined their goals.

The counselor continued to see Donna throughout the school year. Although Donna and her parents worked at improving her study habits and her priorities, on occasion she slipped, and periodically needed to recommit herself to her original plan. The counselor's support was crucial to Donna's eventual success.

COMPETENCY 4
ASSESSMENT

Assessment can take many forms and serve many different purposes. The primary purpose of appraisal is to assist the counselor in helping students recognize their resources, utilize their strengths, and accept their limitations, whether the focus is academic, social, personal, or vocational. Increasingly, tests are used to measure student performance for reasons other than helping individual students with their educational and career goals. It is the task of the counselor to assist students in using all test results for self-understanding and growth.

Formal Assessment Tools

A variety of instruments are used for evaluation purposes. Formal tools with standardized scoring include tests administered by school counselors and other personnel as well as tests administered by the school psychologist. The school psychologist might utilize intelligence tests which assess the ability to learn, as well as other psychological and aptitude tests in order to determine appropriate placement and develop individualized educational plans when needed.

School counselors, teachers, and others may administer achievement tests (which evaluate how much has been learned), state tests measuring student performance, college entrance and preparatory tests (such as SAT, PSAT, and ACT), advanced placement (AP) tests, and others. These tests, while administered at school, are scored offsite by the testing company that prepares and distributes the tests.

Other formal means of appraisal include inventories that measure aptitude, vocational interests, personality traits, and learning styles. The school counselor or other personnel administering the text often score these tests. Counselors may also use assessment tools designed to hone in on behavioral issues such as the incomplete sentence test, lethality inventories, suicide risk assessments, and depression inventories. These need to be used with caution and only with appropriate background and training.

The value of all informal assessment tools lies in their ability to give the counselor information that can enhance his or her work with students and, in many cases, increase the student's self-awareness.

Informal Assessment Tools

School counselors may find they use more informal means of assessment on a more frequent basis than formal means of assessment. These may involve using some of the inventories mentioned above as discussion tools rather than as formal assessments, behavioral observation of the student in the classroom or other settings, feedback forms developed to evaluate specialized guidance programs, behavior surveys, and needs assessments.

Uses of appraisal

Appraisal can be used for the following purposes:

- To help students recognize and utilize the resources within themselves

- To improve self-understanding and enhance self-concepts

- To assess the student's behavior and help the counselor and student anticipate the student's future behavior

- To stimulate the student to consider new interests for further exploration and to develop realistic expectations

- To provide meaningful information that can help the student make intelligent decisions

- To aid the counselor and student in identifying and developing future options

Limitations of appraisal

Appraisal also has limitations, including the following:

- The use of tests can, at times, interfere with the relationship the counselor has developed with the student, especially if the student is sensitive to being evaluated.

- There can be a tendency to allow test results to dictate a course of action without considering many other factors. Care needs to be taken not to make assumptions about the student's abilities and choices based on testing alone.

- If the results of the test are not presented to the student in a manner that promotes self-understanding, more harm than good can result from the test.

- The use of tests tends to put the counselor in the position of an authority, so the student may perceive the test results as the absolute truth.

- Many informal assessment tools, while helpful in generating discussion, can be used subjectively by both the counselor and the student.

Assessment for Other Purposes

Ideally, tests are administered when the student feels the need for additional information for decision making regarding educational or career development planning. If the student makes the decision to take a test, motivation is high, which enhances the test's accuracy. Some tests are administered according to the school district's or the state's mandate. These are primarily performance and achievement tests. The stated purpose of these tests is to assess the effectiveness of the school's educational programs and to identify areas needing improvement, based on student achievement levels.

Conditions Affecting Test Results

Testing room environment

The comfort of the room, desks or tables, and chairs can affect the outcome of the test. The room should be well-lighted, well-ventilated, and free of noise and extraneous sound. A minimum distance should be maintained between desks, alternating seats if possible, and the students should be able to hear the directions clearly. Each desk should be large enough to provide enough writing space for both the test and the answer sheet.

Physical and mental condition of the test taker

The scores obtained on any test depend to a certain extent on the student's physical and mental condition. Tests should never be scheduled to conflict with other school activities. These would include, but are not limited to, exam week for termination of courses in progress, vacations, and extracurricular activities such as proms and sports events. Students tend to overestimate their physical stamina and do not take into consideration the fact that physical exhaustion affects mental function.

Preparation of the test taker

This includes both academic preparation (if an achievement test is to be administered) and the preparation given to the student related to the mechanics of the test. Motivation to do well on the exam is also an important part of preparation.

Validity of the test

If the test does not test what it is supposed to test, there is no reason to administer it. It is not only a waste of the students' and counselor's time, but it is detrimental to the motivation of the student to sit for future tests. There is also the danger of using incorrect and invalid results to determine future goals and placements.

> Ideally, tests are administered when the student feels the need for additional information for decision making regarding educational or career development planning. If the student makes the decision to take a test, motivation is high, which enhances the test's accuracy.

> Related conditions that are beyond the control of the counselor include the stress level of the student, the atmosphere at home, and social interactions between students and their peers.

SKILL 4.2 Procedures Involved in Appraisal Administration

In many cases, test materials are sent to the school counselor (or other administrator) by the company that has devised and will be scoring the test. When the test administrator receives the test materials, they should be counted; the number of tests should be compared to the number on the invoice to ensure that the correct number of tests was received. If possible, the tests should be placed in a safe with a combination lock, the combination to which is known only to a few trusted school personnel. If this is not possible, the tests should be put in locked storage in an area of the school that is not accessible to students and unauthorized personnel.

A day or so before the test is to be administered, the tests should be counted again to confirm that they have been kept secure. The tests should be divided according to the room setup and the number of students to be tested. They should then be put back in the safe location and not taken out until shortly before the test is to be administered. At that time there should be a person in authority present with the tests at all times.

After the test is completed, the following procedures should be followed.

Tests should never be left in a room without a proctor. When the students are given a test break, the tests should be closed and the room locked when the students leave.

Collecting Tests

The proctor should count each test and answer sheet while collecting them. If the tests are numbered, each numbered test should be accounted for in order to ensure that two tests were not given out inadvertently. The students should not leave the room until all the tests and answer sheets are in order.

Storing Tests

The tests should be placed in the safe location until it is time for scoring. If the tests are to be returned to the testing company for scoring, they should be packaged immediately and prepared for mailing. The service selected for transportation should be notified, and a pickup date should be scheduled as soon as possible. In the meantime, the packaged material should be placed in the safe location until picked up for transportation.

Safeguarding Data and Testing Instruments

The testing material should be kept confidential at all times until the counselor is released from the responsibility of protecting the tests or it becomes the responsibility of other professionals. Access to the data results should be available only to authorized personnel. This includes the counselor, the parent/guardian, the student, and possibly a teacher or other school personnel or administrator.

If individuals outside the school community (such as the media or an attorney) want access to the information, permission must be obtained in writing from the student (or parent/guardian if the student is a minor). The information could also be released by a court order if necessary. Legally, the counselor has no authorization to release any information about a student without such permission.

> *The testing material should be kept confidential at all times until the counselor is released from the responsibility of protecting the tests or it becomes the responsibility of other professionals.*

SKILL 4.3 Knowledge of Measurement Concepts

The language of testing is unique, and knowing how to interpret test data is an important part of the appraisal procedure. Some common terms used in testing and measurement are:

- **Correlation coefficient:** A statistical concept in test validity that measures the relationship between two factors.

- **Derived score:** Any score that is not a raw score. It is obtained from a formula that is used to score the raw score data.

- **Norming:** The scores obtained by a randomly selected group of test takers for the purpose of comparison to future groups of test takers to determine uniform levels of success on the tested information.

- **Raw score:** The basic score that is usually obtained by counting the number of right answers. It can also be obtained by counting the number of wrong answers. The authors of the test can determine other ways to define a raw score. The way the score is defined is noted in the test manual.

- **Reliability:** How dependable or consistent the test is. The three types of reliability are:

  1. **Scorer reliability:** How consistently different scorers arrive at the same score; often used as a measurement when grading essays or subjective tests

  2. **Content reliability:** The degree to which the questions measure the content

  3. **Temporal reliability:** How dependable the test is over a long period of time

- **Reliability coefficient:** A statistical concept in test validity that measures how reliable the relationship is between two factors.

> The formula for the standard error of measurement is the square root of 1 minus the reliability coefficient.

- **Standard deviation:** The specific interval between bands of scores; each interval indicates a different level of achievement.

- **Standard error of measurement:** The inaccuracy of a test caused by chance. Every test has some element of inaccuracy or unreliability, so this element of the test is taken into consideration when evaluating the test results. The degree of error is reported in the use of the term standard deviation, which is a band of scores.

- **Standard score:** An indication of the distance between the raw score and the mean of the norm in terms of the standard deviation.

- **Standardization:** Researchers other than the authors of the test have provided the protocol to be used to administer the exam, including the requirement that the test be given and scored in the same way at each administration.

- **Stanine:** An interpretation of placement often used in achievement tests. It is a measurement that runs from 1 to 9 and is a band of about one-half a standard deviation in width. Scores are based on percentile values.

- **Usability:** The consideration given to cost, ease of administration, and time taken to score in the administration of the test.

- **Validity:** The concept of whether the test measures what it is supposed to measure. In other words, how meaningful is the test? There are four types of validity:

  1. **Face validity:** Does the test appear to test what it should? (This is not a very dependable source of information.)

  2. **Content validity:** Is there a close connection between what is taught and what is being tested?

  3. **Construct validity:** What is the statistical relationship between the scores and another variable that should relate to the test?

  4. **Empirical validity:** What is the correlation coefficient between the scores and some standard of performance?

SKILL 4.4 Reporting Assessment Results to Students and Parents

The role of the counselor is not only to supply information to the authorized people concerned with the results of tests, but also to be certain that the test results are interpreted and understood as accurately as possible. The communication of test results should include interacting and responding to the feelings and concerns of the student and his or her parent/guardian(s).

Because counseling is a confidential relationship, the counselor should obtain permission from the student to reveal any information given in confidence. This may sometimes apply to test scores given to parent/guardian(s). At the least, the student should be notified that the parent will be receiving the scores and a verbal approval should be obtained.

Once it is clear that the parent/guardian(s) will receive the test report, the counselor should work with the parents in a counseling relationship. Parent/guardian(s) may not react objectively to a child's test results. If they do not agree that the results are consistent with their concept of the child's ability, it may be difficult for them to accept the results. Nevertheless, parents have a right to know and, to best help their child, need the opportunity to realistically see their child's abilities. When communicating with parents, the counselor must be empathic about the difficulty of accepting new information and recognize the understanding level of the parent and communicate at that level.

> *Test results can be threatening to students and parents who often feel the results are absolutes and reflect a rigid evaluation of the student. Sensitivity to the feelings and needs of students and parents are primary in communicating results.*

Principles of Test Interpretation

The following principles of test interpretation are useful to keep in mind when communicating test results.

The interpretation should be related to the goals of the counseling

All counselor–student relationships are based on the needs of the individual student. Therefore, sharing test data should be framed in this context. The student should be prepared and ready to receive the information and relate it, with the help of the counselor, to the predetermined goals of testing.

The results of the test belong to the student

The goal of testing is to enhance the student's understanding of his or her interests, capabilities, and behavior. The student is entitled to receive the test results in a timely manner, and the counselor should not hesitate to share unfavorable results. Facing the reality of one's abilities is part of the maturation process. This cannot occur if the truth is not communicated or is colored in a manner that could be misinterpreted.

The student's perception of the scores is of the utmost importance

If the testing results conflict with self-perception, the student could have emotional difficulties in accepting the information. This is where the skill and experience of the counselor come into play. The goal of the counselor is to help the student and parents accept the information and build upon this new data. The counselor can enhance the likelihood of acceptance by striving to frame all of the information (even seemingly negative results) as useful and instructive.

Provision should be made for individual interpretation

It is preferable to interpret test results individually, but often the nature of the test and the number of individuals tested do not lend themselves to individual counseling. When group interpretation is required, it is desirable to impress upon the students that individual consultation about their scores is available.

In the group setting, the procedure is limited to explaining the purpose of the test and the norm group to which the students have been compared. Individual results should never be announced in the group. Statistics about which scores are in different stanines or other ranges should be explained so students can evaluate their own results. The counselor should plan on conferring with individual students whose scores are low, students who the counselor knows will be concerned about their scores, or when testing is the result of the counseling process.

> *In the group setting, the procedure is limited to explaining the purpose of the test and the norm group to which the students have been compared. Individual results should never be announced in the group.*

The counselor must be thoroughly familiar with the test

If the counselor does not understand the significance of the test results, accurate interpretation of the results cannot be expected. Therefore, it is imperative for accuracy as well as credibility purposes that the counselor is thoroughly familiar with the test that has been administered.

Interpretation sessions should be structured

The purpose of structuring these sessions is to do away with the mystery of the testing situation, to help the student identify and correct mistaken impressions, and to face some realities the results may reveal. Other issues of concern to the student and the parent/guardian(s) should be addressed at another interview, if possible.

Test results, not scores, should be communicated at a meaningful level to the student

The purpose of reporting test results instead of scores is to help students use the information to form more realistic self-concepts. Scores alone do not impart information about the test taker. The student should understand the implications the results may have for the future. If the student does not understand the information presented, even the most accurate information can be useless.

Objectivity is the goal of the counselor in presenting the information, so counselor judgments and opinions should not be part of the process. It is important for the counselor to explain the language used in the test results, the norm group to which the comparison is being made, and the relationship between the score and the present and future goals of the student.

The student should help in the interpretation of the results

This participation allows the counselor to see if the student understands the test results, encourages the student to contribute new information about himself or herself to the counseling process, and tends to make the results more acceptable to the student.

Test results should, if possible, be verified by other information

These data could consist of information from others who are familiar with the student as well as information from the student himself or herself.

The counselor must present the data and results honestly

If the counselor suspects the student is disappointed with the results, the counselor must make an effort to support the student and explore the student's needs in light of the test results. Additional personal counseling sessions may be in order.

Recording of Test Results

All test results for individual students should be recorded and retained for use at another time, whether for comparison purposes or for meetings with parents and others working with the student. Therefore, a written record or report should be created. Results must be clearly presented in a format that can be understood by the person receiving the report, whether it is someone highly trained in interpretation, moderately trained, or someone with no training at all.

There are many ways a written report can be created. These include, but are not limited to, a narrative format delineating the past and present record of the student, a graph format such as a horizontal or bar graph, or a profile chart. In some cases, recommendations for application of the assessment data may be included. The counselor should incorporate the language of testing in the written report to insure consistency in interpretation by all professionals using the data.

> *It is important for the counselor to explain the language used in the test results, the norm group to which the comparison is being made, and the relationship between the score and the present and future goals of the student.*

> *In all cases, dissemination of test results should be on a "need to know" basis and only with the required permission.*

SKILL 4.5 Interpreting Assessment Data

Assessment data can be used at the micro level (for individual student educational planning) and at the macro level (for overall school and curricular improvement). Some assessment tools yield information that is useful at both levels; other tools are designed to provide specific information for a specific purpose. Clarity about the intent of the tools and methodology to be employed is essential in gathering and utilizing accurate and informative assessment data.

When the goal of testing is school improvement or program development, individual scores are generally less important than the aggregate data. The collective performance of students in a particular grade, class, curricular area, or program is the goal, and results should be reported as such. In these situations, the way the test results are reported and interpreted is generally dictated by the design of the test. However, school counselors, teachers, and administrators may find that a detailed review of the test results can provide insight into avenues for school improvement not necessarily outlined by the general methodology.

Sharing Data with Other Professionals both Inside and Outside the School

The counselor must make every effort to safeguard assessment results. School personnel should not have access to such data unless they are directly involved in providing services to the student, such as the school psychologist, special education teacher, or school social worker. Generally, a need-to-know basis is the guideline. Under most circumstances, clerical staff, teachers, and others should not have access.

While psychotherapists, social workers, and other professionals outside the school who are involved with the student are bound by the ethics of confidentiality by which the counselor is bound, this material cannot be released without the express written permission of the student and/or parent/guardian(s). Once a release is obtained, all material relating to the student sent to these people should contain whatever is necessary for the recipient to help the student.

Test scores can be reported directly, along with the counselor's interpretation of the scores and his or her observations of the student when the scores were presented. This interpretation requires knowledge of the test, its structure and intent, and the scoring guidelines even if the scoring was done offsite. Such information needs to be direct and focused and should not contain speculation or opinion not based on the data. It is particularly important for counselors to be cautious in sharing the results of informal assessment tools.

Test scores can be reported directly, along with the counselor's interpretation of the scores and his or her observations of the student when the scores were presented. This interpretation requires knowledge of the test, its structure and intent, and the scoring guidelines even if the scoring was done offsite.

Interpreting student data from written reports

The counselor quite often is on the receiving end of written reports about students from various sources. These may be from a reading clinic, a psychiatrist or psychologist, a social worker, or a teacher. It is important that the counselor is knowledgeable about the material in the report and, if some of the material is unclear, that he or she investigates further for clarification. If the counselor is to counsel the student based on these written reports, accuracy in interpretation is essential. Often it is appropriate for the counselor to seek a telephone or personal meeting with the writer in order to clarify and consult about the material in the report, as well as collaborate on an action or treatment plan.

DOMAIN II
CONSULTING

PERSONALIZED STUDY PLAN

KNOWN MATERIAL/ SKIP IT

COMPETENCY 5
CONSULTING

Understanding the Needs of Parent/Guardian(s)

After students themselves, parents and legal guardians are the people with whom school counselors are most likely to interact. In fact, without the express consent of parents and guardians, counselors are not permitted to discuss the student with any other family members.

Having an understanding of what parents and guardians need can be helpful in developing and maintaining positive relationships with them. The three basic things that parents need from school counselors are respect, validation and support, and information.

> *The three basic things that parents need from school counselors are respect, validation and support, and information.*

Respect

As noted previously (*see Skill 3.3*), respect is a key element in effective communication. Parents and guardians may or may not be respectful of school personnel. The parents' history with members of the school community, their own experiences as a student, the current stresses in their lives, and their general approach to life may influence how they respond to school counselors. Nonetheless, it is essential that counselors act respectfully in all of their interactions with parents and guardians.

Respect is conveyed through word choice and tone of voice as well as through the content of the speech. Positive, inclusive statements and questions that invite collaboration express respect. A lack of reactivity helps maintain respectful interactions.

Counselors need to remember that some people respond to any contact from someone from their child's school with fear and/or anger. Being nonreactive to the parent's response will aid the counselor in communicating respect and concern and help avoid unnecessary conflict.

Validation and support

*Parents and guardians
need validation and
support from school
counselors, especially
when addressing difficult
issues.*

Parents and guardians need validation and support from school counselors, especially when addressing difficult issues. Direct comments such as, "I know you want the best for your child" and "I'm sure you are doing your best to help your child" can be useful. It also may be helpful to introduce a sensitive concern with, "You probably know this, but I wanted to tell you…" This takes into account that the parent might be aware of what the counselor is going to disclose and communicates that the counselor believes that the parent is tuned into his or her child. While this may not always be the case, it is better to err in this direction.

In spite of any failings, parents and guardians are usually doing their best. From the counselor's perspective, parents may not be meeting the student's needs. They may even be abusive and neglectful. When necessary, the school counselor may have to directly confront a parent or guardian or file an abuse report. However, most of the time, parents and guardians are doing the best they can. Support and validation may also aid them in positively changing their behavior.

Information

The third thing parents and guardians need is clear information. The counselor needs to directly communicate his or her concerns about the student. As noted, the parent may or may not be aware of what has come to the counselor's attention. Parent/guardians have the right to be informed and need to be informed. They also need to hear what the counselor and other school personnel are proposing as an action plan. This information needs to be conveyed in a nonjudgmental way, without direct or implied criticism of the parent, even when the counselor is asking the parent to do something differently.

Consultation as the Model for Interacting with Parents and Guardians

A good way to approach working with parents and guardians is to think about it as a consultation. Interactions with parents and guardians are a two-way street: The counselor has information and concerns to share with the parent or guardian, who also has information and concerns to share with the counselor. A collaborative mindset will aid in eliciting cooperation and engagement with parents and ultimately leads to the best results for the student.

Parent/guardian(s) are a valuable source of information about the student. Issues of family background and information about medical history can be obtained only from parents or those adults who have been privy to family interaction. Such data can be very helpful in generating solutions to the problems a student may be encountering in the school setting.

Uncooperative parents may feel that the school has "not done right by" their child. It is in the best interest of all to permit them to vent their feelings. This may be one of the few times school personnel have listened to them. Emphasize that the school is not giving up on the child, and if past strategies for improvement have not worked, new strategies will be developed.

When consulting with parent/guardians, focus on the issue at hand as soon as possible after allowing them to vent. Explain the concerns and the tentative plan to the parents. Enlist the equal cooperation of parents by asking how they feel about the suggested course of action. Accept ideas for modification when appropriate, and help them see that they are a vital part of making the plan work.

Good counselors are open to possible solutions and modify their action plans as they gather new information from parents. This openness includes being alert to their own assumptions about what is best for the student and what remedies and support are needed. Such an approach will also communicate to parents their significance and value, further aiding true collaboration.

Be careful not to overwhelm parents and guardians by giving them too many tasks, keeping in mind they may have a great deal of stress in their daily lives already. Encourage them to feel that you, collectively, are developing a workable plan that may need modifying as it progresses. It is important to set up checkpoints for contacting them about the progress of the course of action. If additional contact is not made, the parents will be negative about the entire process, and further intervention on the part of the school will be extremely difficult.

On a more general level, another avenue to engage parent/guardians as collaborators is to form a parent advisory committee. This group can serve as a resource for the guidance department and help create open channels of communication between school counselors and parent/guardian(s).

SKILL 5.2 Knowledge of Family Dynamics

Students' families may consist of a variety of people besides a mother, a father, and siblings. This is especially true of families who have experienced the disruption of divorce, death, homelessness, natural disasters, mental illness, addiction problems, and other issues. Being alert to the various configurations of "family" is crucial to effectively serving students and their families. Similarly, sensitivity to and knowledge of various social-cultural groups as they relate to family structure is also important.

Uncooperative parents may have an "attitude" about how the school has "not done right by" their child. It is in the best interest of all to permit them to vent their feelings. This may be one of the few times school personnel have listened to them.

Be careful not to overwhelm parents and guardians by giving them too many tasks, keeping in mind they may have a great deal of stress in their daily lives already.

Being alert to the various configurations of "family" is crucial to effectively serving students and their families. Similarly, sensitivity to and knowledge of various social-cultural groups as they relate to family structure is also important.

Awareness of the issues that particular families face as outlined in Skill 2.1 (Special Populations) is also essential. The stresses on many families impair their ability to support students adequately, and sensitivity on the part of school counselors to these issues can be useful. This awareness can help avoid stigma and further stress as well as serve to ameliorate the existing stress by providing support and resources.

While counselors often find they need to serve as an advocate for students with colleagues, parents, and care providers, school counselors may also need to advocate for parents and guardians at times. Thinking of oneself as an advocate for families as well as for individual students can be beneficial. This stance is useful both in fostering positive relationships with parents and guardians and in producing positive results for the student.

Contributions from the Field of Family Therapy

Family therapy is a branch of counseling that addresses the wellbeing of families. It developed in the 1950s as a way to help families make changes in the way they function. Although it is beyond the scope of the job of school counselors to work with families in a therapeutic context, the field of family therapy has some useful insights for school counselors. This information can help counselors better understand and interact with family members in their efforts to help students succeed in school and life.

Family therapists draw on various theories and counseling approaches, including group dynamics, systems theory, psychodynamic theory and therapy, Gestalt therapy, cognitive-behavioral therapy, object relations, narrative therapy, and solution-focused therapy. They may have a background in child development, social work, or psychology. What they agree on is that the family is the primary group within which each person learns how to behave with others.

Specifically, family therapy suggests that an individual's behavior derives from and is maintained by not only early family and caregiver experiences but also by current experiences with whomever he or she perceives as family.

Specifically, family therapy suggests that an individual's behavior derives from and is maintained by not only early family and caregiver experiences but also by current experiences with whomever he or she perceives as family. Other people's behavior helps keep an individual acting in certain ways. Furthermore, these interactions are often repetitive and circular, reinforcing each other. Therefore, in some cases, interventions need to include family members so that an individual is able to make behavioral changes.

Another contribution from family therapy is the understanding that there are overt and covert roles as well as rules that guide behavior in families. Family members may or may not be consciously aware of these parameters, but their behavior is still affected by them. In rigid families, any deviation from these rules and roles can cause distress in other family members and in the system as a whole.

This reactivity can keep family members, especially children, from changing their behavior, even in settings outside the family.

The way families manage conflict is often a characteristic that defines a particular family. Some families avoid conflict at all costs; others seem to thrive on it. Often, "problem" children or adolescents (known as the "identified patient" in family therapy jargon) serve to keep the parents from addressing underlying issues. This conflict focuses family concern away from a more painful problem, usually one that is grounded in the adult relationship(s).

For more information about family therapy, see these Web sites:

www. familytherapyresources .net/

www.mayoclinic.com

www.en.wikipedia.org/wiki /Family_therapy

SKILL 5.3 **Components of a Consultation Model**

The purpose of all consultation processes is to solve problems. The principals in the process are the consultant, usually the counselor in a school setting (but also possibly simply a person knowledgeable about the problem at hand), and the consultee, often a teacher or other school staff member. The consultee is not usually the student whose problem is the topic of discussion. Although the student has a vital part in the process, the purpose of the consultation is to aid the consultee in solving a problem that usually concerns a student or a group of students.

Most often the consultation process is used to solve an academic problem of a student. However, school problems increasingly involve difficulties of a societal nature that affect the school environment and school population as a whole. School policy issues are often solved by employing the consultation model. Some examples of these issues are dress codes, drug policies, and issues of sudden death in the school community. Different approaches are used depending on the particular goal of the consultant and consultee.

In the school setting, consultees can be one or more school staff members, and consultants can be more than one person with knowledge of the student and/or expertise in the solving of this particular problem.

Role of the Consultant

The consultant can take the role of an advocate by directly presenting evidence and attempting to persuade the consultee to take a particular stand or action. The advocacy can be in support of a student, a group of students, or an idea to be implemented.

The consultant can also act in the capacity of an expert in a particular field. This role is employed when there is a need to inform or educate the consultee in a specialized area. For the school counselor, this may take the form of interpretation of test data, psychological and environmental background information, or placement data.

Another role of the consultant might entail specific training and education in an area such as identifying children "at risk." The goal here is to develop school-wide plans and procedures to improve the drop-out rate, for example.

The counselor's role most often used in the school setting is that of consultant/collaborator, where the consultee and the consultant's roles are equal in attempting to solve the problem. It is a three-pronged relationship involving the counselor/consultant, the teacher/consultee, and the student (and, at times, the student's parents). As a collaborator, the counselor takes part of the responsibility for implementing the plan to solve the problem. The counselor may need to work directly with the student to reinforce behavior change.

The task of fact finding (gathering relevant information, studying it, and presenting it to the consultee) falls on the shoulders of the consultant.

Another role the consultant can take is that of the process specialist. In this role, the counselor outlines the steps needed to reach mutual goals.

Procedures for Consultations

There is a common procedure for all consultations, although the settings in which the consultation takes place may differ. Some of these places include:

- A clinical setting, which can be a mental health facility

- A school setting, with the parent, teacher, or administrator present

- A training setting, for education purposes

- A school or business, with the staff of an organization

Prior to the first session, the consultant should gather certain data. These include background information related to the purpose of the consultation process, political considerations of the process (when applicable), and other facts that may help the consultant understand the dynamics of the situation.

The goals of the consultation should be formulated so that all concerned parties know where the process is headed. The function, role, techniques, and procedures used by the consultant should be formulated after the above issues are determined. The experience of the consultee in the consultation process should be taken into consideration so that if additional education and skill training are required, the consultant is prepared to furnish that training.

Some of the common procedures for all consultation processes are: relationship building, diagnosis and definition of the problem, creation and implementation of a plan, and evaluation and summarization.

Relationship building

Consulting in the school setting usually involves an attempt to change student behavior. For success, the process must obtain the trust and confidence of the student and motivate the student to change. The student also needs to be willing to cooperate in the plans for implementing behavior change. Once the student is on board, the consultant can then proceed to implement the process of consultation by contacting other parties involved, such as the child's parents, teachers, experts in areas of special needs, and any other support personnel deemed important in solving the problem.

Diagnosis and definition of the problem

It should be clear to all participants what has been diagnosed as the problem. Often the consultee and the student see the problem differently, but a plan to solve the problem cannot work if the student and consultee are at odds. In a situation in which a student needs to modify behavior, the model of behavior consultation, based on the theory of social learning, is employed, which seeks specific changes in behavior.

In this model, information regarding the problem is obtained, the problem is defined in detail, goals are set, plan strategies are developed, assessment criteria are agreed upon, and avenues of intervention are explored. Solving the problem depends on the consultee "making it happen"; therefore, it is critical that the consultee has ownership of the plan.

Other models of consultation include organization consultation, in which the problem is in the organizational framework. This is most often used when an expert in a particular area is required. The doctor/patient model is used when an organization knows there is a problem but does not know the nature of the problem. When the interactions of the members of an organization are examined, process consultation is employed. When the mental health of a community can be improved by consulting with other human services professionals in the delivery of their services, mental health consultation is employed.

Creation and implementation of a plan

In creating a plan, the counselor/consultant, together with the student and the consultee (teacher), identify a behavior that is of most concern to all. A plan of action is devised for expediting change with equal input from all participants involved. Techniques of encouragement, logical consequences, praise, and reward are used to reach goals established by all parties. The consultant needs to monitor the process and identify problems with the implementation so the plan can be changed, if necessary.

Evaluation and summarization

Although the initial meeting is usually not the only meeting, a summary of what has transpired during the meeting should be made before terminating the session.

> As far as possible, the student should be included in defining the problem with the consultee, especially at the secondary level, and should also be included in meetings during which the strategies to be used are developed.

> At the conclusion of the initial meeting, each participant should fully understand his or her role in implementing behavior change and should be held responsible for his or her part in the process.

At the conclusion of the initial meeting, each participant should fully understand his or her role in implementing behavior change and should be held responsible for his or her part in the process. Once the behavior change has been accomplished, the consultant should make an evaluation of the process.

SKILL 5.4 Strategies for Effective Collaboration

Assist Participants in Problem Solving

The counselor/consultant should have a plan of action to assist participants in doing their parts to effect change. This might involve teaching specific skills to a teacher with no prior experience in attempting behavior change or helping the teacher devise strategies and sequential plans to deal with the defined behavior problem.

The consultant should be able to help the consultee describe in detail the specific types of behavior that are problematic. If necessary, the consultant should make arrangements for any clerical help needed in order to relieve the teacher/consultee of this task.

Help should also be provided to the student and his or her parent/guardian(s) in order for the consultation to effect the desired change in behavior. This should include frequent contact to evaluate the progress of the process, to ascertain whether more aid is needed, and to check if the student or parent/guardian(s) have additional concerns.

Communicate the Needs of the Student

It is important for the consultant not to assume what the needs of the student are without first clarifying those needs directly with the student. In the case of an adolescent, if this is not done first, trust will not be established and the whole process is likely to fail. Permission to share these needs should be obtained from the student in order to reinforce the trust relationship.

It is always important for the consultant to balance the needs of the student/client with those of the consultee/teacher in order to achieve the best results.

Once this is done, a meeting should be held with the consultee to communicate these needs. If the student can be present, misunderstandings are less likely to occur. Such a meeting can also be a method to open lines of further dialogue between the student and the consultee. In this scenario, the consultant acts in part as the advocate of the student/client, using knowledge gained from past experience.

Involve Parent/Guardian(s) in Consultation

Parent/guardian(s) are a vital part of the consultation process. Consultation works best when the parent/guardian(s) are involved in the consultation process from the beginning. Even in the case of uncooperative parents, the consultant must inform them every step of the way. Often the student's home situation is complicated by divorce or separation, issues of custody, or alienation. The consultant, while respecting the parent/guardian(s)' rights, must always keep in mind that the primary goal is solving the student's problem.

See Skill 5.1 for more information about involving parent/guardian(s) in the consultation process.

Assist in the Use of Data and Resources

The consultant needs to have as much information about the situation and the student as possible. Do not rush into the consultation process without doing an adequate job of gathering data. Some things the consultant can do include:

- Examine the student's permanent record for standardized test scores, patterns of grade fluctuation, weak and strong areas, and attendance record

- Talk with the student's present teacher(s) to ascertain if they are all having the same problem, and, if not, gather insights from any teacher who is not having a problem

- Observe the student in the classroom, if possible

- Administer additional tests, if necessary

- Gather medical, physical, and disciplinary history

Once you have some kind of analysis of the possible problem, compile a list of resources that might be available, both inside and outside the school community, to be used as support mechanisms. This list may include:

- Short-term or long-term personal counseling, both for the student and the family

- Alcohol and other drug counseling

- Academic tutoring

- Referral to the school psychologist for special education testing

- School social worker intervention for family visits and ongoing support

This list should be available when the consultation process begins so that action can be taken immediately.

Identify Procedures for Transition and Follow-Up

When it has been determined that the consultation process has been successful in solving the problem, a formal evaluation of the process is in order. This can

> When it has been determined that the consultation process has been successful in solving the problem, a formal evaluation of the process is in order.

be accomplished by a number of methods. Individual interviews with all parties involved in the process can be conducted or a survey instrument used to determine if the consultee and the student/client have been satisfied with the process. Input concerning the areas they feel need to be continued or modified, the process for the continuation of the plan, and comments relating to the entire procedure should also be solicited.

The consultant becomes increasingly less active in the consultation process during the transition phase, agreeing to decrease and eliminate the need for intervention in a gradual way. As a final step, after the consultant has not been involved for a period of time, a follow-up interview should be conducted regarding the effectiveness of the process. If there is regression on the part of the student/client, it may be appropriate to reinstitute the consultation process or make further referrals.

SKILL 5.5 Referrals to and Use of External Resources

One of the ongoing tasks of school counselors is to help students and families to access and utilize resources outside the school setting. These connections may be a result of counselor or other school personnel making recommendations for referrals, or they may occur when a student or parent/guardian asks for help or expresses a particular need.

Referrals to Outside Agencies and Practitioners

Appropriate referrals for students to professional individuals and agencies are procedural functions of both the school district and the specific school in which the counselor works. There is usually a specific policy that a referring school counselor must follow.

The counselor should use a form to inform the person to whom the student is referred of the nature of the problem, along with background information and standardized test scores, what approaches have already been attempted, and the results of previous attempts. Follow-up and further meetings should be held to determine the outcome of the referral. The person to whom the student is referred should also issue a report on the results.

The first step in getting outside help for the student is to get the informed consent of the student and his or her parent/guardian to make the referral. In the case of abuse by a family or household member, the counselor is mandated to report the incident to the proper authorities as well. If a parent or guardian is the abuser, it

The first step in getting outside help for the student is to get the informed consent of the student and his or her parent/guardian to make the referral.

is not prudent to include that person in the referral process. The mandated state organization will approach the parent or guardian.

In the case of alcohol, drug, or emotional problems, the parent/guardian should be included from the beginning of the referral process. The question of expense or insurance coverage is a significant factor to be considered. In any case of referral, written documentation should be kept. The counselor should make personal contact with the agency or individual receiving the referral. The counselor should be in regular contact with this agency or individual and the student's parents until the problem is resolved or the student is no longer enrolled in the school.

It is often helpful to have a form on which to track referrals to outside agencies and individuals. This creates a useful record for accountability purposes and makes follow-up easier.

Support and Resources for Families

The school counselor is often in the position of helping families to access resources for purposes other than referrals for evaluative or mental health services. Sometimes the counselor will provide the student with information about resources; at other times the counselor will offer referrals to the parents or guardians.

Networking with community agencies, private practitioners, other school districts, professional associations, and local and state education agencies can be useful for gathering resource information. The counselor should maintain a database as well as a file of brochures, business cards, and information packets to draw on as needed. It is also helpful to keep a list of contact people at various agencies and programs in order to facilitate referrals and expedite access for families.

> *Supporting students and families requires knowledge of community and Internet resources on many different topics, including, but not limited to, financial aid, mental health and social service agencies, vocational training programs, food banks, support groups, colleges and universities, advocacy networks, government-sponsored aid programs, and enrichment activities.*

SKILL 5.6 Core Crisis Intervention Concepts and Approaches

Crisis and emergency situations are events beyond the realm of everyday life. They always involve some degree of surprise, shock, loss, and emotion. Crises include death, natural disasters such as earthquakes and hurricanes, vehicular and other accidents, school shootings, and other forms of extreme violence. The unpredictability of crises, the experience of loss that invariably accompanies such situations, and the strong feelings they evoke all make crisis and emergency events particularly potent and challenging for everyone involved.

The Value of Being Prepared

Preplanning and training in basic crisis management skills can be extremely helpful in responding effectively if or when a crisis does occur. Although the events themselves may be unpredictable, there is a body of information about how people react to crises and what responders can do to ameliorate and manage the aftermath of crises. This is particularly important in school settings, where there are a large number of people congregated in one place and contagion is a concern. Anxiety and misinformation can spread like wildfire, exacerbating the short-term and long-term effects of traumatic events.

Designating and training a crisis response team can be beneficial. Comprehensive crisis management training and ongoing refresher courses are necessary for a team to function well. In most cases, the school counselor is an integral part of the crisis team. He or she may or may not be a leader, depending on the structure of the team, the preferences of the administration, and the background of the counselor.

In most cases, the school counselor is an integral part of the crisis team.

In addition to a crisis team, school districts need to have clearly defined crisis response plans. Plans should include as much detail as possible, with specific recommendations for different situations as needed, although a general plan is applicable in many circumstances. Plans should:

- Delineate the school's goals in crisis situations (such as maintaining as normal a school day as possible, or providing timely information)

- Identify key players on the crisis response team

- Specify how communication will be handled

- Describe what interventions will be used with students

- Note how interactions and referrals to outside agencies will be managed

- Detail what follow-up is needed

Further, it helps to have handouts about traumatic stress reactions, sample letters to parents and guardians, press releases (when necessary), and other useful documents ready prior to any event.

The Need for Information

Everyone who experiences a traumatic event needs to be aware of the normal reactions and common feelings of survivors, as well as receive accurate information about the event itself (when this is not known) and what the school is doing in response. This means that the district needs to make clear decisions about the actions the school is taking, including what parents and guardians need to know and do, and communicate these plans succinctly and in a timely manner to everyone in the school community. Information also needs to flow to the larger community. Specific, to-the-point information is essential; rumors should always be avoided.

Intervention for students

Most often, school counselors and other school personnel will be available for crisis counseling and support in a designated room for a day or two after a traumatic event. Some districts will invite local experts in traumatic stress response or grief counseling to come to the school to aid school personnel. Interventions include listening, normalizing the reactions of students, offering to call parents and guardians, and making arrangements for students to go home early when needed. Referrals to outside professionals may also be made.

Self-care during and after an event

A school crisis plan should spell out how responders and other school personnel will receive and give support during the implementation of the crisis management plan. School counselors and other personnel also need to get rest and support after doing crisis response work. This work is very demanding, and the effects on responders may not be immediately apparent. Secondary post-traumatic stress is a concern, particularly when the crisis response team has multiple or ongoing situations to manage. Adequate administrative and personal support, time off, and sufficient training and debriefing are essential.

The following Web sites have information about school crisis management, traumatic stress reactions, and related topics:

www.nctsnet.org/nccts /nav.do?pid=ctr_aud_schl

www.cdc.gov/niosh /docs/2002-107

www.apa.org/practice /traumaticstress.html

www.ed.gov/admins/lead /safety/training /responding/crisis_pg11 .html?exp=2

SKILL 5.7 The School Counselor as Advocate

An **ADVOCATE** is someone who speaks up for another (usually someone lacking power in a situation) with the goal of making sure that person is heard. Schools are complex systems comprising many individuals and groups competing for resources and attention. At times, students and/or parents and guardians may feel that their concerns are not being acknowledged or addressed.

School counselors are in a unique position to serve as advocates for students. They do not grade or evaluate students' academic performance, they do not function as disciplinarians for the school, and they do not make decisions regarding school policies that might affect individual students and families.

ADVOCATE: someone who speaks up for another (usually someone lacking power in a situation) with the goal of making sure that person is heard

Counselors may also observe ongoing issues with groups of students or recognize segments of the student body that are not receiving adequate support or services. In these circumstances, there may be a need for someone to advocate for these individuals or groups.

Furthermore, counselors may be privy to students' personal concerns and have the training and background to understand some of the underlying issues and needs of diverse students. Parents and guardians may also feel that the school counselor is more open to discussing their concerns than other school personnel may be.

Being an advocate requires listening carefully. After hearing someone's concerns or identifying an issue, advocacy requires a frank discussion about what kind of help the student or parent/guardian wants. The school counselor needs to assess the appropriateness of the request for this kind of help and determine a good action plan.

(See Skills 5.1 and 5.2 for more information about consultation.)

When setting goals to advocate for an individual or a group, the advocate needs to ensure that his or her own personal agenda is not driving the need to speak up. Passion about an issue can be valuable, even necessary at times, in effecting change, but taking action on someone's behalf needs to be grounded in accurately assessing the issues at hand and advocating in a professional manner. A good advocate not only speaks with a strong, compassionate voice but also brings clear thinking, a collaborative attitude, and respectful communication to the table.

DOMAIN III
COORDINATING

PERSONALIZED STUDY PLAN

KNOWN MATERIAL/ SKIP IT

COMPETENCY 6
MANAGEMENT AND ORGANIZATION

SKILL 6.1 Components of a Developmental Guidance Program

The ultimate aims of a guidance program include the student's successful acquisition of academic and personal insights in order to make plans for the future with confidence and logic, obtaining personal satisfaction in his or her accomplishments, making appropriate emotional adjustments, being able to solve problems as they inevitably occur in life, and exploring vocational and career possibilities intelligently and knowledgeably.

General Guidelines

In order to achieve these goals, a developmental guidance program should be designed and implemented according to the following five guidelines:

1. The program must be organized, have established systems of operation, and have a stated purpose, along with trained professionals to administer the services provided

2. The guidance service must be an accepted and integral part of the school program

3. The mission statement of the guidance and counseling program should include the promotion of optimum student development and adjustment, with the ultimate goal of developing the student's ability to make intelligent choices and deal with and solve the problems of life

4. The services to be delivered should include, at a minimum, testing and maintaining appropriate records, personal counseling, distribution of educational and vocational information, appropriate placement into school programs, referrals to outside agencies and professionals, and follow-up of the services provided

5. The program should provide for identification, exploration, and development of the potential inherent in all individuals

There are many ways to structure the guidance program. The person leading the program should include the staff in making decisions that are consistent with the mission statement of the department about the types of services to be delivered, the components of those services, and the staff assignments for those components. The staff member who is assigned specific duties should have the freedom to choose the components of those services and the method of their delivery.

> *An important part of the success of the guidance program is an informed and supportive school staff, community, and student population.*

An important part of the success of the guidance program is an informed and supportive school staff, community, and student population. The public relations involved in obtaining this support can be time-consuming but ultimately is both rewarding to the counselor and beneficial to students.

Promoting the Guidance Department

The support of those other than the guidance staff in the delivery of guidance services contributes to the optimum functioning of the department and, ultimately, to the benefit of the students. To promote the guidance department, counselors can do the following:

- Encourage cooperation between and among the guidance staff, the school staff, the community, and the students. A special effort should be made to let teachers and others know that their roles in educating, guiding, and counseling all students are vital to the success of the program.

- Help develop a positive attitude by treating other school colleagues with respect. It may also be helpful to offer workshops and seminars on the functions and specific duties of the guidance staff.

- Have a well-organized program of regular parental contact. This could involve home visits or an advisory committee for the discussion of problems and the exploration of new programs.

- Support community projects with a guidance context related to the needs and welfare of the students.

- Solicit the assistance of community leaders to offer mentoring, job shadowing, and school-to-work programs.

- Cooperate in establishing research projects directly related to proven scientific data for the institution of program decisions and changes.

- Continuously look for opportunities to promote the guidance program in innovative and unique ways.

Vehicles to inform parents/guardians and community members of guidance services

Often, parents and guardians and other members of the community are not aware of the extensive functions of the guidance program. There are a number of techniques that can be used to inform parents and the community of guidance services and programs:

- A guidance newsletter is an excellent vehicle to advertise what is going on in the guidance department and to systematically explain each program on a monthly and ongoing basis.

- Writing a column in the local newspaper is an effective way to reach community members who do not have students in school.

- Individual staff members may take turns speaking to local organizations at their regularly scheduled meetings. These organizations are frequently looking for speakers to attract members to meetings.

- Teas and orientations for parents of students in specific grades allow counselors to explain what programs are planned for their students.

- Participation or attendance at athletic events and other out-of-school functions helps counselors become visible to a greater portion of the school's student population and their parent/guardian(s).

- When counselors invite community leaders to brainstorm on ways to help students succeed in a chosen field, this increases community awareness of the guidance program. Holding a career night is a good example of this type of activity.

SKILL 6.2 Conducting an Orientation Program to the School and Guidance Program

A major change in the life of a child is the transition from home to school. For the student entering school for the first time, as well as the student making the transition from elementary to middle school or from middle school to high school, a smooth and anxiety-reducing procedure can be extremely useful. While the attitude of the parent/guardian is important, the school personnel with whom the child has first contact set the tone for the school experience. Therefore, it is important that the organizers of the first encounter recognize the needs of the child and address them through a student orientation.

While the attitude of the parent/guardian is important, the school personnel with whom the child has first contact set the tone for the school experience.

Orientation Guidelines

Careful planning is essential. A written procedure to eliminate the possibility of omitting details that are important to the success of the orientation helps. Details include:

1. Parents receive advance notification of the time, date, and place of the orientation. The notice should include a student handbook with the school regulations clearly spelled out as well as penalties for infractions of the school rules.

2. The meeting is set for the early evening and lasts no more than an hour and a half.

3. The agenda for the meeting is carefully delineated both ahead of time and again at the meeting.

4. The principal and other school administrators are introduced and their roles in the school community explained.

5. The guidance department introduces its staff members and explains the functions and programs of the department, including the procedures for seeing a counselor.

6. There should be a question-and-answer period that is restricted in duration.

7. At the middle and high school levels, discuss scheduling and give all students copies of their schedules. Additional copies should be available on the first day of school for students who have not brought their copy to school.

8. An upper-class student can conduct a tour of the facilities to help the new students familiarize themselves with the building and the rooms in which their classes will be held.

9. If possible, refreshments should be served, allowing parents, students, and staff to mingle in an informal atmosphere.

SKILL 6.3 Developing Special Programs to Meet Identified Needs

Although many of the school counselor's tasks are designated by the overall plan of the guidance program, there is occasionally a need to develop special programs to cope with an emerging problem or respond to a particular group of students. Such a need might be identified by a formal needs assessment or, more commonly, by a classroom management problem, teachers' observations, or the counselor's direct knowledge.

Two examples of special programs are the Lunch Bunch and an anger management mini group. The Lunch Bunch is an opportunity for new students to meet with other students new to the district plus the counselor in a small group at lunch time. Meeting in a somewhat informal setting while eating lunch can be useful and non-threatening for new students by addressing the discomfort some students feel at lunchtime when longtime friends sit together. It helps build peer relationships as well as a connection with the school counselor. It can, after a few meetings, include returning students to help the students build bridges into the larger school community. The Lunch Bunch should only meet short term—for example, once a week at the same time for four to six weeks—in order to facilitate this process of integration.

> A specific program to address the needs of an underserved student population, for example, can be a creative solution and serve to prevent an escalation of the problem.

A psychoeducational group focused on anger management can be an opportunity for violence and bullying prevention as well as an intervention strategy. In this setting (which is more formal than the Lunch Bunch, for example), the school counselor meets with a small group of students (six to eight) who need help with anger management skills. They can be self-selected or identified by the counselor, teachers, and other staff. In this group, the counselor can share information, teach skills, and employ behavior modification approaches. Students can also discuss their concerns about and struggles with anger and other emotions.

> A psychoeducational group focused on anger management can be an opportunity for violence and bullying prevention as well as an intervention strategy.

Ideally, the school counselor has students complete evaluation forms following their involvement in such special programs in order to assess the programs' effectiveness. This information can be used in deciding whether to offer the program again, modify the program, or develop new programs. Other staff members and teachers who were involved in the program or are able to observe the effects of the program can also be solicited for their feedback.

SKILL 6.4 Basic Prevention Concepts and Other Curricular Strategies

In addition to providing counseling after a problem has been identified, it is the job of the school counselor to contribute to the school's effort to prevent difficulties before they arise. Central to the notion of prevention is the importance of creating a positive school environment (*see Skill 9.1*). Further, as noted previously, attending to issues of bullying, prejudice, aggression, and violence in the school setting are key to preventing problems. Teaching communication, self-awareness, and conflict resolution skills to students are effective prevention approaches.

There are several other key prevention concepts.

Maintain an Open-Door Policy

Students need to know that the school counselor is there to help. An attitude of openness and positive communication can encourage students to seek assistance when something concerns them before it escalates into a larger problem.

Create a Student Assistance Team (SAT)

By designating and training a group of teachers and staff (counselors, psychologist, nurse, social worker, etc.) as people students can go to when they are experiencing difficulties, the school offers students the opportunity to get the help they need to be successful in school. SATs provide early intervention and referrals, and have the advantage of being interdisciplinary and collaborative.

Implement Innovative Programs

Implement programs that involve students in the school community in innovative ways. When students are engaged in programs beyond the scope of the classroom and traditional guidance functions, they become invested in the larger school community.

Implement programs that involve students in the school community in innovative ways. When students are engaged in programs beyond the scope of the classroom and traditional guidance functions, they become invested in the larger school community. This enhances their self-esteem and helps forge new bonds among students. At times, peers are able to help students when adults are less able to do so. Attention needs to be given to recruitment of students for such programs, and adequate orientation, training, and supervision must be provided.

Such programs might include the following:

1. Cross-age teaching: Have high school students help with programs for elementary and middle school students. This could involve tutoring, conflict resolution, peer mediation, or orientation for students moving from one school building to the next.

2. New-student welcoming committee: Establish a group of students who are willing to mentor students new to the district. They can sit with their mentees at lunch and share information about the school. New friendships may develop, and both mentors and mentees have the chance to meet people who may be different from them.

3. Service clubs: Sponsor or help start a service club dedicated to helping students implement projects that improve the school and community environment. Some examples are a recycling project within the school, a holiday gift program for needy families, or a volunteer program to help the elderly in the community or to bring seasonal artwork to nursing home patients.

4. Student involvement in the guidance program: Invite students to help out with guidance activities such as Career Day or Financial Aid Night.

COMPETENCY 7
INFORMATION ACQUISITION AND DISSEMINATION

There are many sources of information that can support counseling activities. Some useful sources are detailed below.

Current Professional Journals

The counselor should belong to professional organizations such as the local and state branches of the American Counseling Association (ACA) and the American School Counselor Association (ASCA), teachers' organizations that relate to their work in developmental areas such as reading and special education, and other broad educational organizations such as Phi Delta Kappa (PDK). The journals that these organizations publish have a wealth of information about current trends, theories, and practices in the field.

Commercial Advertising

It is important that the counselor is aware of these programs and evaluates them. Often students look to the counselor to determine the legitimacy of these offers. Advertisements for scholarship searches, tutoring services, and computer programs for academic improvement are some of the ways advertisers entice parents and students to buy their products.

Students and parents are bombarded with commercial advertising that often involves education programs.

Publications

Once the counselor is registered as a licensed professional, he or she will receive solicitations for new publications, new programs, and memberships in various organizations. While there is a tendency to toss all this information into the recycling bin, some of it is valuable and should at least be perused. The counseling staff can devise a system in which each counselor is responsible for specific information and can share pertinent material at staff meetings.

College and Military Base Visits

In order to keep up with new programs colleges are offering to students and to become familiar with the admissions staff at the different institutions, it is important for the counselor to visit these schools and, at least once a year, take an out-of-area visit to schools in which some of his or her students have taken an interest. The armed forces offer trips to military installations to familiarize counselors with the educational programs of the particular branch of the service represented. These are usually free or low-cost trips. The school district may be persuaded to provide funds from the guidance budget for some of these visits.

Students are often unable to visit a school before applying, and the counselor visitation may help a particular student by providing information about the characteristics of that school.

College Night

A joint college night sponsored by all the schools in the county can be both a service to the students and a possible fund-raiser. If the colleges are charged a small fee for presenting, and if a dinner is provided, counselors can raise money for scholarships for needy and deserving students. It is also good public relations for the department when they can present a scholarship to a student at the awards night program.

Visits to Other School Programs

Counselors can learn from innovative programs instituted by other schools by visiting these programs and evaluating their good and bad aspects. After a program has been in place for a period of time, the originators of the program are aware of improvements that should be made. If your school is interested in starting the program, it can be beneficial to learn from the mistakes of others and to be able to offer an improved version of the program.

Workshops and conventions are a valuable resource for new ideas and innovative practices. They are also a vehicle for learning new state and federal rules and regulations.

Workshops and Conventions

When a counselor belongs to professional organizations, information about coming events is mailed to the counselor well in advance of events. The counselor can then choose the event he or she wishes to attend, depending on his or her interest and expertise. In addition, counselors who have expertise in a particular area can present at these programs. This gives them the chance to share their ideas with others and also lends a degree of prestige to the school in which they are employed.

Local opportunities should not be excluded; nearby colleges or agencies may offer relevant continuing education programs as well as the chance to network with potential referrals.

SKILL 7.2 Evaluating and Identifying Educational and Vocational Materials

Appropriate materials are instrumental in helping students make educational decisions in relation to their career goals. Finding good materials is part of the school counselor's task. The National Career Development Association (NCDA) has formulated guidelines for the preparation and evaluation of career and occupational literature. These guidelines are appropriate for both publishers and users of all vocational and educational materials. They also serve as the basis for ratings of career and occupational literature by the Career Information Review Service of NCDA in the *Career Development Quarterly*.

The National Career Development Association (NCDA) has formulated guidelines for the preparation and evaluation of career and occupational literature.

Areas of Evaluation

General areas of evaluation should include:

- Dates of publication in order to determine if the material is current. Material more than five years old should be discarded, because new information is usually available.

- Accuracy of information, which should be free from distortion and advertising. The content should be reviewed by trained experts and should reflect different points of view. Data should be based on current and reliable research.

- The format should be clear, concise, and interesting.

- The vocabulary should be appropriate to the age and level of the target group. Age ranges should be defined in the material. Material targeted for young high school students, for example, should reflect appropriate language and style. Be sure the material does not use sexist language.

- The purpose of the information should be presented in the introduction to the material, and the target population should be clearly indicated.

- Bias and stereotyping of individuals with disabilities or based on gender, race, social status, ethnicity, age, or religion should be carefully reviewed and deleted. Vocabulary should be gender-neutral, and persons of both sexes should be represented equally.

- The use of graphics is valuable, but they should be presented in a manner that is accurate, current, and unbiased.

Content of Career Materials

The content of all career materials should:

- Describe the duties and nature of the work in a clear and interesting fashion. Literature describing the field should include the importance of the occupation in a global sense; the availability of occupations in the field; the skills, knowledge, and abilities of people in the field; the different levels of occupations in the field; and the nature of any specializations.

- Portray the work setting and conditions of the work environment in terms of the physical and mental duties of the work, the hours, required travel, and any aspects of the work that might be considered undesirable.

- Include the preparation required for entrance into the occupation, together with the training, knowledge, skills, and abilities of those who are successful in the occupation. The levels of preparation required for each level of the occupation should also be described.

- Delineate special requirements or considerations needed for employment in the occupation. These include bona fide physical requirements, licensing, and certification or membership requirements. Social and psychological factors that have an impact on one's lifestyle should also be addressed.

- Describe a variety of methods of entry into the occupation.

- Include information about earnings and benefits.

- Portray advancement possibilities and the criteria for advancement.

- Address the long-term employment outlook. This is a particularly important part of the evaluation.

- Include opportunities for experience and exploration to ascertain if that field is appropriate for a specific individual.

- Describe related occupations that share similar requirements.

- Offer additional sources of information.

The National Career Development Association publishes a Career and Occupational Literature Reviewer's Rating Form that is available from NCDA, 5999 Stevenson Avenue, Alexandria, VA, 20034. The guidance department can use this form to rate material that is being considered for purchase for the guidance department or the library.

Finding Appropriate Materials

The counselor must be able to readily access useful information for different students and varying needs. Becoming familiar with available references can help, and the counselor should also regularly monitor these references for new information. Career and occupational materials change quickly due to frequent shifts in the world of work and technological advances, so the school counselor must stay abreast of current materials.

Federal Government Sources

O*NET OnLine is a Web site run by the U.S. Department of Labor that provides users with helpful information about career trends at no cost. This site can be accessed through the Department of Labor's Web site for Education and Training Administration at *www.doleta.gov/*. Other sites and useful documents can be accessed here as well:

- Employment and Training Administration, Department of Labor, Dictionary of Occupational Titles (DOT); this is a comprehensive source of information about occupations and characteristics of the workers in various occupations

- Employment and Training Administration, Department of Labor, Selected Characteristics of Occupations Defined in the Dictionary of Occupational Titles

- Employment and Training Administration, Department of Labor, Guide for Occupational Exploration

- Bureau of Labor Statistics, Department of Labor, Occupational Outlook Handbook (available online at *www.bls.gov/oco/*; updated every two years)

- Bureau of Labor Statistics, Department of Labor, Occupational Outlook Quarterly (available online at *www.bls.gov/opub/ooq/ooqhome.htm*)

- Department of Defense, Military Career Guide

- Office of Federal Statistical Policy and Standards, Department of Commerce, Standard Occupational Classification Manual

- Office of Management and Budget, Executive Office of the President, Standard Industrial Classification Manual

- National Center for Education Statistics, Department of Education, A Classification of Industrial Programs

- Bureau of the Census, Department of Commerce, U.S. Census of Population 1990, Classified Index of Industries and Occupations

Other Governmental and Commercial Sources

Regional sources include the Bureau of Labor Statistics regional centers. Local sources include chambers of commerce, employment and rehabilitative services offices, community colleges and four-year colleges and universities, private industry councils, and civic or service organizations.

Many commercial publishers also specialize in providing information about careers and vocations. Always evaluate their products using the guidelines noted earlier in this section before utilizing these materials. Also be aware of the intent of the source, which is likely meant to sell a particular product or program.

SKILL 7.3 Locating and Securing Scholarship and Financial Aid Assistance

The guidance department should have a collection of books and information to help students locate and secure scholarships and financial aid. There are printed guides available, although many students and parent/guardian(s) find using the Internet most helpful.

There are many resources online. Although some commercial sites may provide useful information, they may not be the best or most unbiased sources, and some charge a fee. Most colleges and technical schools provide detailed information about financial aid on their individual Web sites.

Searching for specific scholarships is also a good idea. The race, gender, or sexual orientation of the student, his or her area of study, membership in certain organizations, and other factors can lead to specialized financial aid options. One helpful resource in this area is *The Higher Education Money Book for Women and Minorities*, published by Young, Matthews & Cox. Local public and college libraries can be good sources of information as well.

The financial aid workshops offered by many colleges and universities to interested high schools free of charge are an excellent resource for counselors. It is the counselor's job to organize and advertise these workshops, which are provided by college staff members who are experts in financial aid. Sponsoring a Financial Aid Night is an excellent way for students and parent/guardian(s) to gain useful information about aid options and build relationships with the counselors. It is also another chance for the school to promote the guidance program.

Two free noncommercial sites with good information on scholarships and financial aid are:

www.finaid.org

www.studentaid.ed.gov

It is important for the counselor to attend workshops explaining the new regulations involving federal funding sources such as the Pell Grant and other federal sources for educational loans.

COMPETENCY 8
PROGRAM EVALUATION

Purposes of Research

Basic research

This is research done for knowledge without a stated practical application. It is often the result of a professional researcher's desire to obtain more knowledge about certain phenomena and is usually done in a clinical or scientific laboratory setting. Application of the results is not considered.

Applied research

The techniques used in applied research are the same as those used in basic research. This is research done for the purpose of applying the results to the improvement of methods of delivering education to enhance the learning process.

Action research

This is research that is directed at a specific problem to be solved. It is done with the immediate goal of applying the results to a specific problem, not to develop a theory or to create generalizations.

Types of Research

Historical research

This is a type of research designed to apply the scientific method to describing and analyzing the past in order to understand the present and perhaps predict the future.

Descriptive research

This is research in which analysis of the relationships between uncontrolled variables and the development of generalizations based on these uncontrolled variables is the goal. The formation of generalizations, often used in educational research, can lead to false results because the variables cannot be controlled, human subjects cannot be utilized, and the causes of the problem are often more complicated than the result of a single variable. Two elements of descriptive research are:

- Assessment: The description given to such types of studies as surveys, polls, activity analysis, and trends. No value judgments, explanations of reasons or causes, or recommendations are given.

- Evaluation: A value judgment with regard to the effectiveness, desirability, or utility of a research project. Some examples of evaluation studies are school surveys (e.g., about students' use of drugs) and follow-up studies. The application of findings to solving the particular problem is included in the study without any attempt to generalize.

Experimental and quasi-experimental research

This is a logical and systematic way of answering the question, "If this is done under carefully controlled conditions, what will happen?" This type of research is complicated and does not lend itself easily to use in a school setting.

Single-subject experimental research

This is a type of research that focuses on the individual and not on the results of group experimentation. It is used to test hypotheses of the effect of a particular treatment on one or more behaviors or phenomena.

Qualitative research

This is a type of holistic educational research that focuses on in-depth interviews, observations, and document analysis. Methods used include document and content analysis, case studies, and cultural anthropology. This type of research interprets data without the use of numerical analysis.

Basic Steps in Research

All research is based on the use of the scientific method. This is the attempt to control as many variables of a problem as possible in order to separate out the influences of individual and specific elements of the problem.

Selecting the research problem

The practicing counselor usually has no problem selecting a problem that needs to be solved in the setting in which his or her work is conducted. The main consideration is determining what can actually be studied; that is, can the desired variable be observed and measured? Is there an instrument available to measure this variable? If not, can one be designed?

Developing the research problem

The importance of this step in research cannot be too strongly emphasized. Research cannot be conducted on a problem that has not been fully developed. Various parts of the problem should be defined with the help of those familiar with the problem by talking about the problem with colleagues and thinking about all aspects of the problem.

Review of the literature is one of the more important ongoing activities in which the researcher can engage. In addition to scholarly works, the reference section of the library contains many sources of information about current public interests and concerns. Incorporating public interest in the project gives the work added benefit.

Formulate the research question

This step includes formulating all aspects of the question the researcher seeks to answer. It specifically defines the population involved, gives a general description of the situation under which the research will be conducted, and always states the groups to be compared. It is posed in the form of a question. It includes the following three elements:

> The researcher must identify factors, variables, and assumptions that will have an impact on the outcome of the problem. These variables are an integral part of the research project.

1. Purpose statement: This statement describes what the study intends to do and how it will aid the researcher in answering the question(s) posed. In proposals, this statement is written in the present tense; in completed research, this statement is written in the past tense.

2. Procedural statement: This statement follows naturally from the purpose statement. It tells the reader what actions were taken to obtain the results of the study.

3. Hypothesis: This is the statement of what the researcher believes will be the relationship between the variables. The research hypothesis is what the researcher believes will be found as a result of the research. The null hypothesis is the statistical and logical opposite of the research hypothesis. Because we cannot often predict what will happen, sometimes we can predict what will not happen. This is the purpose of the null hypothesis. The alternative hypothesis is a statement of the possibility of other variables not specifically addressed in the design.

Organize the plan for the research report

The research report has the following components:

1. Introduction

2. Hypothesis

3. Review of the literature

4. Method used in conducting the research (research design)

5. Results

6. Conclusions

7. Discussion

8. References

Basic Steps in Evaluation and Follow-Up

An unbiased party should evaluate the research.

Some of the following questions should be asked in the critique:

- Does the title of the research report clearly reflect the research done?

- Are the problem and hypothesis clearly defined and testable?

- Are all the relevant terms defined?

- Is the related literature summarized adequately, relative to the problem?

- Is the research well organized, and are important findings emphasized?

- Is the research design described adequately?

- Are variables and samples described?

- Are controls and data-gathering instruments and procedures appropriate?

- Can the research be replicated?

- Do the results of the research use appropriate statistics, tables, and charts, and is the analysis of the relationship of the data logical and objective?

- Finally, is the discussion of the research clear and objective, and are the findings justified by the data presented?

LONGITUDINAL STUD- IES: studies done to see if an established program is still effective after a period of time

The follow-up procedure is done after the program has been in effect for an established period of time. LONGITUDINAL STUDIES can be done to see if the program established by the research is still effective after a period of time. A survey instrument can be used in follow-up studies to ascertain if the participants felt there was a significant change from before the study and to see if the results of the program established from the research study are long-lasting.

Interpretation of Results of Research, Evaluation, and Follow-Up

In the discussion portion of any research project, the research reports the level of significance of the study. This is most often used to determine the effectiveness of the research with evaluation and follow-up of the procedures used. The attainment of statistical significance (usually reported as 0.05 or less, meaning the results were unlikely to be due to chance) is not always the determining factor of the worth of a program. The evaluator of the program must interpret what the results mean, the influence of the variables on those results, and the relation of each statistical analysis to the hypothesis formulated at the beginning of the study.

Practical significance is another criterion for judging the contribution of the study to everyday practice. Implications for possible change derived from the practical application of the results may be valuable for the improvement of the program. Shortcomings in the research may become clear; in this case, additional research should be considered.

SKILL 8.2 Needs Assessment and Program Evaluation Techniques

Needs Assessment

NEEDS ASSESSMENT is an extensive preliminary study of the real and perceived wants and requirements of a population, community, or group. A series of complete and extensive questions is formulated to submit to all elements of the population involved. The design of the needs assessment study should be carefully formulated so the results can be analyzed in relation to the purpose of the study.

> **NEEDS ASSESSMENT:** an extensive preliminary study of the real and perceived wants and requirements of a population, community, or group

For example, a needs assessment of a school community would include community taxpayers, community leaders, parents, school administrators, teachers, support staff, and students. Other individuals may come forward who wish to participate in the study, and they should be included if they have a connection with the purpose of the study.

Program Evaluation Techniques

Program evaluation is often a requirement of funding sources or of administrators. Sometimes there is a sincere wish to see if a program is producing the desired results; at other times the demand for an evaluation is the result of political pressure, either to discredit opponents of the program or to strengthen proponents' evidence of the value of the program. Finances influence the requirement of a program evaluation in a multitude of ways.

There are two broad types of program evaluation: formative and summative.

Formative evaluation

This type of evaluation involves the collection of data while a program is in the developmental, implementational, or operational stage. In the developmental stage the evaluator tries to determine the general goals, the specific outcomes or behaviors to be attained, and the current performance level of the population of the program to be evaluated. In the implementational stage the evaluator tries to determine if the program is implemented appropriately and the identified population is participating in the program. In the operational stage the evaluator looks at how well the program is running.

Other information included in the evaluation is whether the staff is adequate and well trained and whether any unanticipated difficulties have surfaced.

Summative evaluation

This type of evaluation involves the collection of data after a program has been in place for a period of time. The summative evaluation is often done after one year of operation. This may not be an adequate amount of time to determine the effectiveness of the program, depending on the nature of the program. The summative evaluation often is used to determine if the program will be continued.

Evaluation models

Models used in evaluation can be classified in the following manner:

The CIPP model
This model of evaluation has four stages:

1. **C**ontext evaluation identifies the elements of a setting and the discrepancies between what exists and what is desirable.

2. **I**nput evaluation is the analysis of available resources and methods for the selection of the most appropriate course of action.

3. **P**rocess evaluation is the collection of data about the progress of the program.

4. **P**roduct evaluation is the process of determining the extent to which the program has achieved its goals. In this model, the evaluator gathers the information needed to make a decision in each stage and presents this material to the administrator for decision making.

PROGRAM STANDARDS: the criteria the developers of the program identified for utilization of resources, procedural operations, program management, and final outcomes

PROGRAM PERFORMANCE: what actually occurred when the program was operational in the educational setting

Discrepancy evaluation
The evaluator compares the degree of agreement between program standards and program performance. **PROGRAM STANDARDS** are the criteria the developers of the program identified for utilization of resources, procedural operations, program management, and final outcomes. **PROGRAM PERFORMANCE** is what actually

occurred when the program was operational in the educational setting. The five questions the evaluator answers are:

1. Are standards defined in measurable terms?

2. Are behavioral objectives stated clearly?

3. What instruments have been developed or selected to measure the standards?

4. What data have been collected on performance?

5. Have the data been used to determine the discrepancy between standards and performance?

The findings of the evaluator are then submitted in a report.

Adversarial evaluation

The evaluator and the administrator, with the help of the personnel involved in the program, compile a list of issues to evaluate. Selected personnel form teams to either support or oppose the program, gathering information to support their stand and prepare arguments for their side of the issue. The teams present their arguments before a panel of decision makers who make the final decision regarding the modification, elimination, or retention of the program.

SKILL 8.3 Developing Objectives and Determining Outcomes Based on Data

All programs in the guidance curriculum need to be based on clear objectives and evaluated effectively. The school counselor must assess new programs before implementing them.

Factors to consider are:

- Will this program be acceptable to the community?

- What will be the cost to the school district?

- Can grant money be obtained to initiate the program?

- Will that money be available on a continuous basis or will it run out after a period of time?

A needs assessment of the school community might be in order to see if the program is acceptable. For example, the health department might feel that a smoking cessation program would be beneficial to students. In a needs assessment survey,

New and innovative programs and methods are sometimes introduced without careful consideration of their value for the setting in which they are to be used.

however, students might indicate that they would not attend this type of program. It might be more advantageous for the health department to develop an academic unit about the damage smoking causes to the individual's health in later life.

Before adding a program to the guidance and counseling curriculum, how this task will be accomplished should be evaluated. Will new staff be needed, or can existing staff handle this program? If the latter is the case, will other programs now in existence suffer, or can an ineffective program be eliminated to allow time for the new program? Can the staff view the proposed new program in operation in another school? If so, the counselors at the other school should be questioned regarding the strengths and weaknesses of the program, how they would change it, and what benefits students have gained from it.

After all evaluative data have been compiled and analyzed, the person in charge of the program determines the degree to which program objectives have been met. If formulation of the program objectives was done carefully and there is indisputable evidence that the objectives have not been reached, it is ethical to eliminate the program and start again from scratch. If the program objectives have clearly been met, then the program should be retained, with possible further plans for expansion.

Problems can arise when there is no clear evidence that program objectives have been attained or if some of the objectives have been attained but others, considered more important, have not been. In this case, it is clear that modification of the program is in order.

The task of coming up with new methods to reach the stated objectives should begin with a new perspective of what needs to be done to improve the program. Perhaps people who did not have initial input into the program should be recruited to help in the revision of the program. Perhaps the original objectives of the program were unrealistic. These can be difficult questions to resolve and require thought and effort.

Program objectives should be developed before the adoption of any program. These objectives are based on the needs of the population to be served and can be drawn from the needs assessment. Program objectives should be written with measurable goals and a clear methodology for evaluating the achievement or lack of achievement of the goals.

DOMAIN IV

PROFESSIONAL ISSUES

PERSONALIZED STUDY PLAN

KNOWN MATERIAL/ SKIP IT

COMPETENCY 9
PROFESSIONAL ISSUES

SKILL 9.1 **Professional Standards of the American School Counseling Association (ASCA) and American Counseling Association (ACA)**

The ACA Code of Ethics and Standards of Practice were first developed in 1961 and revised in 1974. Since then, they have been revised approximately every seven years, with the latest revision in 2005. These codes are detailed below.

The Counseling Relationship

The relationship between counselors and clients is based on trust and respect. Therefore, the counselor is responsible for respecting the dignity of all clients and always being mindful of clients' welfare. The counselor must keep appropriate records, get informed consent, maintain professional boundaries, be culturally and developmentally competent, and always be vigilant about avoiding harm to clients.

Confidentiality

It is important that counselors provide their services in a culturally competent manner that respects the rights of the client. Clients must be provided with information and guidelines about when the counselor may breech confidentiality. This informed consent may need to be reviewed throughout the counseling relationship. Records containing sensitive information about clients should be handled with great care, and discretion must be exercised in terms of where records are stored. At all times, the counselor must make every effort to protect the information the client has disclosed within the confines of the trust-based relationship.

> Exceptions to confidentiality may include when clients are in danger of harming themselves or someone else and when the counselor's work with the client is court-ordered, with disclosure being a condition of the counseling.

Professional Responsibility

Counselors must have a working knowledge of their ethical responsibilities as they work with clients. To best serve their clients, counselors need to know the limits of their competence (i.e., know when to refer a client to another provider), be involved with continued professional development, clearly and realistically publicize their services, fairly represent their professional qualifications, monitor the effectiveness of services rendered, and rigorously practice codes of conduct that are nondiscriminatory.

Relationships with Other Professionals

Consultation is a powerful tool in the counseling practice. No counselor is expected, nor should be expected, to know how to work with all populations, cases, and challenges that could be presented. Establishing relationships with other professionals and specialists allows counselors to discuss the effectiveness of case management, maintain confidentiality, and increase overall effectiveness of the services provided to the client.

Evaluation, Assessment, and Interpretation

Assessments may be related to education, career, or psychological issues. The intended use of any assessment instrument must be disclosed to the client. Multicultural considerations must be taken into account to avoid assessments that are inappropriate due to a biased empirical background. Part of counselors' continued professional development is to ensure that any assessment used is the most recent version available. Legal proceedings for forensic evaluations can include the professional opinion of the counselor as well as written or court-ordered consent.

Teaching, Training, and Supervision

Consultation with professionals allows supervising counselors to ethically monitor the work of counselors-in-training. Before serving as a supervisor, counselors undergo extensive training in policies and procedures in the areas of appraisal and evaluation. Supervisors have an ethical obligation to the clients of the supervisee to ensure that the services provided are appropriate. Supervisors need to encourage counselors-in-training to refrain from providing counseling and related services when the trainees' physical, mental, and emotional wellbeing are called into question.

Research and Publications

It is imperative that counselors establish and maintain ethical standards when conducting research. Participants must be notified of the purpose of a study and how their input or results will be used, and they must receive information about the results of the overall project. Researchers must firmly adhere to both federal and state laws as well as institutional regulations.

Resolving Ethical Issues

Following ethical and professional standards is critical to the work counselors do with their clients. Ethical standards not only prevent harm to the client, but also protect the counselor from making unfounded and unintentional mistakes.

Counselors need to consult with other counseling professionals about any situation or case that warrants an ethical question or decision.

The eight topics addressed cover the most common questions in ethical practice. They are by no means all-inclusive; instead, they are guidelines for basic ethical behavior. Although the ethics guidelines are more specific than standards of practice, they cannot possibly include all situations. Standards of practice are, by their nature, more generic and provide basic behavior standards for all counselors. These codes identify areas of concern, but do not provide a "cookbook recipe" for standards of conduct or the resolution of specific ethical situations.

When an ethical issue arises in the counselor's practice in any context (i.e., in private practice, a school setting, or an agency), it is wise to have one's own process of determining a course of action. Referring to the ACA Code of Ethics would be the first step in resolving the problem. Additionally, after formulating a course of action, all of the ramifications of that course of action should be weighed. If there are any doubts about the ethics of this course of action, colleagues, attorneys, and specialists should be consulted.

In the past, divisions of ACA—such as ASCA—had their own codes of ethics, but in 1997, with the revision of the code, divisions were asked to dissolve their codes and develop best practice guidelines as a basic coverage with specific codes that apply to their specialty areas.

Should a counselor suspect a colleague of ethical misconduct, ACA expects counselors to follow the protocol described in the ACA Policies and Procedures for Processing Complaints of Ethical Violations.

To review ASCA standards, go to:
www.schoolcounselor .org/content .asp?contentid=173

To view ACA's code of ethics or access resources related to ethical dilemmas, go to:
www.counseling.org /Resources/CodeOfEthics /TP/Home/CT2.aspx

SKILL 9.2 Legal Rights of Students and Parents Concerning Student Records and Assessment Data

School employees may have access to student records on a need-to-know basis. These employees may include principals, assistant principals, school psychologists, school counselors, and special education professionals. Regardless of his or her position, each employee must maintain the confidentiality of student information.

FERPA

In 1973, Congress passed a federal statute called FERPA to clarify the legal rights of students and parent/guardian(s) concerning access to student records. Also known as the Buckley Amendment, FERPA stands for Family Educational Rights and Privacy Act (20 U.S.C. § 1232g; 34 CFR Part 99).

Schools that receive funds from the federal government must comply with FERPA. The rights afforded by FERPA apply to parent/guardian(s) of students

For more information about FERPA, go to:
www.nces.ed.gov/forum /FERPA_links.asp

under the age of eighteen. Once a student turns eighteen, these rights are then transferred to the "eligible" student.

Under 34 CFR Part 99.7, FERPA states that parent/guardian(s) must be notified on an annual basis about their rights to have access to or to review their student's records. The following information must be included in the annual notification:

- Parent/guardian(s) have the right to review their child's records

- Parent/guardian(s) can advocate for changes to be made to the record should any information be incorrect

- Parent/guardian(s) can provide or withhold consent for the disclosure of personal information located with their child's record

- How a parent/guardian can file a complaint with the Department of Education concerning a school or institution's failure to comply with FERPA

- Which school officials may have access to school records

All assessment data are considered student records and must be kept confidential.

A good resource for issues related to student privacy and confidentiality can be found at:

nces.ed.gov/pubs2006 /stu_privacy/intro.asp

Schools can use a variety of ways to inform parents about their rights, such as the school or community newspaper, bulletin boards, and student handbooks. Schools are not required to individually inform parents of their rights.

Schools must procure parental consent to share students' personal information. For example, a high school counselor must have a consent form on file before providing information to a college concerning a student's academic background. An ethical counselor will not provide personal information (except for information that has been published publicly, for example, in a student directory) to colleges, military recruiters, and coaches without gaining consent of the parent or guardian.

All assessment data are considered student records and must be kept confidential. Legally and ethically, only the students and/or their parent/guardian(s) have the right to access their records unless they have specifically signed a waiver or requested that the information be shared with colleges, outside professionals, or other personnel such as attorneys.

SKILL 9.3 Legislation Regarding Exceptional Students

Special education law is filled with abbreviations. In the explanations of the laws in this section, the abbreviations are used instead of the actual names of the acts or authorities. The following is a list of these abbreviations for easy reference. See www.ed.gov for more information.

EDGAR	Education Department General Administrative Regulations
EAHCA	Education for all Handicapped Children Act
EHA	Education for the Handicapped Act
FAPE	Free Appropriate Public Education
IEP	Individualized Education Program
IFSP	Individualized Family Service Plan
IDEA	Individuals with Disabilities Education Act
ITDA	Infants and Toddlers with Disabilities Act
LEA	Local Education Authority
OCR	Office of Civil Rights (U.S. Department of Education).
OSERS	Office of Special Education and Rehabilitative Services (U.S. Department of Education)
OSEP	Office of Special Education Programs (U.S. Department of Education)
SEA	State Education Authority

In 1975 Congress signed into law the Individuals with Disabilities Education Act (IDEA), or Public Law 94-142, making local and state education entities responsible for providing children with disabilities a "free and appropriate public education." This act was a turning point in the education of children with disabilities, providing that these children have a right to FAPE and also providing for procedural protections to ensure that they received it. Subsequently, Section 504 of the Rehabilitation Act of 1993 was enacted, which also affected the educational rights of children with disabilities.

There are overlapping provisions as well as differences between these laws. Section 504 is broad and general, and includes a wider range of discrimination, while IDEA is more specific and detailed. Other acts delineate the procedures for the delivery of education services to children with disabilities.

Brown vs. Board of Education and Mills vs. Board of Education were two important legal decisions that helped hasten the enactment of education protections for children with disabilities. Section 504 of the Rehabilitation Act of 1993 provided

In 1975 Congress signed into law the Individuals with Disabilities Education Act (IDEA), or Public Law 94-142, making local and state education entities responsible for providing children with disabilities a "free and appropriate public education."

that "no otherwise qualified handicapped individual... shall solely by reason of his handicap be excluded from participation in, be denied the benefits of, or be subjected to discrimination under any program or activity receiving federal assistance." The subsequent amendments provided for payment of attorney's fees and damages to parents if they proved successful in legal suits brought against educational institutions for not providing their children with a FAPE.

IDEA is a funding vehicle of the federal government for a SEA to provide a FAPE to all children with disabilities. In addition, if a state opts to provide a FAPE for children from ages 3 to 5 and 18 to 21, it must, under IDEA, provide that opportunity for all children with disabilities in those age groups. In addition, if any children without disabilities in those age groups are provided with educational services, then a proportionate share of those with disabilities must also be provided with the same educational services. The funding is provided by a complicated formula that takes into account the number of children in a given state who have been classified as disabled.

> Section 504 of the Rehabilitation Act of 1993 provided that "no otherwise qualified handicapped individual... shall solely by reason of his handicap be excluded from participation in, be denied the benefits of, or be subjected to discrimination under any program or activity receiving federal assistance."

Each state monitors the devising and implementation of its own FAPE. The main provision enacted by Congress was the requirement that each child classified be provided with an IEP on an annual basis. Procedural protections include that the child be identified, that the child be evaluated by a multidisciplinary team, that eligibility for special education be determined, and that an IEP be developed with parental participation.

SKILL 9.4 Laws Regarding Child Abuse and Neglect

> Although the confidentiality of the counselor–client relationship might be violated, the school counselor has a duty to protect the minor child from harm.

Every state has laws that require the reporting of suspected abuse and neglect of children under the age of 18. The counselor should investigate the state laws as well as the policies of the school district in which he or she will be working in order to become familiar with the definitions of abuse in a particular state, the mandate to report, and the procedures to follow when reporting suspected cases.

Although the confidentiality of the counselor–client relationship might be violated, the school counselor has a duty to protect the minor child from harm. Most often, though, the child who is a victim of such abuse, and who reports it to the counselor, is seeking help. The skillful counselor will seek the consent of the child to report the incident or incidents in an effort to maintain a trusting relationship with the child.

SKILL 9.5 Using Technology Effectively

The core of a school counselor's job involves communication and connection with students, parents/guardians, teachers, administrators, other school personnel, and outside professionals. The personal relationship between counselors and others cannot be supplanted by technology. However, because communication and information are central to a school counselor's work, technology can be utilized very effectively to enhance the school counselor's job.

There are several areas in which school counselors need to be technologically proficient. One is in basic computer skills, such as keyboarding, word processing, and using e-mail. Many schools have computerized most student data and scheduling, and counselors must be able to access and utilize this information efficiently. E-mail is the primary form of communication in many school districts, and counselors, like all faculty and staff, must be able to communicate using e-mail.

Increasingly, parents and guardians are also using e-mail to communicate with school personnel. Some school districts have created specific interactive programs on the school's Web site to facilitate the sharing of information with parents, guardians, community members, teachers, and other school personnel.

A second area in which school counselors are increasingly required to be technologically savvy is in the use of the Internet to access information. While there are many types of Internet information that may be relevant to school counselors' work, of particular importance is information about career development, higher education, training programs, and financial aid.

Third, counselors need to be able to use software to develop presentations and graphics for the classroom, at conferences or meetings, for reports, and with colleagues. Most professional fields require such capacity, and school counselors need to stay current with the opportunities that technology offers. This may also involve a working knowledge of the hardware used for presentations.

> *Relevant state statutes can be searched at:*
>
> www.childwelfare.gov /systemwide/laws_policies /state/
>
> *State departments of education also have useful information regarding child protection laws.*

> *Students and many parents/guardians use the Internet as their primary source for gathering data. This requires that counselors have not only a facility in using Internet browsers and search engines, but also the capacity to assess the value and utility of different Web sites.*

SKILL 9.6 Professional Development

Licensure

Professional counselors can be certified in different areas by the National Board for Certified Counselors (NBCC) (www.nbcc.org), as well as licensed by many states. These certifying agents have their own codes of ethics to which members are accountable. The counselor who holds each specific certification or license is ethically bound and accountable to know and abide by the ethical code of the certifying body. Violations can and should be reported to these monitoring agencies.

Continuing Education

All licensing and certifying bodies require a requisite number of hours of continuing education. Regardless, all school counselors have a professional and ethical responsibility to stay abreast of current developments in the field. Attending conferences and seminars can provide professional nourishment and also be helpful in preventing burnout in what can be a very demanding career. In addition to going to programs geared specifically to school counseling and guidance, counselors may find it interesting and helpful to participate in workshops and training programs designed for mental health professionals, educators, social workers, and administrators. Attending meetings of the local, state, and national counselor associations can also be informative.

Attending conferences and seminars can provide professional nourishment and also be helpful in preventing burnout in what can be a very demanding career.

For more information about professional development opportunities, including the state and national conferences, go to:

www.schoolcounselor.org /content.asp?pl=325&sl =129&contentid=129

BIBLIOGRAPHY

Best, J. W., and J. V. Kahn. 1996. *Research in Education,* 7th Edition. Boston: Allyn and Bacon, Inc.

Bragstad, B. J., and S. M. Stumpf. 1987. *A Guidebook for Teaching Study Skills and Motivation,* 2nd Edition. Boston: Allyn and Bacon, Inc.

Brownell, J. 1986. *Building Active Listening Skills.* Englewood Cliffs, NJ: Prentice-Hall, Inc.

Bukstein, O. G. 1995. *Substance Abuse: Adolescent Assessment and Prevention.* Hoboken, NJ: John Wiley and Sons.

Burley-Allen, M. 1982. *Listening: The Forgotten Skill.* Hoboken, NJ: John Wiley and Sons, Inc.

Cartwright, D., and A. Zander, eds. 1968. *Group Dynamics: Research and Theory,* 3rd Edition. New York: Harper & Row.

Cates, W. M. 1985. *A Practical Guide to Educational Research.* Englewood Cliffs, NJ: Prentice-Hall, Inc.

Corey, G. 1991. *Manual for Theory and Practice of Counseling and Psychotherapy,* 4th Edition. Pacific Grove, CA: Brooks/Cole Publishing Co.

Corey, G. 1996. *Instructor's Manual for Theory and Practice of Counseling and Psychotherapy,* 5th Edition. Pacific Grove, CA: Brooks/Cole Publishing Co.

Corey, G. 1996. *Student Manual for Theory and Practice of Counseling and Psychotherapy,* 5th Edition. Pacific Grove, CA: Brooks/Cole Publishing Co.

Corey, G., 1990. *Theory and Practice of Group Counseling,* 3rd Edition. Pacific Grove, CA: Brooks/Cole Publishing Co.

Cottle, W. C. 1968. *Guidance Monograph Series, Series 111, Testing, Interest and Personality Inventories.* Boston: Houghton Mifflin Co.

Dougherty, A. M. 1995. *Case Studies in Human Services Consultation.* Pacific Grove, CA: Brooks/Cole Publishing Co.

Downing, L. N. 1968. *Guidance and Counseling Services: An Introduction.* New York: McGraw-Hill Book Co.

Dreshman, J. L., C. L. Crabbe, and S. Tarasevich. 2001. *Caring in Times of Crisis: A Crisis Management/Postvention Manual for Administrators, Student Assistance Teams and Other School Personnel K-12.* Chapin, SC: Youthlight, Inc.

Dunn, R., and K. Dunn. 1978. *Teaching Students Through Their Individual Learning Styles: A Practical Approach.* Reston, VA: Reston Publishing Co.

Erikson, E. H. 1963. *Childhood and Society*, 2nd Edition. New York: W. W. Norton and Co. Inc.

Forum Guide to the Privacy of Student Information: A Resource for Schools (NFES 2006–805). (2006). U.S. Dept of Education. Washington, DC: National Center for Education Statistics.

Goldman, L. 1961. *Century Psychology Series: Using Tests in Counseling*. New York: Appleton-Century Crofts.

Gressard, C. F., and L. Keel. "Ethics in Counseling." *Counseling Today*. (February 1998): 16.

Guernsey, T. F. and K. Klare. 1993. *Special Education Law*. Durham, NC: Carolina Academic Press.

Hazler, R. J. 1996. *Breaking the Cycle of Violence*. Washington, DC: Accelerated Development.

Hergenhahn, B. R. 1988. *An Introduction to Theories of Learning*, 3rd Edition. Englewood Cliffs, NJ: Prentice-Hall, Inc.

Johnson, D. W., and R. T. Johnson. 1995. *Reducing School Violence Through Conflict Resolution*. Alexandria, VA: Association for Supervision and Curriculum Development.

Johnson, D. W., and F. P. Johnson. 1975. *Joining Together: Group Theory and Group Skills*. Englewood Cliffs, NJ: Prentice-Hall, Inc.

Kemp, C. G. 1964. *Perspectives on the Group Process*. Boston: Houghton Mifflin Co.

Lyman, H. B. 1968. *Guidance Monograph Series, Series 111 Testing, Intelligence, Aptitude and Achievement Testing*. Boston: Houghton Mifflin Co.

Mahler, C., and E. Caldwell. 1961. *Group Counseling in Secondary Schools*. Chicago, IL: Science Research Associates.

Mahler, C. 1969. *Group Counseling in the School*. Boston: Houghton Mifflin Co.

McDaniels, C., and C. G. Norman. 1992. *Counseling for Career Development*, 1st Edition. San Francisco: Jossey-Bass Publishers.

Meyering, R. A. 1968. *Guidance Monograph Series, Series 11 Counseling, Use of Test Data in Counseling*. Boston: Houghton Mifflin Co.

Osipow, S. H. 1968. *Theories of Career Development*. New York: Century Psychology Series, Appleton-Century Crofts, Educational Division of Meredith Corp.

Osipow, S. H., and L. F. Fitzgerald. 1996. *Theories of Career Development*, 4th Edition. Boston: Allyn and Bacon.

Osipow, S. H., and W. B. Walsh. 1970. *Strategies in Counseling for Behavior Change*. New York: Century Psychology Series, Appleton-Century Crofts.

Patterson, C. H. 1966. *Theories of Counseling and Psychotherapy.* New York: Harper & Row.

Reeves, E. T. 1970. *The Dynamics of Group Behavior.* New York: American Management Association, Inc.

Rogers, D. 1969. *Readings in Child Psychology.* Pacific Grove, CA: Brooks/Cole Publishing Co.

Shaw, M. E. 1976. *Group Dynamics: The Psychology of Small Group Behavior,* 2nd Edition. New York: McGraw-Hill Book Co.

Sims, R. R., and S. J. Sims. 1995. *The Importance of Learning Styles.* Westport, CT: Greenwood Press.

Vandracek, R. M., M. R. Lerner, and J. E. Schulenberg. 1986. *Career Development: A Life Span Developmental Approach.* Hillsdale, NJ: Lawrence Erlbaum Associates.

White, J., F. Mullis, G. B. Earle, and G. Brigman. 1995. *Consultation in Schools: The Counselor's Role.* Portland, ME: J. Weston Walch.

Yalom, I.D., and M. Leszcz. 2005. *The Theory and Practice of Group Psychotherapy, 5th Edition.* NY: Basic Books.

Zebrowitz, L. A. 1990. *Social Perception.* Pacific Grove, CA: Brooks/Cole Publishers.

Zunker, V. G. 1994. *Using Assessment Results for Career Development,* 4th Edition. Pacific Grove, CA: Brooks/Cole Publishers.

SAMPLE TEST

SAMPLE TEST

Section One: Listening Section

For the listening section of the test, the candidate will be given a CD to listen to and will then answer written questions based on what they have heard. The CD will contain client statements and responses and various extended interactions between counselors and clients. The questions will evaluate the candidate's ability to identify the client's feeling or problems and to evaluate the appropriateness of the counselor's response to those feelings and problems. The candidate will have 40 minutes to complete this portion of the test and will be given the questions and answer choices but not a written script of the taped material.

At this time, XAMonline does not offer an accompanying CD for the listening section.

Questions 1–19: Read the excerpt and select the word or phrase that best describes the client's feelings, needs, or attitudes.

1. Student: "I want to drop my history class. I don't get along with Ms. Jones and I don't need the credit to graduate. What do you think I should do?"

    A. Confidence

    B. Fear

    C. Arrogance

    D. Uncertainty

    E. Apathy

2. Student: "I don't know why my mom is giving me such a hard time about my grades. I have mostly Bs, with a couple of As. I try so hard and I really study a lot."

    A. Confusion

    B. Anger

    C. Hurt

    D. Fear

    E. Arrogance

3. Student: "I am sick of being teased by those girls. If you don't do something, I am going to do something bad. I can't take it anymore. I really can't."

    A. Anger

    B. Frustration

    C. Hurt

    D. Uncertainty

    E. Shame

4. Student: "My daddy says I'm dumb because I didn't do so well on my spelling test. But I just can't remember certain words. Do you think I'm dumb?"

    A. Sadness

    B. Frustration

    C. Fear

    D. Anxiety

    E. Inadequacy

5. Mother: "I want to talk with you about how Jackie is doing in math. She always loved it until she got to middle school. Is there something going on with the teacher or in the class that her father and I should know about? What can we do to help?"

   A. Anger

   B. Frustration

   C. Concern

   D. Irritation

   E. Arrogance

6. Teacher: "I'm glad I caught you. I really need to talk about that new boy. He is not fitting in and I really don't know what to do about it. He seems to like causing trouble with the other boys. It's driving me crazy!"

   A. Anger

   B. Frustration

   C. Concern

   D. Irritation

   E. Arrogance

7. Student: "I hate Mr. Allison. He's mean and he's out to get me. It doesn't matter what I do. I've had it."

   A. Anger

   B. Frustration

   C. Concern

   D. Irritation

   E. Arrogance

8. Teacher: "Thanks for the feedback about my reading group. They are a handful, and I think your suggestions might work. I'll let you know what happens."

   A. Worry

   B. Frustration

   C. Concern

   D. Relief

   E. Appreciation

9. Student: "Thanks for your help. I really don't know what to tell my dad about what happened in gym, and I'm afraid of his reaction. But at least I have a few ideas about what to say. What if he gets mad at me?"

   A. Worry

   B. Frustration

   C. Concern

   D. Relief

   E. Appreciation

10. Father: "Thanks for letting me know about Zelda. She isn't always the easiest kid to work with, and I am so glad she seems to be getting along with her teachers this year."

    A. Worry

    B. Frustration

    C. Concern

    D. Relief

    E. Appreciation

11. Student: "I don't know what to do about the future. I didn't score so well on my SATs. My parents want me to go to a four-year college, but I really want to do the graphic design program at the community college. That would be really cool."

    Counselor: "It sounds like you know what you want but you're not sure how to talk with your parents about what you want."

    A. Judgmental

    B. Empathetic

    C. Concerned

    D. Perceptive

    E. Uncaring

12. Parent: "I can't believe you didn't call me immediately when my daughter's friends told you she was cutting herself yesterday. Why did you wait until today?"

    Counselor: "I'm sorry you are upset. I can understand that. I felt I needed to speak directly with your daughter first and make sure it wasn't just gossip. I called you as soon as your daughter and I talked."

    A. Judgmental

    B. Empathic

    C. Concerned

    D. Perceptive

    E. Uncaring

13. Student: "I really wonder if I should be in this advanced math class. I'm not very good with pressure and there is a lot of homework."

    Counselor: "It sounds like you probably shouldn't put yourself through that if you can't deal with the pressure. That is a high-powered class. Maybe you should drop the course."

    A. Judgmental

    B. Empathic

    C. Concerned

    D. Perceptive

    E. Uncaring

14. Student: "Thanks, again, for helping me with my schedule. I feel like I've got the right courses now."

    Counselor: "You're very welcome. I'm glad the courses feel like a fit. Let me know if I can help you out in the future—that's what I'm here for."

    A. Grateful

    B. Solicitous

    C. Concerned

    D. Perceptive

    E. Curious

15. Student: "Hey, Ms. Cortez. Guess what? I'm going to the rink with Maria and Josie. That's the first time they ever asked me. Pretty cool, huh?"

Counselor: "Very cool. Sounds like you're starting to make friends. I'm so glad, Emma."

A. Supportive

B. Empathic

C. Concerned

D. Perceptive

E. Condescending

16. Teacher: "Can I talk with you for a few minutes about Frankie? He's having a tough time in English, and I wondered how he was doing in his other classes."

Counselor: "Sure. Thanks for letting me know. I'll check with his other teachers. I'm free fifth period if you want to talk more. Let me know."

A. Supportive

B. Empathic

C. Concerned

D. Perceptive

E. Responsive

17. Student: "I don't know what to do about the future. I didn't score so well on my SATs. My parents want me to go to a four-year college, but I really want to do the graphic design program at the community college. That would be really cool."

Counselor: "It sounds like you're feeling that you're in a dilemma and aren't sure what to do. Would you like to talk about this more?"

A. Judgmental

B. Empathic

C. Concerned

D. Perceptive

E. Uncaring

18. Student: "What do you want now? You are always bugging me and pulling me out of class for stuff!"

Counselor: "It sounds like you're upset with me. Talk to me, Carrie. What's up?"

A. Judgmental and empathic

B. Empathic and concerned

C. Concerned and frustrated

D. Perceptive and frustrated

E. Supportive and judgmental

19. Student: "I can't stand talking about this anymore! Every time I come to you, you say we are going to work it out. But it never gets worked out."

    Counselor: "It sounds like you're fed up with the whole thing—and so am I. I keep trying to get something done but I'm not succeeding, am I?"

    A. Judgmental and empathic

    B. Empathic and concerned

    C. Concerned and frustrated

    D. Perceptive and frustrated

    E. Supportive and judgmental

Questions 20–25: Read the excerpt and select the answer that best describes *how the client is most likely to react to the counselor's response.*

20. Student: "What do you want now? You are always bugging me and pulling me out of class for stuff!"

    Counselor: "It sounds like you're upset with me. Talk to me, Carrie. What's up?"

    A. Feeling criticized, the student will become silent.

    B. Feeling the counselor's care and concern, the student will open up about being upset and tell the counselor what is going on.

    C. The student will lash out further at the counselor.

    D. The student will change the subject and ask the counselor why she was called to the counselor's office.

    E. The student will turn around and walk out.

21. Student: "I'm afraid of what I am going to do. My friends have all started using drugs—nothing heavy, just pot. But I don't want to do it and yet I don't want to stop being friends with them. What should I do?"

    Counselor: "I'm so glad you felt you could come to me and that you could tell me what's going on. You're pretty strong to be able to do that. Let's talk more about this, okay?"

    A. The student will show frustration that the counselor doesn't immediately tell her what to do.

    B. The student will become worried that the counselor will get her friends in trouble, and stop talking.

    C. The student will share more about her dilemma and feelings.

    D. The student will become curious and ask the counselor if he ever used drugs.

    E. The student will express fear about what the counselor is going to do.

22. Student: "I'm crying because Joey hit me. He always does that at recess."

    Counselor: "I'm so sorry, Freddie. He's not supposed to hit. Are you hurt? Can I help you?"

    A. The student will stop crying and tell the counselor about what's been happening at recess.

    B. The student will cry more.

    C. The student will run off, afraid of getting in trouble.

    D. The student will defend Joey, saying he's his best friend.

    E. The student will become silent, cross his arms, and just sit.

23. Mother: "Thanks so much for calling me. What is happening with Serena? Why is she there? She's been so upset lately. Is she in trouble?"

Counselor: "I'm glad I reached you. Serena is here with me and I think it would be best for her to tell you in her own words what is happening. Would that be alright with you? She'd really like to talk with you herself."

A. The mother will insist on having the counselor tell her what is happening with her daughter.

B. The mother will become angry that the counselor refuses to talk with her.

C. The mother will accuse the counselor of hiding things from her.

D. The mother will become silent and wait for the counselor to speak.

E. The mother will agree and ask to talk with her daughter.

24. Student: "I wondered if I could help you with those papers. I like to help and would be happy to put all that stuff together and staple it. I have a free period."

Counselor: "Well, maybe that's a good idea. But what's going on? Is something up? Would you like to talk with me?"

A. Feeling that her help was rejected, the student will become silent and just walk away.

B. Uncertain about the counselor's response, the student will insist everything is fine and ask again if she can help with the paperwork.

C. Feeling the counselor's care and concern, the student will acknowledge that she would like to talk.

D. Feeling judged, the student will lash out, saying she just offered to help.

E. The student will change the subject and ask the counselor if she is going to the football game on Friday.

25. Student: "I have been trying to get my essay done for my college applications and it's just not coming out right. I don't know how to say what I want to say, and Ms. Huntley said I can't spend any more time on it in English. My dad's really pressuring me to get it done. I can't do this."

Counselor: "You sound kind of discouraged, Sam, and under a lot of pressure. Would it help to talk with me about it? Maybe we could figure out who might be able to work with you on it to help you clarify what you really want to say."

A. The student will express relief at being heard and then begin complaining further about his father and Ms. Huntley.

B. The student will express relief at being heard and talk further with the counselor about how to get his essay done.

C. Feeling the counselor's care and concern, the student will ask the counselor to write the essay for him.

D. The student will express frustration that the counselor is not willing to work on the essay with him.

E. The student will ask the counselor to read the essay.

Questions 26–28: Read the excerpt and choose the answer that best describes *the appropriateness of the counselor's response.*

26. Counselor: "Hi, Timmy. Wow, that's quite a bruise on your arm. Does it hurt? Are you okay?"

Student: "Why are you asking me these questions about my arm? I just banged it on my bike handlebar."

Counselor: "I was just kind of worried— I wanted to make sure you were okay. Sometimes it's hard for kids to tell adults about getting hurt, especially if someone else hurt them and they're afraid of getting in trouble. You're not in any trouble. And it's okay to talk about things."

A. Appropriate, because the counselor conveys concern and invites the student to talk about things that might be difficult to discuss

B. Appropriate, because the counselor is being friendly and concerned

C. Inappropriate, because there is no reason for the counselor to ask a student about injuries not sustained in the school setting

D. Inappropriate, because the counselor is suggesting child abuse to the student

E. Inappropriate, because the student did not bring the issue to the counselor

27. Counselor (to a teacher): "Do you mind if I ask you something about Shandra? She came to me with something personal and I wasn't sure what I should do. Can we talk?"

A. Appropriate, because the teacher knows Shandra and her family quite well and may provide some insight

B. Appropriate, because the counselor needs to get a second opinion to do her job well

C. Inappropriate, because counselors should know what to do without talking with teachers or other staff except in extreme situations

D. Inappropriate, because counselors need to respect students' privacy and not discuss personal matters with teachers; an appropriate consult would be with another counselor

E. Inappropriate, because the teacher knows the student personally

28. Student: "Is it okay to talk with you about something private? I mean, do you have to tell someone else anything I tell you? This is really important."

Counselor: "I'm glad you came to me. I keep everything students tell me private, unless you are in danger of hurting yourself or someone else. Then I have to tell someone—that's the law. But let's see what's going on. I really would like to help you."

Student: "But you might have to tell someone. Maybe I shouldn't talk to you."

Counselor: "I will do my best to keep this between us. And I will tell you first if I need to go to someone else, including your parents. In fact, if I call your parents, I would like you to be in the room with me. How's that? We will only go to someone else if we have to. I really want to help."

A. Appropriate, because she tells the student that she really wants to help her no matter what

B. Appropriate, because the counselor is both reassuring about the importance of privacy and honest about the need to disclose certain information to parents and others

C. Inappropriate, because the counselor creates anxiety by mentioning the law and possible disclosure

D. Inappropriate, because counselors should never keep important information about students private

E. Inappropriate, because the student will feel betrayed by the possible need to disclose the information

Questions 29–31: Read the excerpt, then choose the best answer for the questions that follow.

Counselor: "I understand that you and Sarah had an argument in Ms. Tucker's room during class today. Can you tell me what happened?"

Student: "Sarah has been my best friend all this year in seventh grade. She told James that I like him after she promised she wouldn't tell him. Now he knows and everyone is laughing at me."

Counselor: "So, what I'm hearing you say is that you shared your secret with Sarah, thinking that you could trust her, and she shared your secret with other people. Is this how the argument started?"

Student: "No, we started fighting because she whispered something to James and they started laughing at me. So I told her to shut up and then she yelled at me, and that's what happened."

Counselor: "And, in the meantime, you disrupted Ms. Tucker's teaching."

Student: "I didn't really think about that…"

Counselor: "How do you think you could handle this type of situation in the future so that you don't end up in a fight with your friend, and you don't disrupt class?"

29. **The student's response to the counselor's initial statement indicates which of the following?**

   A. The student feels as though she is being blamed for the situation.

   B. The student recognizes her responsibility in the problem.

   C. The student does not recognize her responsibility in the problem.

   D. The student sees the problem as an issue between herself and her best friend.

   E. She is too traumatized to return to the class with Sarah and James.

30. **The counselor's behavior throughout the session indicates that his objective was to facilitate:**

   A. Conflict resolution between the student and Sarah

   B. A better understanding of the student's responsibility for the problem

   C. Modeling appropriate classroom behavior

   D. Helping the student learn whom she can and cannot trust

   E. A healthier understanding of the counseling process

31. **Based on the overall tone of the session, which of the following is the student MOST likely to do in the future?**

   A. Return to class and resume the argument with Sarah

   B. Avoid returning to the counselor's office to resolve a problem

   C. Tell Sarah's secrets to retaliate against her

   D. Apologize to Ms. Tucker for disrupting class

   E. Think about this experience before sharing additional personal information with Sarah

Questions 32–34: Read the excerpt, then choose the best answer for the questions that follow.

Counselor: "When we talked the other day, you shared with me that you overheard your parents discussing a divorce, and I know that was a very, very difficult thing for you to hear. How are you feeling today?"

Student: "I'm really angry at both of them, and I wish they would stop trying to pretend everything is okay."

Counselor: "You mentioned that you felt more comfortable talking with your mom about the situation than your dad. Have you had an opportunity to talk with her about it?"

Student: "No, not yet. I just don't know what to say to her."

Counselor: "Why don't we practice that today? Let's try this: Turn your chair to face this empty chair, and pretend that your mom is sitting right here in front of you. How do you feel about trying that?"

Student: "I don't know. It seems kind of weird, but I guess we could try."

32. **The student's response to the counselor's initial question indicates which of the following?**

   A. The student and counselor have established a comfortable rapport with one another.

   B. The student does not have an accurate understanding of the situation between his parents.

   C. The student is avoiding his own concerns by blaming the situation on his parents.

   D. The student's anger at his parents hinders his ability to address school-related issues.

   E. The student's intent is for the counselor to intervene with his parents.

33. **The counselor's behavior throughout the session indicates that her objective was to:**

   A. Encourage the student to take responsibility for his part in the problem

   B. Help the student learn to mediate the problems between his parents

   C. Learn more personal information about the student in order to address school-related issues

   D. Help the student communicate his concerns more effectively to his parents

   E. Help the student work through his anger toward his parents

34. **Suggesting the empty chair technique indicated that the counselor's objective was to do which of the following?**

   A. Give the student a safe environment in which to express his concerns to his mother

   B. Help the student practice working through his anger toward his mother before the actual confrontation

   C. Show the student how irrational his behavior has become

   D. Give the student a safe environment in which to work through his anger toward his parents

   E. Gain a better understanding of the situation between the student's parents

Questions 35–37: Read the excerpt, then choose the best answer for the questions that follow.

Counselor: "You mentioned that you have some concerns about your coursework in terms of the colleges to which you are applying. Walk me through your concerns, and we'll address them one at a time."

Student: "Well, first of all, I was thinking that I only had to complete three social studies credits to graduate, but it looks like all of my college choices require four credits. What am I going to do to make up the fourth credit? I already have my schedule for next year, and I have seven classes already selected."

Counselor: "Let's take a look at your schedule and see what we need to do. I see that you're planning to take Art and Choir next year, and from what I remember, you really enjoy fine arts courses."

Student: "I really do want to take those fine arts classes. I think I may major in art education in college. I don't really want to drop either of those classes."

Counselor: "I understand that you want to take both, so you're going to need to make a choice based on your goals and on what's best for you. You can take both art classes next year and possibly go to summer school for a social studies credit, or…"

Student: "No, I definitely don't want to go to summer school!"

Counselor: "Okay, we could look at colleges that only require three credits, or we could change one fine arts class to a Contemporary Issues or Psychology/Sociology course. If we do that, you would be able to meet your fourth requirement for social studies for your colleges. What do you think?"

Student: "Well, I really want to participate in both arts classes, but I think this is more important. I sing in my church choir, and I'm a member of the art club. I guess I'll just take art and change my choir class to Contemporary Issues. I've heard that's a great class."

Counselor: "That's an excellent choice. You'll really enjoy that class. What an easy fix! So, what's next?"

35. The student's response to the counselor's initial suggestion for schedule changes indicates which of the following:

A. The student is unwilling to consider the counselor's suggestions at this time.

B. The student is interested only in having fun.

C. The student is focusing more on minute details than on choices that directly affect his college plans.

D. The student sees the arts classes as more important to his future than the social studies classes.

E. The student believes that the counselor is not interested in what is best for the student.

36. The counselor's objective throughout the session is which of the following:

    A. To help the student recognize his mistakes

    B. To help the student take responsibility for his decisions

    C. To influence the student to make choices based on the counselor's wishes

    D. To empower the student to make the best decision for himself based on several options

    E. To influence the student to make choices based on his parents' wishes

37. Which of the following is MOST likely to occur following the counselor's final statement in the session?

    A. Based on the success of his previous decision, the student will feel confident in making additional choices about his schedule.

    B. The student will feel as though the counselor is patronizing him.

    C. The student will make the rest of his decisions without input from the counselor.

    D. The student will feel obligated to ask for the counselor's help in making scheduling decisions in the future.

    E. The counselor will try to influence the student's future scheduling decisions.

Questions 38–40: Read the excerpt, then choose the best answer for the questions that follow.

Counselor: "I was really surprised to see your Biology grade. What kinds of problems are you having in the class?"

Student: "Ms. Jackson doesn't like me. I want to switch my schedule."

Counselor: "What has given you the impression that she doesn't like you?"

Student: "She is always giving me bad grades on everything. I just don't want to be in her class any more. I want to take study hall instead."

Counselor: "I'm looking at your grades in Biology, and I see several missing assignments. Talk to me about the missing work."

Student: "I told her I was going to turn that stuff in, and she just gave me zeros on everything. She always does that."

Counselor: "I hear you saying that Ms. Jackson is at fault for your problems in Biology. What are some things that you could do to help yourself in her class?"

Student: "I don't know."

Counselor: "At this point, I'm not going to switch your schedule. I think we need to discuss some things that you can do to improve both your grades and your relationship with Ms. Jackson."

38. The student's response to the counselor's initial question indicates which of the following?

    A. The student refuses to accept responsibility for her behavior.

    B. The student is resistant to the counseling process.

    C. The student is ready to discuss the problems she is experiencing with Ms. Jackson.

    D. The best way to solve the issue is to immediately change the student's schedule.

    E. At this point in the session, the counselor must work toward a positive rapport with the student.

39. The counselor's behavior throughout the session indicates that her objective was to facilitate:

    A. Empathy for the student

    B. Empathy for Ms. Jackson

    C. Disciplinary action against the student

    D. Having the student take responsibility for her part in the problem

    E. Unconditional positive regard for the student and her behavior

40. The student's behavior throughout the session indicates all of the following EXCEPT:

    A. Resistance to the counseling process

    B. Refusal to accept responsibility for her behavior in the classroom

    C. Blaming the counselor for the problem because the counselor refuses to change her schedule

    D. Blaming the teacher for the student's lack of success in the classroom

    E. Refusal to consider changes that the student could make

Section Two: Pencil-and-Paper Test

Counseling and Guidance

(Average) (Skill 1.1)

41. The process of an active organism exhibiting controlled behavior is called:

    A. Operant conditioning

    B. Modeling

    C. Counterconditioning

    D. Transference

    E. Control

(Easy) (Skill 1.1)

42. The stages of life in Erik Erikson's psychosocial theory include all of the following EXCEPT:

    A. Innocence vs. generativity

    B. Basic trust vs. basic mistrust

    C. Identity vs. role confusion

    D. Ego integrity vs. despair

    E. Autonomy vs. shame and doubt

(Average) (Skill 1.1)

43. **Which of the following is the definition of cognitive restructuring?**

   A. Teaching skills and techniques for dealing with difficult situations in ways that are direct, firm, and clear

   B. The process the therapist evokes in making an evaluation of the client's level of functioning at the beginning of the therapy and subsequently adjusting procedures and techniques to the goals of the client

   C. A specific response to a behavior that increases the probability of that behavior being repeated

   D. The attempt to block out negative thoughts by refusing to acknowledge them

   E. The process of identifying and understanding the impact of negative behavior and thoughts and learning to replace them with more realistic and appropriate actions and beliefs

(Average) (Skill 1.1)

44. **Borderline Personality Disorder can be defined as follows:**

   A. The unconscious process that operates to protect the individual from threatening and anxiety-producing thoughts, feelings, and impulses

   B. The pathology that develops when an individual fails to adequately develop in the separation-individuation phase

   C. The pathology caused by unconscious sexual feelings of a daughter toward her father, coupled with hostility toward her mother

   D. A personality disorder characterized by extreme self-love and an exaggerated sense of self-importance

   E. An ego-defense mechanism of reverting to a less mature stage of development

(Average) (Skill 1.1)

45. **Freud's concept of the ego can be defined as which of the following?**

   A. The part of the personality that is ruled by the pleasure principle; the center of the instincts, which are largely unconscious

   B. The part of the personality that mediates between the unconscious instincts and the environment

   C. The part of the personality that resists change of any kind

   D. The part of the personality that determines what is right and wrong and strives to "be good"

   E. The part of the personality responsible for a sense of humor

(Average) (Skill 1.3)

46. **The process of learning is not affected by:**

   A. Past experiences

   B. Environmental factors

   C. Psychosexual stages

   D. Mental processes

   E. Social factors

(Easy) (Skill 1.3)

47. **Stages of human development as outlined by Jean Piaget include all of the following except:**

   A. Sensorimotor stage

   B. Concrete operational stage

   C. Preoperational stage

   D. Cultural and environmental stage

   E. Formal operational stage

(Rigorous) (Skill 1.4)

48. **A student who needs the emotional element of structure as a condition of the learning environment must have which of the following:**

    A. Specific rules for completing an assignment (i.e., time limits, restriction of options, a specific way of responding)

    B. Individualized program of choices, teaming, or self-evaluation

    C. Taped instruction, games, small groups, or structured multi-sensory learning packets

    D. Short assignments and the experience of success in order to continue to achieve

    E. Open-ended assignments that allow the student to self-determine the pace and rigor level of his or her involvement

(Rigorous) (Skill 1.4)

49. **Individual learning styles can be expressed in relation to all of the following except:**

    A. Environmental factors

    B. Emotional factors

    C. Intelligence quotients

    D. Sociological elements

    E. Physical elements

(Average) (Skill 1.5)

50. **Stressors that may affect a student's school performance include all of the following except:**

    A. Mental health issues

    B. Homelessness

    C. Losing a parent to death or divorce

    D. Being harassed at school

    E. Having a single parent

(Easy) (Skill 1.7)

51. **Mood swings, personality changes, excessive irritability, secretive behavior, and a sudden change in friends can be a sign of which of the following?**

    A. General irritability

    B. Substance abuse

    C. Malnutrition

    D. An eating disorder

    E. Borderline Personality Disorder

(Average) (Skill 1.8)

52. **Which of the following facts about teen suicide is NOT accurate?**

    A. Depression increases the risk of a first suicide attempt

    B. A majority of young people who commit suicide abuse substances

    C. Young men attempt suicide more frequently than young women

    D. Four times as many men as women commit suicide

    E. Firearms are used in a little more than half of all youth suicides

(Average) (Skill 1.8)

53. **When students self-injure, they:**

    A. Are suicidal

    B. Are overly focused on what others think of them

    C. Do it primarily to get attention

    D. Are expressing emotional pain in a physical way

    E. Don't know what they are doing

(Rigorous) (Skill 2.1)

54. **Why is it important for counselors to be aware of developmental theories and milestones?**

    A. Because all children progress along these developmental milestones at exactly the same rate

    B. Such knowledge provides a background against which they are better able to determine if a child or adolescent is developmentally delayed

    C. Because children should be encouraged to meet these milestones at the appropriate time

    D. Because counselors teach these theories to children

    E. In order to make expectations clear

(Easy) (Skill 2.2)

55. **Positive school environments have all of the following characteristics except:**

    A. Strict rules

    B. Clear adult leadership

    C. Respect for diversity

    D. Policies and procedures to ensure the safety of everyone in the school community

    E. A philosophical commitment to certain values

(Average) (Skill 2.2)

56. **A positive school environment:**

    A. Is the primary responsibility of the school counselor

    B. Cannot be effectively determined without good testing instruments

    C. Is created by an attitude of collaboration and care

    D. Is difficult to achieve in today's world

    E. Exists primarily in small schools

(Rigorous) (Skill 2.3)

57. **Effects of stereotyping and prejudice on victims do NOT include:**

    A. Confrontation of the perpetrator by the victim

    B. The development of a sense of inferiority

    C. The development of a persecution complex

    D. Thoughts of violence toward the perpetrator

    E. Strong emotional reactions

(Rigorous) (Skill 2.4)

58. **Violence prevention programs do not include:**

    A. Conflict resolution seminars

    B. Behavior modification programs

    C. Training faculty and staff to intervene before violent confrontations occur

    D. Teaching students about diversity issues

    E. Instituting a boxing program to train students to protect themselves

(Average) (Skill 3.1)

59. **With regard to counseling, it is beyond the scope of the school counselor's role to:**

    A. Provide individual and group counseling

    B. Provide crisis intervention

    C. Provide family consultation

    D. Provide mental health evaluations

    E. Provide career counseling

(Rigorous) (Skill 3.2)

60. **The thinking through of irrational thoughts that have resulted in emotional problems is the basis of this theory:**

    A. Reality therapy

    B. Rational emotive behavior therapy

    C. Gestalt therapy

    D. Existential therapy

    E. Person-centered therapy

(Easy) (Skill 3.2)

61. **Questions of freedom, choice, and responsibility are addressed in:**

    A. Reality therapy

    B. Existential therapy

    C. Cognitive-behavioral therapy

    D. Person-centered therapy

    E. Psychoanalytic therapy

(Rigorous) (Skill 3.2)

62. **The WDEP model in reality theory includes all of the following except:**

    A. Direction

    B. Wants

    C. Evaluation

    D. Evaluation

    E. Planning and commitment

(Average) (Skill 3.3)

63. **The keys to effective communication include all of the following except:**

    A. Listening carefully to the speaker's words

    B. Paying attention to nonverbal communication

    C. Asking for clarification

    D. Expressing oneself clearly and directly

    E. Being able to anticipate what the speaker is going to say

(Easy) (Skill 3.3)

64. **Good responding skills include all of the following EXCEPT:**

    A. Ability to show your feelings without inhibitions

    B. Reflecting back the other person's feelings

    C. Giving constructive feedback

    D. Maintaining eye contact

    E. Asking good questions

(Easy) (Skill 3.4)

65. The ability to create rapport and meaningful relationships with students is the sign of an effective counselor. Which of the following is the most important ingredient in fostering open communication with students?

    A. Maintaining a monthly newsletter about teen-related issues so that student's know you are in tune with the issues they are facing

    B. Attending school extracurricular and sporting events to show support for the student's outside interests

    C. Being familiar with the movies and shows that are popular with students

    D. Keeping information confidential, within the limits of the need for parental notification and school policies

    E. Never interrupting them when they are talking about their feelings

(Average) (Skill 3.5)

66. A disadvantage of group counseling is:

    A. The presence of a built-in support system

    B. A non-threatening atmosphere

    C. The ability to substitute the group for the real world, permitting the client unlimited time to make adjustments

    D. The counselor can reach more clients

    E. The client's chance to learn from others

(Average) (Skill 3.5)

67. All of the following are limitations of group counseling EXCEPT:

    A. Often the individual members need different theoretical approaches and/ or extended follow up

    B. Members can test their attitudes and beliefs against those of other members of the group

    C. People sometimes function poorly in groups

    D. Individuals in the group can justify their present status by reinforcement from the group

    E. Scheduling a convenient time for everyone can sometimes be a problem

(Rigorous) (Skill 3.6)

68. Group dynamics include all of the following EXCEPT:

    A. A political ideology built on the concept of the organization and management of groups

    B. The employment of specific techniques and concepts to keep the group vitalized

    C. A branch of knowledge concerned with groups and their interactions, and interactions with other groups and individuals

    D. A way of describing individual behavior

    E. The ways in which individuals respond to other individuals in a group context

(Rigorous) (Skill 3.7)

69. The occupational environments/personality types of Holland's theory do NOT include:

    A. Artistic

    B. Conventional

    C. Investigative

    D. Hostile

    E. Social

(Average) (Skill 3.7)

70. Which of the following accurately describes the trait-factor theories of career development?

    A. The circumstances of society, beyond the control of the individual, are the contributing factors in career choice

    B. As an individual grows older, self-concept changes along with the view of the reality of his or her vocational choice

    C. There is a direct relationship between an individual's interests and abilities and vocational choices

    D. Individuals tend to go into the same vocation as their most important role model

    E. People with similar personalities choose the same types of vocations

(Rigorous) (Skill 3.8)

71. What are the four stages of the anticipation phase of decision making, as defined by Tiedman and O'Hara?

    A. Exploration, crystallization, choice, and clarification

    B. Choice, crystallization, induction, and reformation

    C. Induction, reformation, crystallization, and integration

    D. Crystallization, exploration, reformation, and clarification

    E. Reformation, integration, crystallization, and choice

(Rigorous) (Skill 3.9)

72. The major steps in Zunker's model for using assessment results in developmental career counseling are all of the following EXCEPT:

    A. Determining the instruments to be used

    B. Analyzing needs

    C. Establishing the purpose of the testing

    D. Administering a complete battery of tests

    E. Utilizing the results of assessment

(Average) (Skill 3.10)

73. In helping students to make decisions, steps in the process do NOT include:

    A. Defining the problem

    B. Listing all options

    C. Exploring barriers to options

    D. Formulating goals in relation to outcomes

    E. Surveying family, friends, and peers

(Average) (Skill 3.11)

74. **In preparing job shadowing opportunities for students, what is an important step to ensuring future participation of local businesses?**

    A. Choosing only local businesses that are already active in local issues

    B. Selecting only students who have prior work experience

    C. Recognizing their contribution of time and resources with a small token of thanks

    D. Preparing a questionnaire for the businessperson in order to understand his or her expectations and general practices

    E. Making sure the student is fully committed to pursuing the same career as the individual he or she is job shadowing

(Average) (Skill 3.11)

75. **Which of the following would provide students with the exposure to the greatest number of potential career choices?**

    A. Apprenticeship

    B. Career days

    C. School-to-work programs

    D. Job shadowing

    E. On the job training

(Rigorous) (Skill 3.11)

76. **Through the Reserve Officers' Training Corps (ROTC) program, students can receive up to a full scholarship for:**

    A. Two years of study in exchange for time served in the military before college

    B. Two years of study in exchange for time served in the military during college

    C. Two years of study in exchange for an extended time in the military

    D. Four years of study in exchange for time served in the military during college

    E. Four years of study in exchange for an extended time in the military

(Easy) (Skill 4.1)

77. **Which of the following is NOT a form of assessment administered by school counselors?**

    A. Achievement tests

    B. Interest inventories

    C. Intelligence tests

    D. College entrance exams

    E. Performance tests

(Rigorous) (Skill 4.1)

78. **All of the following are disadvantages of testing EXCEPT:**

   A. Using the test to predict future behavior

   B. The possibility of results being used improperly

   C. The possibility of the student misinterpreting the test results

   D. The inherent subjectivity of tests administered for counseling purposes

   E. Some students simply do not do well on standardized tests

(Average) (Skill 4.1)

79. **Informal forms of assessment include all of the following except:**

   A. Behavioral observation

   B. Learning styles inventories

   C. Sentence completion

   D. Interviewing peers

   E. Needs assessments

(Rigorous) (Skill 4.2)

80. **In the administration of tests, procedures should include all of the following except:**

   A. Safeguarding the tests

   B. Informing the students about the nature of the test by giving them questions from the test

   C. Guarding the tests in the exam room when students have access to the room

   D. Guarding the tests by not leaving them where students and unauthorized personnel have access

   E. Following the appropriate procedures for packaging and mailing the completed tests back to the scoring company

(Rigorous) (Skill 4.3)

81. **The inaccuracy of some test results that is caused by chance is called:**

   A. Standardization

   B. Standard error of measurement

   C. Standard score

   D. Derived score

   E. Standard deviation

(Rigorous) (Skill 4.3)

82. **A statistical concept that measures the relationship between two factors in test validity is:**

   A. Reliability coefficient

   B. Standard deviation

   C. Raw score

   D. Correlation coefficient

   E. Standard error of measurement

(Easy) (Skill 4.4)

83. **If test results need to be interpreted in a group, the counselor should NOT:**

   A. Announce individual test scores

   B. Explain the norm group to which the students have been compared

   C. Provide for private individual interpretation for students

   D. Explain statistics related to the test so students can understand the meaning of their scores

   E. Discuss the possible uses of the test scores

(Average) (Skill 4.4)

84. In interpreting test results, the counselor should NOT:

A. Relate the results to the goals that had previously been determined

B. Provide for individual interpretation

C. Wait to interpret the test results when the student is scheduling the following year's courses

D. Give the student input into the interpretation of the test results

E. Ask for the student's response to the results

(Average) (Skill 4.5)

85. In interpreting test results to other professionals and parents, the counselor does NOT always have to:

A. Be thoroughly familiar with the test

B. Understand the scoring procedure

C. Notify the student that the counselor will be sharing the results with his or her parent/guardian(s)

D. Work with the parents in a counseling relationship to help them understand their child's abilities

E. Let other staff members see the results of the test

Consulting

(Average) (Skill 5.1)

86. In interactions with school counselors and other school officials, parents and guardians need respect, information, and:

A. Positive feedback on their behavior

B. Confirmation that they are doing a great job with their child

C. Validation and support

D. Detailed descriptions of their child's interactions with peers and teachers

E. A complete review of their child's grades

(Easy) (Skill 5.1)

87. In working with parents, a good model to utilize is:

A. Collaborative consultation

B. Mental health consultation

C. Family counseling

D. Advising

E. Medical model consultation

(Rigorous) (Skill 5.1)

88. The consultation process with parents does NOT include:

A. Allowing them to vent their frustrations about the school and school officials

B. Getting to the issue at hand as soon as possible

C. Inviting the parents' opinion about the issue

D. Clearly delineating the next steps the parents need to take

E. Taking care not to make too many suggestions and overwhelm them

(Rigorous) (Skill 5.2)

89. **Elements of family dynamics include all of the following EXCEPT:**

    A. Rules and roles within the family

    B. The reinforcement of individual behavior patterns via family interactions

    C. An "identified patient" who serves to divert the family from underlying problems

    D. The parents' childhood backgrounds

    E. The ways in which shared values and conflicts are seen in family interactions

(Average) (Skill 5.3)

90. **The role of consultants in problem-solving processes does not include functioning as:**

    A. An advocate

    B. An expert in a particular area

    C. A school official

    D. A collaborator

    E. A process specialist

(Average) (Skill 5.3)

91. **Procedures in the consultation process include all of the following EXCEPT:**

    A. Relationship building

    B. Monitoring the process of behavior change by a neutral party

    C. Evaluation and summarization

    D. Diagnosis of the problem

    E. Gathering information

(Average) (Skill 5.4)

92. **The role the counselor can take in assisting participants in the consultation process does NOT include:**

    A. Demonstrating classroom behavior management techniques

    B. Describing the nature of the problem

    C. Teaching specific skills

    D. Helping devise strategies to change behaviors

    E. Eliciting possible solutions from others

(Average) (Skill 5.4)

93. **In the consultation process, communicating a student's needs to others does NOT include:**

    A. The counselor making a judgment to others regarding what is best for the student

    B. Clarifying the needs of the student with the student

    C. Opening lines of communication between the consultee and the student by having open dialogue

    D. Balancing the needs of the student and the consultee so each can understand the other's position

    E. Asking the consultee to reflect back what he or she has heard

(Average) (Skill 5.4)

94. **Procedures for successful communication with parents/guardian(s) in the consultation process do NOT include:**

    A. Informing parents frequently about progress on the resolution of the problem

    B. Using parents as a valuable source of information about the student

    C. Involving the parent/guardian(s) in the consultation process from the beginning

    D. Frequent contact to ascertain whether more aid is needed and to check if the student or parent/guardian(s) have additional concerns

    E. Explaining the problem in simple language because parents are probably unaware of all ramifications

(Rigorous) (Skill 5.5)

95. **In the case of abuse by a family or household member, which of the following steps is mandated?**

    A. Reporting the incident to the proper authorities

    B. Maintaining regular contact with outside agencies until the problem is resolved

    C. Including the parent/guardian in the referral process as soon as possible

    D. Getting informed consent of the student and his or her parent/guardian prior to making a referral to an outside agency or practitioner

    E. Waiting 48 hours before reporting the suspected abuse

(Easy) (Skill 5.5)

96. **School counselors may provide information about which of the following resources for families?**

    A. Mental health referrals

    B. Food banks and government aid programs

    C. Local support groups

    D. Community organizations

    E. All of the above

(Easy) (Skill 5.6)

97. **All but which of the following are important aspects of crisis intervention?**

    A. Accurate information for those affected by the situation

    B. The latest news reports about the crisis

    C. A school crisis response plan

    D. A systematic way to inform school personnel about the actions to be taken

    E. Debriefing for crisis responders

(Rigorous) (Skill 5.7)

98. **An effective advocate does NOT:**

    A. Raise issues that may cause discomfort

    B. Speak up for those who may not have a voice or may not have been heard in the past

    C. Try to facilitate change

    D. Watch for trends that may indicate underserved populations

    E. Share all information gathered about a particular situation

Coordinating

(Rigorous) (Skill 6.1)

99. The goals of the guidance program should NOT include:

   A. Acquisition of academic skills by the student population commensurate with their abilities

   B. Acquisition of personal insights by students

   C. Learned ability to make intelligent choices

   D. Capacity to cope with life's stressors

   E. Selection of a lifetime career

(Easy) (Skill 6.2)

100. Components of an orientation program should include each of the following EXCEPT:

   A. Advance notice by mail

   B. Invitations to the entire community

   C. A tour of the facilities

   D. Introduction of counselors and administrators to students and parents, with a description of their roles

   E. A planned agenda

(Rigorous) (Skill 6.3)

101. The need for specialized programs may be indicated by all of the following EXCEPT:

   A. Classroom management problems

   B. Targeted grant money

   C. A formal needs assessment

   D. Teachers' or counselors' observations

   E. Identification of underserved students

(Average) (Skill 6.4)

102. All of the following are good prevention approaches EXCEPT:

   A. Informing parent/guardian(s) about their child's behavior in the school setting

   B. Programs on conflict resolution and communication skills

   C. Anger management groups

   D. An open-door policy

   E. Engaging students in community activities

(Average) (Skill 6.4)

103. Which of the following is a key prevention concept?

   A. Creating a positive school environment

   B. Attending to issues of bullying, prejudice, aggression, and violence

   C. Teaching communication, self-awareness, and conflict resolution skills

   D. Maintaining an open door policy

   E. All of the above

(Average) (Skill 7.2)

104. In evaluating the content of career information, all of the following areas should be included EXCEPT:

   A. The impressions of the reader, as indicated by filling out an evaluation form

   B. The preparation required for entry-level jobs

   C. The work setting and conditions of the career

   D. The long-term employment outlook

   E. The skills and aptitude needed for a particular career

(Average) (Skill 7.3)

105. Financial aid specifically earmarked for women and minorities is LEAST likely to be found in:

   A. Minority and women's organizations

   B. Local organizations committed to higher education for women and minorities

   C. General financial aid references

   D. The publication The Higher Education Money Book for Women and Minorities

   E. Local minority houses of worship

(Average) (Skill 8.1)

106. Which of the following best describes qualitative research?

   A. Applies the scientific method to describing and analyzing the past in order to understand the future

   B. Focuses on the individual and not on the results of group experimentation

   C. Focuses on in-depth interviews, observations, and document analysis

   D. Interprets data using numerical analysis

   E. Involves carefully controlled laboratory experiments

(Rigorous) (Skill 8.2)

107. The research evaluation stages of the CIPP model do NOT include:

   A. Context evaluation

   B. Process evaluation

   C. Input evaluation

   D. Product evaluation

   E. Program evaluation

(Rigorous) (Skill 8.2)

108. Formative evaluation does NOT involve:

   A. Collection of data in the developmental stage of research

   B. Collection of data in the implementation stage of research

   C. Collection of data prior to the setting of objectives

   D. Collection of data after a program has been in place for a period of time

   E. Collection of data when the research is in the operational stage

(Rigorous) (Skill 8.2)

109. The following individuals should be included when conducting a program needs assessment:

   A. Students only

   B. Administrators only

   C. People in the community who have no students in school

   D. The community, students, staff, administrators, and parents

   E. Anyone who has an opinion about the program

(Rigorous) (Skill 8.3)

110. Factors that determine the value of a program do NOT include:

   A. How well the program fits preconceived ideas of intended outcomes

   B. Statistical significance

   C. Interpretation of the meaning of the results

   D. The practicality of implementing the program for everyday use

   E. The value of the program to those benefiting from the program

(Rigorous) (Skill 8.3)

111. **Program objectives are:**

    A. Created to fit the outcomes of the research

    B. Readjusted as the need arises

    C. Determined after the program has been operational for a period of time

    D. Necessary only when formal research is being conducted

    E. Formulated before the research is instituted

(Rigorous) (Skill 8.3)

112. **In evaluating a newly created program, the counselor should:**

    A. Ask the guidance staff if they think the program is working

    B. Ask students informally what they think of the program

    C. Conduct an extensive evaluation of all involved that includes surveys, questionnaires, and observations

    D. After three months, evaluate the program and make a recommendation

    E. Consult with parents to see if the program is working

(Rigorous) (Skill 8.3)

113. **Before introducing new and innovative programs to the guidance curriculum, the counselor should first:**

    A. Ask the administration for a budget for the program

    B. Conduct a needs assessment survey

    C. Arrange for a pilot program

    D. Contact Board of Education members to get them to agree on the implementation of the program

    E. Determine program objectives

Professional Issues

(Rigorous) (Skill 9.1)

114. **Guidelines for ethical behavior written in the ACA Code of Ethics and Standards of Practice include all of the following areas EXCEPT:**

    A. Client records

    B. Penalties for specific ethical violations

    C. Confidentiality

    D. Resolution of ethical issues

    E. Relationships with other professionals

(Easy) (Skill 9.1)

115. **When an ethical issue arises in a counselor's practice, the counselor should:**

    A. Refer to the ACA Code of Ethics

    B. Decide what to do immediately so the problem will not linger

    C. Ask the client what to do

    D. Consult with the Board of Education

    E. Consult with an attorney

(Rigorous) (Skill 9.2)

116. **Parents, guardians, and students have a right to all of the following records EXCEPT:**

    A. Copies of all records relating to the student

    B. Copies of all student records containing comparisons of the student with other students

    C. All of the student's records maintained by public institutions

    D. A list of all types of records directly related to the student

    E. The student's complete transcript

(Average) (Skill 9.2)

117. **Written permission to release assessment data must be obtained from:**

   A. The counselor

   B. The company that scored the test

   C. The student who is over 18 or the student's parent or guardian

   D. The Board of Education

   E. The teacher who generated the assessment data

(Rigorous) (Skill 9.3)

118. **The intent of the Individuals with Disabilities Education Act of 1975 was all of the following EXCEPT:**

   A. To provide guidelines for assessing disabilities

   B. To give children with disabilities a free and appropriate education

   C. To provide for the needs of children with disabilities

   D. To prevent discrimination against children with disabilities

   E. To give children with disabilities special services to make up for past discrimination

(Average) (Skill 9.5)

119. **School Web sites can be helpful to school counselors because they allow the counselor to:**

   A. Maintain a personal relationship with students

   B. Research information about higher education and financial aid

   C. Develop presentations for conferences

   D. Share information within the school district and the community

   E. Assess the value of Web sites used by students and parents/guardians

(Easy) (Skill 9.6)

120. **Continuing professional development is important for school counselors for all of the following reasons EXCEPT:**

   A. To keep abreast of changes in professional practices and standards

   B. To utilize all available monies in the budget for staff development

   C. To be refreshed and renewed as a professional

   D. To further develop counseling skills

   E. To learn about new programs and techniques

Answer Key

ANSWER KEY							
1. D	16. E	31. E	46. C	61. B	76. E	91. B	106. C
2. C	17. B	32. A	47. D	62. A	77. C	92. A	107. E
3. B	18. B	33. D	48. A	63. E	78. A	93. A	108. D
4. E	19. D	34. A	49. C	64. A	79. D	94. E	109. D
5. C	20. B	35. C	50. E	65. D	80. B	95. A	110. A
6. D	21. C	36. D	51. B	66. C	81. B	96. E	111. E
7. A	22. A	37. A	52. C	67. B	82. D	97. B	112. C
8. E	23. E	38. E	53. D	68. D	83. A	98. E	113. B
9. A	24. C	39. D	54. B	69. D	84. C	99. E	114. B
10. D	25. B	40. C	55. A	70. C	85. E	100. B	115. A
11. D	26. A	41. A	56. C	71. A	86. C	101. B	116. B
12. B	27. D	42. A	57. A	72. D	87. A	102. A	117. C
13. A	28. B	43. E	58. E	73. E	88. D	103. E	118. E
14. B	29. D	44. B	59. D	74. D	89. D	104. A	119. D
15. A	30. B	45. B	60. B	75. B	90. C	105. C	120. B

RIGOR TABLE	
Rigor level	**Questions**
Easy 20%	42, 47, 51, 55, 61, 64, 65, 77, 83, 87, 96, 97, 100, 115, 120
Average 40%	41, 43, 44, 45, 46, 50, 52, 53, 56, 59, 63, 66, 67, 70, 73, 74, 75, 79, 84, 85, 86, 90, 91, 92, 93, 94, 102, 103, 104, 105, 106, 117, 119
Rigorous 40%	48, 49, 54, 57, 58, 60, 62, 68, 69, 71, 72, 76, 78,80, 81, 82, 88, 89, 95, 98, 99, 101, 107, 108, 109, 110, 111, 112, 113, 114, 116, 118

SAMPLE TEST WITH RATIONALES

Section One: Listening Section

For the listening section of the test, the candidate will be given a CD to listen to and will then answer written questions based on what they have heard. The CD will contain client statements and responses and various extended interactions between counselors and clients. The questions will evaluate the candidate's ability to identify the client's feeling or problems and to evaluate the appropriateness of the counselor's response to those feelings and problems. The candidate will have 40 minutes to complete this portion of the test and will be given the questions and answer choices but not a written script of the taped material.

At this time, XAMonline does not offer an accompanying CD for the listening section.

Questions 1–19: Read the excerpt and select the word or phrase that best describes the client's feelings, needs, or attitudes.

1. Student: "I want to drop my history class. I don't get along with Ms. Jones and I don't need the credit to graduate. What do you think I should do?"

    A. Confidence

    B. Fear

    C. Arrogance

    D. Uncertainty

    E. Apathy

Answer: D. Uncertainty

Although the student might convey some arrogance initially, she is not really sure what to do.

2. Student: "I don't know why my mom is giving me such a hard time about my grades. I have mostly Bs, with a couple of As. I try so hard and I really study a lot."

    A. Confusion

    B. Anger

    C. Hurt

    D. Fear

    E. Arrogance

Answer: C. Hurt

The student is hurt by the pressure her mother is putting on her and of the mother's lack of acknowledgement of the her efforts.

3. Student: "I am sick of being teased by those girls. If you don't do something, I am going to do something bad. I can't take it anymore. I really can't."

    A. Anger

    B. Frustration

    C. Hurt

    D. Uncertainty

    E. Shame

Answer: B. Frustration

The student might also be feeling hurt, shame, and anger, but frustration is the primary emotion expressed in her statements.

4. Student: "My daddy says I'm dumb because I didn't do so well on my spelling test. But I just can't remember certain words. Do you think I'm dumb?"

A. Sadness

B. Frustration

C. Fear

D. Anxiety

E. Inadequacy

Answer: E. Inadequacy

Again, the student may be feeling other things as well, but inadequacy is the core emotion.

5. Mother: "I want to talk with you about how Jackie is doing in math. She always loved it until she got to middle school. Is there something going on with the teacher or in the class that her father and I should know about? What can we do to help?"

A. Anger

B. Frustration

C. Concern

D. Irritation

E. Arrogance

Answer: C. Concern

The mother is concerned about her daughter and wants to help.

6. Teacher: "I'm glad I caught you. I really need to talk about that new boy. He is not fitting in and I really don't know what to do about it. He seems to like causing trouble with the other boys. It's driving me crazy!"

A. Anger

B. Frustration

C. Concern

D. Irritation

E. Arrogance

Answer: D. Irritation

The teacher might be frustrated and concerned as well, but her irritation comes through most strongly in this example.

7. Student: "I hate Mr. Allison. He's mean and he's out to get me. It doesn't matter what I do. I've had it."

A. Anger

B. Frustration

C. Concern

D. Irritation

E. Arrogance

Answer: A. Anger

The student's anger is clear. This emotion is stronger than irritation or frustration.

8. Teacher: "Thanks for the feedback about my reading group. They are a handful, and I think your suggestions might work. I'll let you know what happens."

   A. Worry

   B. Frustration

   C. Concern

   D. Relief

   E. Appreciation

   Answer: E. Appreciation

   The teacher is thankful for the counselor's help and appreciates the support. She may also feel relieved, but that is not apparent in her statement.

9. Student: "Thanks for your help. I really don't know what to tell my dad about what happened in gym, and I'm afraid of his reaction. But at least I have a few ideas about what to say. What if he gets mad at me?"

   A. Worry

   B. Frustration

   C. Concern

   D. Relief

   E. Appreciation

   Answer: A. Worry

   Although the student is expressing appreciation, he is clearly concerned about what to say to his father and what his father's reaction will be.

10. Father: "Thanks for letting me know about Zelda. She isn't always the easiest kid to work with, and I am so glad she seems to be getting along with her teachers this year."

    A. Worry

    B. Frustration

    C. Concern

    D. Relief

    E. Appreciation

    Answer: D. Relief

    The father is grateful and perhaps also concerned, but his primarily feeling is relief that his daughter is doing well.

11. Student: "I don't know what to do about the future. I didn't score so well on my SATs. My parents want me to go to a four-year college, but I really want to do the graphic design program at the community college. That would be really cool."

    Counselor: "It sounds like you know what you want but you're not sure how to talk with your parents about what you want."

    A. Judgmental

    B. Empathic

    C. Concerned

    D. Perceptive

    E. Uncaring

Answer: D. Perceptive

The counselor conveys empathy and concern to the student, but she also picks up on the student's uncertainty about how to discuss the matter with his parents. This shows the counselor is not just empathic but also perceptive about the student's needs.

12. Parent: "I can't believe you didn't call me immediately when my daughter's friends told you she was cutting herself yesterday. Why did you wait until today?"

    Counselor: "I'm sorry you are upset. I can understand that. I felt I needed to speak directly with your daughter first and make sure it wasn't just gossip. I called you as soon as your daughter and I talked."

    A. Judgmental

    B. Empathic

    C. Concerned

    D. Perceptive

    E. Uncaring

Answer: B. Empathic

The counselor empathizes with the upset parent and also tries to explain her actions, hoping that this will help the parent feel reassured.

13. Student: "I really wonder if I should be in this advanced math class. I'm not very good with pressure and there is a lot of homework."

    Counselor: "It sounds like you probably shouldn't put yourself through that if you can't deal with the pressure. That is a high-powered class. Maybe you should drop the course."

    A. Judgmental

    B. Empathic

    C. Concerned

    D. Perceptive

    E. Uncaring

Answer: A. Judgmental

Although the counselor is empathizing with the student's feelings, he also conveys judgment about what the student should do. It would be more helpful to empathize and then explore options with the student, as well as discuss issues related to the pressure the student is feeling.

14. Student: "Thanks, again, for helping me with my schedule. I feel like I've got the right courses now."

    Counselor: "You're very welcome. I'm glad the courses feel like a fit. Let me know if I can help you out in the future—that's what I'm here for."

    A. Grateful

    B. Solicitous

    C. Concerned

    D. Perceptive

    E. Curious

Answer: B. Solicitous

The counselor makes an effort to let the student know he is there for the student, should the need arise in the future.

15. Student: "Hey, Ms. Cortez. Guess what? I'm going to the rink with Maria and Josie. That's the first time they ever asked me. Pretty cool, huh?"

Counselor: "Very cool. Sounds like you're starting to make friends. I'm so glad, Emma."

A. Supportive

B. Empathic

C. Concerned

D. Perceptive

E. Condescending

Answer: A. Supportive

The counselor's simple, but important, response will be supportive and affirming to the student.

16. Teacher: "Can I talk with you for a few minutes about Frankie? He's having a tough time in English, and I wondered how he was doing in his other classes."

Counselor: "Sure. Thanks for letting me know. I'll check with his other teachers. I'm free fifth period if you want to talk more. Let me know."

A. Supportive

B. Empathic

C. Concerned

D. Perceptive

E. Responsive

Answer: E. Responsive

Although the counselor also expresses concern and support, the overriding attitude is one of being responsive to the teacher's concern and need.

17. Student: "I don't know what to do about the future. I didn't score so well on my SATs. My parents want me to go to a four-year college, but I really want to do the graphic design program at the community college. That would be really cool."

Counselor: "It sounds like you're feeling that you're in a dilemma and aren't sure what to do. Would you like to talk about this more?"

A. Judgmental

B. Empathic

C. Concerned

D. Perceptive

E. Uncaring

Answer: B. Empathic

The counselor's response here is primarily one of empathy. When this example was used earlier (question 11), the counselor took it a step further (by being perceptive). In this case, the counselor is focused on reflecting back the student's sense of being in a dilemma, conveying empathy.

18. Student: "What do you want now? You are always bugging me and pulling me out of class for stuff!"

    Counselor: "It sounds like you're upset with me. Talk to me, Carrie. What's up?"

    A. Judgmental and empathic

    B. Empathic and concerned

    C. Concerned and frustrated

    D. Perceptive and frustrated

    E. Supportive and judgmental

    Answer: B. Empathic and concerned

    The counselor's first statement communicates empathy; the subsequent comments express concern and invite the student to talk more with the counselor. Overall, empathy and concern are both present.

19. Student: "I can't stand talking about this anymore! Every time I come to you, you say we are going to work it out. But it never gets worked out."

    Counselor: "It sounds like you're fed up with the whole thing—and so am I. I keep trying to get something done but I'm not succeeding, am I?"

    A. Judgmental and empathic

    B. Empathic and concerned

    C. Concerned and frustrated

    D. Perceptive and frustrated

    E. Supportive and judgmental

    Answer: D. Perceptive and frustrated

    The counselor is perceptive about what is going on with the student and also expresses her own frustration with the situation.

Questions 20–25: Read the excerpt and select the answer that best describes *how the client is most likely to react to the counselor's response.*

20. Student: "What do you want now? You are always bugging me and pulling me out of class for stuff!"

    Counselor: "It sounds like you're upset with me. Talk to me, Carrie. What's up?"

    A. Feeling criticized, the student will become silent.

    B. Feeling the counselor's care and concern, the student will open up about being upset and tell the counselor what is going on.

    C. The student will lash out further at the counselor.

    D. The student will change the subject and ask the counselor why she was called to the counselor's office.

    E. The student will turn around and walk out.

    Answer: B. Feeling the counselor's care and concern, the student will open up about being upset and tell the counselor what is going on.

    The combination of empathy and invitation on the counselor's part are likely to encourage the student to drop the irritated bravado and talk about her underlying feelings.

21. Student: "I'm afraid of what I am going to do. My friends have all started using drugs—nothing heavy, just pot. But I don't want to do it and yet I don't want to stop being friends with them. What should I do?"

Counselor: "I'm so glad you felt you could come to me and that you could tell me what's going on. You're pretty strong to be able to do that. Let's talk more about this, okay?"

A. The student will show frustration that the counselor doesn't immediately tell her what to do.

B. The student will become worried that the counselor will get her friends in trouble, and stop talking.

C. The student will share more about her dilemma and feelings.

D. The student will become curious and ask the counselor if he ever used drugs.

E. The student will express fear about what the counselor is going to do.

Answer: C. The student will share more about her dilemma and feelings.

The counselor's response is very affirming, nonjudgmental, and inviting. This kind of response is likely to elicit a positive and open response from the student.

22. Student: "I'm crying because Joey hit me. He always does that at recess."

Counselor: "I'm so sorry, Freddie. He's not supposed to hit. Are you hurt? Can I help you?"

A. The student will stop crying and tell the counselor about what's been happening at recess.

B. The student will cry more.

C. The student will run off, afraid of getting in trouble.

D. The student will defend Joey, saying he's his best friend.

E. The student will become silent, cross his arms, and just sit.

Answer: A. The student will stop crying and tell the counselor about what's been happening at recess.

The student's tears are probably an honest expression of hurt and an effort to get some help with a difficult situation. Once the counselor responds positively to Freddie, he is likely to stop crying and tell the counselor more about the situation.

23. Mother: "Thanks so much for calling me. What is happening with Serena? Why is she there? She's been so upset lately. Is she in trouble?"

    Counselor: "I'm glad I reached you. Serena is here with me and I think it would be best for her to tell you in her own words what is happening. Would that be alright with you? She'd really like to talk with you herself."

    A. The mother will insist on having the counselor tell her what is happening with her daughter.

    B. The mother will become angry that the counselor refuses to talk with her.

    C. The mother will accuse the counselor of hiding things from her.

    D. The mother will become silent and wait for the counselor to speak.

    E. The mother will agree and ask to talk with her daughter.

    Answer: E. The mother will agree and ask to talk with her daughter.

    Most parents will be eager to talk with their child when the school counselor calls, especially if the counselor is clear in communicating the child's interest in talking with the parent. This is a good approach for many issues, though at times the counselor may decide to talk about the issue at hand with the parent prior to having the student talk with his or her parent.

24. Student: "I wondered if I could help you with those papers. I like to help and would be happy to put all that stuff together and staple it. I have a free period."

    Counselor: "Well, maybe that's a good idea. But what's going on? Is something up? Would you like to talk with me?"

    A. Feeling that her help was rejected, the student will become silent and just walk away.

    B. Uncertain about the counselor's response, the student will insist everything is fine and ask again if she can help with the paperwork.

    C. Feeling the counselor's care and concern, the student will acknowledge that she would like to talk.

    D. Feeling judged, the student will lash out, saying she just offered to help.

    E. The student will change the subject and ask the counselor if she is going to the football game on Friday.

    Answer: C. Feeling the counselor's care and concern, the student will acknowledge that she would like to talk.

    The student's offer to help is very likely an indirect way of asking to talk. The counselor could have simply accepted the help and gradually allowed the talking to unfold. With some students this might be the best approach. However, in this scenario, the counselor is more direct, though still inviting and concerned.

25. Student: "I have been trying to get my essay done for my college applications and it's just not coming out right. I don't know how to say what I want to say, and Ms. Huntley said I can't spend any more time on it in English. My dad's really pressuring me to get it done. I can't do this."

Counselor: "You sound kind of discouraged, Sam, and under a lot of pressure. Would it help to talk with me about it? Maybe we could figure out who might be able to work with you on it to help you clarify what you really want to say."

A. The student will express relief at being heard and then begin complaining further about his father and Ms. Huntley.

B. The student will express relief at being heard and talk further with the counselor about how to get his essay done.

C. Feeling the counselor's care and concern, the student will ask the counselor to write the essay for him.

D. The student will express frustration that the counselor is not willing to work on the essay with him.

E. The student will ask the counselor to read the essay.

Answer: B. The student will express relief at being heard and talk further with the counselor about how to get his essay done.

The counselor is empathic and then moves to an action suggestion. She is clear about the ways in which she can help Sam, which provides focus for something that the student feels is overwhelming.

Questions 26–28: Read the excerpt and choose the answer that best describes *the appropriateness of the counselor's response.*

26. Counselor: "Hi, Timmy. Wow, that's quite a bruise on your arm. Does it hurt? Are you okay?"

Student: "Why are you asking me these questions about my arm? I just banged it on my bike handlebar."

Counselor: "I was just kind of worried—I wanted to make sure you were okay. Sometimes it's hard for kids to tell adults about getting hurt, especially if someone else hurt them and they're afraid of getting in trouble. You're not in any trouble. And it's okay to talk about things."

A. Appropriate, because the counselor conveys concern and invites the student to talk about things that might be difficult to discuss

B. Appropriate, because the counselor is being friendly and concerned

C. Inappropriate, because there is no reason for the counselor to ask a student about injuries not sustained in the school setting

D. Inappropriate, because the counselor is suggesting child abuse to the student

E. Inappropriate, because the student did not bring the issue to the counselor

Answer: A. Appropriate, because the counselor conveys concerns and invites the student to talk about things that might be difficult to discuss

The counselor has a responsibility to be alert to possible child abuse but also to be cautious in not leading children when asking questions. The counselor's response is appropriate because it conveys concern, which should be reassuring to the student, and also gives the student permission to talk about difficult things without suggesting abuse directly.

27. **Counselor (to a teacher): "Do you mind if I ask you something about Shandra? She came to me with something personal and I wasn't sure what I should do. Can we talk?"**

    A. Appropriate, because the teacher knows Shandra and her family quite well and may provide some insight

    B. Appropriate, because the counselor needs to get a second opinion to do her job well

    C. Inappropriate, because counselors should know what to do without talking with teachers or other staff except in extreme situations

    D. Inappropriate, because counselors need to respect students' privacy and not discuss personal matters with teachers; an appropriate consult would be with another counselor

    E. Inappropriate, because the teacher knows the student personally

Answer D. Inappropriate, because counselors need to respect students' privacy and not discuss personal matters with teachers; an appropriate consult would be with another counselor

Keeping confidences in a school community can be difficult when many teachers and students know each other outside the school setting. Counselors have a duty to maintain appropriate boundaries. Option E is partially correct, but even if the teacher did not know the student, the counselor should seek a consult with another counselor, not a teacher.

28. Student: "Is it okay to talk with you about something private? I mean, do you have to tell someone else anything I tell you? This is really important."

Counselor: "I'm glad you came to me. I keep everything students tell me private, unless you are in danger of hurting yourself or someone else. Then I have to tell someone—that's the law. But let's see what's going on. I really would like to help you."

Student: "But you might have to tell someone. Maybe I shouldn't talk to you."

Counselor: "I will do my best to keep this between us. And I will tell you first if I need to go to someone else, including your parents. In fact, if I call your parents, I would like you to be in the room with me. How's that? We will only go to someone else if we have to. I really want to help."

A. Appropriate, because she tells the student that she really wants to help her no matter what

B. Appropriate, because the counselor is both reassuring about the importance of privacy and honest about the need to disclose certain information to parents and others

C. Inappropriate, because the counselor creates anxiety by mentioning the law and possible disclosure

D. Inappropriate, because counselors should never keep important information about students private

E. Inappropriate, because the student will feel betrayed by the possible need to disclose the information

Answer: B. Appropriate, because the counselor is both reassuring about the importance of privacy and honest about the need to disclose certain information to parents and others

Counselors need to balance their efforts to invite students to talk with them with their legal and ethical responsibilities. Not telling the student early on that the counselor must disclose certain information will ultimately lead to a greater sense of betrayal for the student. To be up-front about this issue and inviting at the same time can actually build trust.

Questions 29–31: Read the excerpt, then choose the best answer for the questions that follow.

Counselor: "I understand that you and Sarah had an argument in Ms. Tucker's room during class today. Can you tell me what happened?"

Student: "Sarah has been my best friend all this year in seventh grade. She told James that I like him after she promised she wouldn't tell him. Now he knows and everyone is laughing at me."

Counselor: "So, what I'm hearing you say is that you shared your secret with Sarah, thinking that you could trust her, and she shared your secret with other people. Is this how the argument started?"

Student: "No, we started fighting because she whispered something to James and they started laughing at me. So I told her to shut up and then she yelled at me, and that's what happened."

Counselor: "And, in the meantime, you disrupted Ms. Tucker's teaching."

Student: "I didn't really think about that…"

Counselor: "How do you think you could handle this type of situation in the future so that you don't end up in a fight with your friend, and you don't disrupt class?"

29. The student's response to the counselor's initial statement indicates which of the following?

   A. The student feels as though she is being blamed for the situation.

   B. The student recognizes her responsibility in the problem.

   C. The student does not recognize her responsibility in the problem.

   D. The student sees the problem as an issue between herself and her best friend.

   E. She is too traumatized to return to the class with Sarah and James.

Answer: D. The student sees the problem as an issue between herself and her best friend.

At this point, the only thing being discussed is the issue that brought the student to the counselor's office. There has been no mention of responsibility for the problem. The student does not feel as though she is being blamed, so A would not be an appropriate choice.

30. The counselor's behavior throughout the session indicates that his objective was to facilitate:

   A. Conflict resolution between the student and Sarah

   B. A better understanding of the student's responsibility for the problem

   C. Modeling appropriate classroom behavior

   D. Helping the student learn whom she can and cannot trust

   E. A healthier understanding of the counseling process

Answer: B. A better understanding of the student's responsibility for the problem

The counselor's objective was to point out to the student that her behavior disrupted Ms. Tucker's class. Options C, D, and E are possible residual effects of the session. There was no mention of conflict resolution during the session, which would require the presence of both the student and her friend Sarah.

31. Based on the overall tone of the session, which of the following is the student MOST likely to do in the future?

   A. Return to class and resume the argument with Sarah

   B. Avoid returning to the counselor's office to resolve a problem

   C. Tell Sarah's secrets to retaliate against her

   D. Apologize to Ms. Tucker for disrupting class

   E. Think about this experience before sharing additional personal information with Sarah

Answer: E. Think about this experience before sharing additional personal information with Sarah

Developmentally, a seventh grade student is not typically mature enough to apologize to a teacher for disrupting a class. The tone of the session does not indicate that the student wishes to continue the argument with Sarah or to retaliate against her. The session seems comfortable for the student, so it is unlikely that she will avoid additional visits to the counselor's office.

Questions 32–34: Read the excerpt, then choose the best answer for the questions that follow.

Counselor: "When we talked the other day, you shared with me that you overheard your parents discussing a divorce, and I know that was a very, very difficult thing for you to hear. How are you feeling today?"

Student: "I'm really angry at both of them, and I wish they would stop trying to pretend everything is okay."

Counselor: "You mentioned that you felt more comfortable talking with your mom about the situation than your dad. Have you had an opportunity to talk with her about it?"

Student: "No, not yet. I just don't know what to say to her."

Counselor: "Why don't we practice that today? Let's try this: Turn your chair to face this empty chair, and pretend that your mom is sitting right here in front of you. How do you feel about trying that?"

Student: "I don't know. It seems kind of weird, but I guess we could try."

32. The student's response to the counselor's initial question indicates which of the following?

A. The student and counselor have established a comfortable rapport with one another.

B. The student does not have an accurate understanding of the situation between his parents.

C. The student is avoiding his own concerns by blaming the situation on his parents.

D. The student's anger at his parents hinders his ability to address school-related issues.

E. The student's intent is for the counselor to intervene with his parents.

Answer: A. The student and counselor have established a comfortable rapport with one another.

The ease with which the student shares with the counselor indicates that a previous session has helped to establish rapport between student and counselor. Very few details have been discussed at this point; therefore, answers A, C, D, and E are not appropriate choices.

33. **The counselor's behavior throughout the session indicates that her objective was to:**

    A. Encourage the student to take responsibility for his part in the problem

    B. Help the student learn to mediate the problems between his parents

    C. Learn more personal information about the student in order to address school-related issues

    D. Help the student communicate his concerns more effectively to his parents

    E. Help the student work through his anger toward his parents

Answer: D. Help the student communicate his concerns more effectively to his parents

The counselor's objective is never to learn personal information about a student for alternative purposes. This situation does not indicate that the student has any responsibility for the problem, and the counselor would never encourage a student to attempt to mediate a situation between divorcing parents. While the session may help the student work through anger, the primary objective is to help the student communicate more effectively.

34. **Suggesting the empty chair technique indicated that the counselor's objective was to do which of the following?**

    A. Give the student a safe environment in which to express his concerns to his mother

    B. Help the student practice working through his anger toward his mother before the actual confrontation

    C. Show the student how irrational his behavior has become

    D. Give the student a safe environment in which to work through his anger toward his parents

    E. Gain a better understanding of the situation between the student's parents

Answer: A. Give the student a safe environment in which to express his concerns to his mother

Answers C and E are irrelevant. The objective is to give the student an opportunity to express his concerns in a safe environment because he may or may not have an actual follow-up conversation with his mother. Answer D is incorrect because the student already stated that he feels more comfortable talking to his mother. Answer B is incorrect because the counselor does not wish to encourage the student to engage in a confrontation.

Questions 35–37: Read the excerpt, then choose the best answer for the questions that follow.

Counselor: "You mentioned that you have some concerns about your coursework in terms of the colleges to which you are applying. Walk me through your concerns, and we'll address them one at a time."

Student: "Well, first of all, I was thinking that I only had to complete three social studies credits to graduate, but it looks like all of my college choices require four credits. What am I going to do to make up the fourth credit? I already have my schedule for next year, and I have seven classes already selected."

Counselor: "Let's take a look at your schedule and see what we need to do. I see that you're planning to take Art and Choir next year, and from what I remember, you really enjoy fine arts courses."

Student: "I really do want to take those fine arts classes. I think I may major in art education in college. I don't really want to drop either of those classes."

Counselor: "I understand that you want to take both, so you're going to need to make a choice based on your goals and on what's best for you. You can take both art classes next year and possibly go to summer school for a social studies credit, or…"

Student: "No, I definitely don't want to go to summer school!"

Counselor: "Okay, we could look at colleges that only require three credits, or we could change one fine arts class to a Contemporary Issues or Psychology/Sociology course. If we do that, you would be able to meet your fourth requirement for social studies for your colleges. What do you think?"

Student: "Well, I really want to participate in both arts classes, but I think this is more important. I sing in my church choir, and I'm a member of the art club. I guess I'll just take art and change my choir class to Contemporary Issues. I've heard that's a great class."

Counselor: "That's an excellent choice. You'll really enjoy that class. What an easy fix! So, what's next?"

35. The student's response to the counselor's initial suggestion for schedule changes indicates which of the following:

A. The student is unwilling to consider the counselor's suggestions at this time.

B. The student is interested only in having fun.

C. The student is focusing more on minute details than on choices that directly affect his college plans.

D. The student sees the arts classes as more important to his future than the social studies classes.

E. The student believes that the counselor is not interested in what is best for the student.

Answer: C. The student is focusing more on minute details than on choices that directly affect his college plans.

At this point in the session, the student is looking at details rather than the big picture. He is not interested only in having fun, he is not resistant to or unwilling to consider the counselor's suggestions, and he does not believe that the counselor is not looking out for his best interest. Answer D is a good answer, but C is the best option.

36. **The counselor's objective throughout the session is which of the following:**

   A. To help the student recognize his mistakes

   B. To help the student take responsibility for his decisions

   C. To influence the student to make choices based on the counselor's wishes

   D. To empower the student to make the best decision for himself based on several options

   E. To influence the student to make choices based on his parents' wishes

Answer: D. To empower the student to make the best decision for himself based on several options

The counselor's job is never to influence a student to make decisions based on anyone else's wishes. The student is not having difficulty taking responsibility for his decisions. The counselor wants to give the student the most information possible so that the student can make an informed decision with outcomes in his own best interest.

37. **Which of the following is MOST likely to occur following the counselor's final statement in the session?**

   A. Based on the success of his previous decision, the student will feel confident in making additional choices about his schedule.

   B. The student will feel as though the counselor is patronizing him.

   C. The student will make the rest of his decisions without input from the counselor.

   D. The student will feel obligated to ask for the counselor's help in making scheduling decisions in the future.

   E. The counselor will try to influence the student's future scheduling decisions.

Answer: A. Based on the success of his previous decision, the student will feel confident in making additional choices about his schedule.

The counselor helped the student to see the "big picture" while making his decisions about schedule changes. The student made the decisions independently, with encouragement from the counselor, so it is likely that he will feel inclined to consult with the counselor in the future. However, he has been empowered to make decisions on his own.

Questions 38–40: Read the excerpt, then choose the best answer for the questions that follow.

Counselor: "I was really surprised to see your Biology grade. What kinds of problems are you having in the class?"

Student: "Ms. Jackson doesn't like me. I want to switch my schedule."

Counselor: "What has given you the impression that she doesn't like you?"

Student: "She is always giving me bad grades on everything. I just don't want to be in her class any more. I want to take study hall instead."

Counselor: "I'm looking at your grades in Biology, and I see several missing assignments. Talk to me about the missing work."

Student: "I told her I was going to turn that stuff in, and she just gave me zeros on everything. She always does that."

Counselor: "I hear you saying that Ms. Jackson is at fault for your problems in Biology. What are some things that you could do to help yourself in her class?"

Student: "I don't know."

Counselor: "At this point, I'm not going to switch your schedule. I think we need to discuss some things that you can do to improve both your grades and your relationship with Ms. Jackson."

38. The student's response to the counselor's initial question indicates which of the following?

A. The student refuses to accept responsibility for her behavior.

B. The student is resistant to the counseling process.

C. The student is ready to discuss the problems she is experiencing with Ms. Jackson.

D. The best way to solve the issue is to immediately change the student's schedule.

E. At this point in the session, the counselor must work toward a positive rapport with the student.

Answer: E. At this point in the session, the counselor must work toward a positive rapport with the student.

At the beginning of the session, the student appears to have a negative attitude. However, so early in the process, it is the responsibility of the counselor to work toward a positive rapport with the student.

39. The counselor's behavior throughout the session indicates that her objective was to facilitate:

A. Empathy for the student

B. Empathy for Ms. Jackson

C. Disciplinary action against the student

D. Having the student take responsibility for her part in the problem

E. Unconditional positive regard for the student and her behavior

Answer: D. Having the student take responsibility for her part in the problem

The counselor does not have unconditional positive regard for the student's negative behaviors, and it is not the counselor's responsibility to take disciplinary action against the student. In addition, while the counselor should always have empathy for both the student and Ms. Jackson, it is most important to point out to the student that she is partially responsible for the problems that she is having in the classroom.

40. **The student's behavior throughout the session indicates all of the following EXCEPT:**

    A. Resistance to the counseling process

    B. Refusal to accept responsibility for her behavior in the classroom

    C. Blaming the counselor for the problem because the counselor refuses to change her schedule

    D. Blaming the teacher for the student's lack of success in the classroom

    E. Refusal to consider changes that the student could make

Answer: C. Blaming the counselor for the problem because the counselor refuses to change her schedule

While blaming the counselor may occur before the end of the session, the student has not blamed the counselor up to this point.

Section Two: Pencil-and-Paper Test

Counseling and Guidance

(Average) (Skill 1.1)
41. **The process of an active organism exhibiting controlled behavior is called:**

    A. Operant conditioning

    B. Modeling

    C. Counterconditioning

    D. Transference

    E. Control

Answer: A. Operant conditioning

Counterconditioning is the process of replacing the behaviors that have caused the problem and engaging in new behaviors that can eliminate the problem. Transference is a process in which the client projects feelings related to past interactions onto the therapist in the counseling relationship. Modeling involves observing the behavior of those we wish to imitate and then copying the behaviors we have observed.

(Easy) (Skill 1.1)
42. **The stages of life in Erik Erikson's psychosocial theory include all of the following EXCEPT:**

    A. Innocence vs. generativity

    B. Basic trust vs. basic mistrust

    C. Identity vs. role confusion

    D. Ego integrity vs. despair

    E. Autonomy vs. shame and doubt

Answer: A. Innocence vs. generativity

Innocence is not one of Erikson's stages. Generativity vs. Stagnation is the stage when maturity is achieved. The task here is to establish and guide the next generation and come to terms with one's dreams and accomplishments.

(Average) (Skill 1.1)

43. **Which of the following is the definition of cognitive restructuring?**

    A. Teaching skills and techniques for dealing with difficult situations in ways that are direct, firm, and clear

    B. The process the therapist evokes in making an evaluation of the client's level of functioning at the beginning of the therapy and subsequently adjusting procedures and techniques to the goals of the client

    C. A specific response to a behavior that increases the probability of that behavior being repeated

    D. The attempt to block out negative thoughts by refusing to acknowledge them

    E. The process of identifying and understanding the impact of negative behavior and thoughts and learning to replace them with more realistic and appropriate actions and beliefs

Answer: E. The process of identifying and understanding the impact of negative behavior and thoughts and learning to replace them with more realistic and appropriate actions and beliefs

Cognitive restructuring begins with identifying and understanding how negative thoughts and/or behaviors can impact various aspects of one's life. Over time, the goal is to be able to consciously replace these negative thoughts and behaviors with thoughts and behaviors that lead to a more positive impact.

(Average) (Skill 1.1)

44. **Borderline Personality Disorder can be defined as follows:**

    A. The unconscious process that operates to protect the individual from threatening and anxiety-producing thoughts, feelings, and impulses

    B. The pathology that develops when an individual fails to adequately develop in the separation-individuation phase

    C. The pathology caused by unconscious sexual feelings of a daughter toward her father, coupled with hostility toward her mother

    D. A personality disorder characterized by extreme self-love and an exaggerated sense of self-importance

    E. An ego-defense mechanism of reverting to a less mature stage of development

Answer: B. The pathology that develops when an individual fails to adequately develop in the separation-individuation phase

Borderline Personality Disorder is a pathology that develops when an individual fails to adequately develop in the separation-individuation phase and is characterized by instability, irritability, self-destruction, impulsive anger, and extreme mood shifts.

(Average) (Skill 1.1)

45. Freud's concept of the ego can be defined as which of the following?

A. The part of the personality that is ruled by the pleasure principle; the center of the instincts, which are largely unconscious

B. The part of the personality that mediates between the unconscious instincts and the environment

C. The part of the personality that resists change of any kind

D. The part of the personality that determines what is right and wrong and strives to "be good"

E. The part of the personality responsible for a sense of humor

Answer: B. The part of the personality that mediates between the unconscious instincts and the environment

The ego is the arbitrator between external reality and internal impulses and experiences.

(Average) (Skill 1.3)

46. The process of learning is not affected by:

A. Past experiences

B. Environmental factors

C. Psychosexual stages

D. Mental processes

E. Social factors

Answer: C. Psychosexual stages

Psychosexual stages are a concept in psychoanalytic theory and are not included in discussions of learning theories.

(Easy) (Skill 1.3)

47. Stages of human development as outlined by Jean Piaget include all of the following except:

A. Sensorimotor stage

B. Concrete operational stage

C. Preoperational stage

D. Cultural and environmental stage

E. Formal operational stage

Answer: D. Cultural and environment stage

While cultural and environmental factors may play a role throughout one's development, it is not a stage as defined by Piaget.

(Rigorous) (Skill 1.4)

48. **A student who needs the emotional element of structure as a condition of the learning environment must have which of the following:**

    A. Specific rules for completing an assignment (i.e., time limits, restriction of options, a specific way of responding)

    B. Individualized program of choices, teaming, or self-evaluation

    C. Taped instruction, games, small groups, or structured multi-sensory learning packets

    D. Short assignments and the experience of success in order to continue to achieve

    E. Open-ended assignments that allow the student to self-determine the pace and rigor level of his or her involvement

Answer: A. Specific rules for completing an assignment (i.e., time limits, restriction of options, a specific way of responding)

Different students need different amounts of structure depending on their learning style and their ability to make decisions. The motivated, responsible, and persistent student needs little structure while the unmotivated student with learning problems needs the most structure to achieve success. The student who needs structure must have specific rules for completing assignments. These include time limits, restriction of options, and a specific way of responding.

(Rigorous) (Skill 1.4)

49. **Individual learning styles can be expressed in relation to all of the following except:**

    A. Environmental factors

    B. Emotional factors

    C. Intelligence quotients

    D. Sociological elements

    E. Physical elements

Answer: C. Intelligence quotients

Individual learning styles include environmental, emotional, sociological, and physical elements. Learning styles do not measure and are not based on intelligence quotients.

(Average) (Skill 1.5)

50. **Stressors that may affect a student's school performance include all of the following except:**

    A. Mental health issues

    B. Homelessness

    C. Losing a parent to death or divorce

    D. Being harassed at school

    E. Having a single parent

Answer: E. Having a single parent

Being the child of a single parent is not a stressor in and of itself. Losing a parent to death or divorce, coping with mental health or addiction issues at home, experiencing difficulties at school with peers, child abuse, and other issues generally are stressors for children that affect school performance.

(Easy) (Skill 1.7)

51. **Mood swings, personality changes, excessive irritability, secretive behavior, and a sudden change in friends can be a sign of which of the following?**

    A. General irritability

    B. Substance abuse

    C. Malnutrition

    D. An eating disorder

    E. Borderline Personality Disorder

Answer: B. Substance abuse

The job of the school counselor is to recognize the signs of addiction and substance abuse in students and, with the cooperation of the student's parents/guardians, make referrals to the proper agency for treatment. Some of the indicators of substance abuse are an inability to perform at school and at home in spite of apparent cognitive capacity and the lack of other interfering factors; excessive sleepiness or irritability; mood swings or apparent personality changes; secretive behavior; and a sudden change in friends.

(Average) (Skill 1.8)

52. **Which of the following facts about teen suicide is NOT accurate?**

    A. Depression increases the risk of a first suicide attempt

    B. A majority of young people who commit suicide abuse substances

    C. Young men attempt suicide more frequently than young women

    D. Four times as many men as women commit suicide

    E. Firearms are used in a little more than half of all youth suicides

Answer: C. Young men attempt suicide more frequently than young women

Although four times as many men as women commit suicide, young women attempt suicide three times more frequently than young men.

(Average) (Skill 1.8)

53. **When students self-injure, they:**

    A. Are suicidal

    B. Are overly focused on what others think of them

    C. Do it primarily to get attention

    D. Are expressing emotional pain in a physical way

    E. Don't know what they are doing

Answer: D. Are expressing emotional pain in a physical way

Self-injury is an attempt to convey and release emotional pain and tension through cutting, hitting, or other forms of self-harm. While students who self-injure may need attention or help, they generally don't self-injure just to get attention, nor are they suicidal. They may or may not be concerned with what others think of them. Although they may dissociate from the pain, they are generally aware of their behavior.

(Rigorous) (Skill 2.1)

54. **Why is it important for counselors to be aware of developmental theories and milestones?**

    A. Because all children progress along these developmental milestones at exactly the same rate

    B. Such knowledge provides a background against which they are better able to determine if a child or adolescent is developmentally delayed

    C. Because children should be encouraged to meet these milestones at the appropriate time

    D. Because counselors teach these theories to children

    E. In order to make expectations clear

    Answer: B. Such knowledge provides a background against which they are better able to determine if a child or adolescent is developmentally delayed

    Stage theories and lists of developmental milestones need to be considered as markers to guide the observer, not absolute standards within which all children will neatly fit. However, school counselors and other professionals need to be aware of developmental theories and milestones, as they provide a background against which they are better able to determine if a child or adolescent is developmentally delayed or needs assistance in reaching his or her full potential.

(Easy) (Skill 2.2)

55. **Positive school environments have all of the following characteristics EXCEPT:**

    A. Strict rules

    B. Clear adult leadership

    C. Respect for diversity

    D. Policies and procedures to ensure the safety of everyone in the school community

    E. A philosophical commitment to certain values

    Answer: A. Strict rules

    While clear policies and strong leadership are essential, strict rules generally do not contribute to creating positive school environments. At times, they may even have a detrimental effect, depending on the nature of the rules.

(Average) (Skill 2.2)

56. **A positive school environment:**

    A. Is the primary responsibility of the school counselor

    B. Cannot be effectively determined without good testing instruments

    C. Is created by an attitude of collaboration and care

    D. Is difficult to achieve in today's world

    E. Exists primarily in small schools

    Answer: C. Is created by an attitude of collaboration and care

    A caring approach and an actively collaborative style are major contributors to positive school environments. While school counselors must be a part of this process, it is not their primary responsibility, nor can they effect such change alone.

(Rigorous) (Skill 2.3)

57. **Effects of stereotyping and prejudice on victims do NOT include:**

    A. Confrontation of the perpetrator by the victim

    B. The development of a sense of inferiority

    C. The development of a persecution complex

    D. Thoughts of violence toward the perpetrator

    E. Strong emotional reactions

    Answer: A. Confrontation of the perpetrator by the victim

    To confront a perpetrator could lead to a potentially dangerous altercation between the victim and the perpetrator, although in some structured situations and with sufficient planning this can be a healing event for victim and/or perpetrator. However, such an interaction is not an effect of stereotyping and prejudice.

(Rigorous) (Skill 2.4)

58. **Violence prevention programs do not include:**

    A. Conflict resolution seminars

    B. Behavior modification programs

    C. Training faculty and staff to intervene before violent confrontations occur

    D. Teaching students about diversity issues

    E. Instituting a boxing program to train students to protect themselves

Answer: E. Instituting a boxing program to train students to protect themselves

Students can be taught to respect the rights of others through programs of cooperation and conflict resolution. The violence prevention program should not promote, encourage, or prepare students to engage in physical retaliation. A boxing program is outside the scope of violence prevention.

(Average) (Skill 3.1)

59. **With regard to counseling, it is beyond the scope of the school counselor's role to:**

    A. Provide individual and group counseling

    B. Provide crisis intervention

    C. Provide family consultation

    D. Provide mental health evaluations

    E. Provide career counseling

Answer: D. Provide mental health evaluations

Although school counselors may identify the need for a mental health evaluation, it is beyond the scope of their role and often their knowledge base to actually perform mental health evaluations. Referral to a community agency or private practitioner is most appropriate to meet students' mental health evaluation needs.

(Rigorous) (Skill 3.2)

60. **The thinking through of irrational thoughts that have resulted in emotional problems is the basis of this theory:**

    A. Reality therapy

    B. Rational emotive behavior therapy

    C. Gestalt therapy

    D. Existential therapy

    E. Person-centered therapy

Answer: B. Rational emotive behavior therapy

The key phrase here is "thinking through irrational thoughts." Reality therapy and Gestalt therapy involve therapeutic practices that analyze rational versus irrational thoughts. Existential therapy is concerned with larger issues of personal freedoms and choice. Person-centered therapy may or may not address the client's thought patterns. The correction of these irrational thoughts and the identification of the reality of the moment is the basis of rational emotive behavior therapy.

(Easy) (Skill 3.2)

61. **Questions of freedom, choice, and responsibility are addressed in:**

    A. Reality therapy

    B. Existential therapy

    C. Cognitive-behavioral therapy

    D. Person-centered therapy

    E. Psychoanalytic therapy

Answer: B. Existential therapy

Existentialism differs from the psychodynamic and behavior therapies in that it does not rely on a deterministic view of human nature such as being controlled by irrational actions, past occurrences, or the unconscious.

(Rigorous) (Skill 3.2)

62. **The WDEP model in reality theory includes all of the following except:**

    A. Direction

    B. Wants

    C. Evaluation

    D. Evaluation

    E. Planning and commitment

Answer: A. Direction

The WDEP model is about defining behaviors to target for intervention, setting related goals, and executing practices to facilitate behavior change. Doing, not direction, is the step in the model when the therapist explores what clients are doing and what direction they are taking in their behavior to obtain those wants and needs.

(Average) (Skill 3.3)

63. **The keys to effective communication include all of the following EXCEPT:**

    A. Listening carefully to the speaker's words

    B. Paying attention to nonverbal communication

    C. Asking for clarification

    D. Expressing oneself clearly and directly

    E. Being able to anticipate what the speaker is going to say

    Answer: E. Being able to anticipate what the speaker is going to say

    Focusing on what you think the speaker is going to say interferes with your ability to actually listen to what the speaker is saying.

(Easy) (Skill 3.3)

64. **Good responding skills include all of the following EXCEPT:**

    A. Ability to show your feelings without inhibitions

    B. Reflecting back the other person's feelings

    C. Giving constructive feedback

    D. Maintaining eye contact

    E. Asking good questions

    Answer: A. Ability to show your feelings without inhibitions

    Responding should be about the client, not the counselor.

(Easy) (Skill 3.4)

65. **The ability to create rapport and meaningful relationships with students is the sign of an effective counselor. Which of the following is the most important ingredient in fostering open communication with students?**

    A. Maintaining a monthly newsletter about teen-related issues so that student's know you are in tune with the issues they are facing

    B. Attending school extracurricular and sporting events to show support for the student's outside interests

    C. Being familiar with the movies and shows that are popular with students

    D. Keeping information confidential, within the limits of the need for parental notification and school policies

    E. Never interrupting them when they are talking about their feelings

    Answer: D. Keeping information confidential within the limits of the need for parental notification and school policies

    When the counselor has the trust of the student, the student is much more likely to listen to and act on the counselor's suggestions. Keeping information confidential, within the limits of the need for parental notification and other school policies, is essential to building trust.

(Average) (Skill 3.5)

66. **A disadvantage of group counseling is:**

    A. The presence of a built-in support system

    B. A non-threatening atmosphere

    C. The ability to substitute the group for the real world, permitting the client unlimited time to make adjustments

    D. The counselor can reach more clients

    E. The client's chance to learn from others

Answer: C. The ability to substitute the group for the real world, permitting the client unlimited time to make adjustments

The key words to focus on are substitute and unlimited. The group experience is one that provides individuals in the group the opportunity to disclose and confront problems as well as practice new skills. Due to a variety of possible constraints, it should never be assumed that the opportunity of counseling is unlimited. Group counseling creates an alternative environment on which clients sometimes begin to depend, to the exclusion of other aspects of their lives, further distorting views of reality.

(Average) (Skill 3.5)

67. **All of the following are limitations of group counseling EXCEPT:**

    A. Often the individual members need different theoretical approaches and/or extended follow up

    B. Members can test their attitudes and beliefs against those of other members of the group

    C. People sometimes function poorly in groups

    D. Individuals in the group can justify their present status by reinforcement from the group

    E. Scheduling a convenient time for everyone can sometimes be a problem

Answer: B. Members can test their attitudes and beliefs against those of other members of the group

Answer B is not a limitation of group counseling, but rather one of the benefits of group counseling. Members can test their attitudes and beliefs against those of other members of the group. They can receive feedback and discover how others view them. Through group counseling, they can achieve some of the goals of becoming emotionally involved without the threat of rejection.

(Rigorous) (Skill 3.6)

68. **Group dynamics include all of the following EXCEPT:**

    A. A political ideology built on the concept of the organization and management of groups

    B. The employment of specific techniques and concepts to keep the group vitalized

    C. A branch of knowledge concerned with groups and their interactions, and interactions with other groups and individuals

    D. A way of describing individual behavior

    E. The ways in which individuals respond to other individuals in a group context

    Answer: D. A way of describing individual behavior

    Focusing on individual behavior misses out on the dynamics of the group experience.

(Rigorous) (Skill 3.7)

69. **The occupational environments/personality types of Holland's theory do NOT include:**

    A. Artistic

    B. Conventional

    C. Investigative

    D. Hostile

    E. Social

    Answer: D. Hostile

    While some occupational settings may in fact be hostile, this adjective does not describe one of the occupational environments defined by Holland.

(Average) (Skill 3.7)

70. **Which of the following accurately describes the trait-factor theories of career development?**

    A. The circumstances of society, beyond the control of the individual, are the contributing factors in career choice

    B. As an individual grows older, self-concept changes along with the view of the reality of his or her vocational choice

    C. There is a direct relationship between an individual's interests and abilities and vocational choices

    D. Individuals tend to go into the same vocation as their most important role model

    E. People with similar personalities choose the same types of vocations

    Answer: C. There is a direct relationship between an individual's interests and abilities and vocational choices

    The trait-factor theories assume there is a direct relationship between an individual's interests and abilities and vocational choices. When interests and abilities are matched, the individual has found his or her future vocation. Interest inventories, aptitude tests, and the general field of vocational testing have been generated from this theory.

(Rigorous) (Skill 3.8)

71. **What are the four stages of the antici-pation phase of decision making, as defined by Tiedman and O'Hara?**

    A. Exploration, crystallization, choice, and clarification

    B. Choice, crystallization, induction, and reformation

    C. Induction, reformation, crystalliza-tion, and integration

    D. Crystallization, exploration, reforma-tion, and clarification

    E. Reformation, integration, crystalliza-tion, and choice

    Answer: A. Exploration, crystallization, choice, and clarification

    Tiedman and O'Hara describe a decision-making process that is divided into two phases: the anticipation phase (made up of exploration, crystallization, choice, and clarification stages) and the accom-modation phase (made up of induction, reformation, and integration stages).

(Rigorous) (Skill 3.9)

72. **The major steps in Zunker's model for using assessment results in developmen-tal career counseling are all of the follow-ing EXCEPT:**

    A. Determining the instruments to be used

    B. Analyzing needs

    C. Establishing the purpose of the testing

    D. Administering a complete battery of tests

    E. Utilizing the results of assessment

Answer: D. Administering a complete battery of tests

Zunker, with influence from other theorists, established a model for the use of assessment results in developmental career counseling. There are four major steps: analyzing needs, establishing the purpose of testing, determining the instruments to be used, and utilizing the results in decision making about training and education. Identifying specific tests is more useful than using a whole battery of tests.

(Average) (Skill 3.10)

73. **In helping students to make decisions, steps in the process do NOT include:**

    A. Defining the problem

    B. Listing all options

    C. Exploring barriers to options

    D. Formulating goals in relation to outcomes

    E. Surveying family, friends, and peers

Answer: E. Surveying family, friends, and peers

Surveying denotes a process of informa-tion gathering from friends and family; it is not a step in the decision-making process.

(Average) (Skill 3.11)

74. **In preparing job shadowing opportunities for students, what is an important step to ensuring future participation of local businesses?**

    A. Choosing only local businesses that are already active in local issues

    B. Selecting only students who have prior work experience

    C. Recognizing their contribution of time and resources with a small token of thanks

    D. Preparing a questionnaire for the businessperson in order to understand his or her expectations and general practices

    E. Making sure the student is fully committed to pursuing the same career as the individual he or she is job shadowing

Answer: D. Preparing a questionnaire for the businessperson in order to understand his or her expectations and general practices

The community businessperson should fill out a form before students engage in job shadowing. Questions such as what the business expects to get from the experience, how much time they are willing to spend with the student, and what their general practices are should be included. A bad experience on the part of the community businessperson might mean he or she will not participate in the program the following year.

(Average) (Skill 3.11)

75. **Which of the following would provide students with the exposure to the greatest number of potential career choices?**

    A. Apprenticeship

    B. Career days

    C. School-to-work programs

    D. Job shadowing

    E. On the job training

Answer: B. Career days

Career days give students exposure to many different potential vocations. The students gather a wealth of occupational information and can hone in on the areas that interest them the most. Additionally, community business institutions are willing to participate in career-day programs because they are eager to influence young people to enter their professions in order to create a pool of future applicants.

(Rigorous) (Skill 3.11)

76. **Through the Reserve Officers' Training Corps (ROTC) program, students can receive up to a full scholarship for:**

    A. Two years of study in exchange for time served in the military before college

    B. Two years of study in exchange for time served in the military during college

    C. Two years of study in exchange for an extended time in the military

    D. Four years of study in exchange for time served in the military during college

    E. Four years of study in exchange for an extended time in the military

Answer: E. Four years of study in exchange for an extended time in the military

The Reserve Officers' Training Corps (ROTC) program offers students the opportunity to receive up to a full scholarship for four years of study in exchange for an extended time in the military.

(Easy) (Skill 4.1)

77. **Which of the following is NOT a form of assessment administered by school counselors?**

    A. Achievement tests

    B. Interest inventories

    C. Intelligence tests

    D. College entrance exams

    E. Performance tests

Answer: C. Intelligence tests

Intelligence tests are generally administered by school psychologists, psychologists in agencies, or psychologists in the private sector who are trained to do psychological testing.

(Rigorous) (Skill 4.1)

78. **All of the following are disadvantages of testing EXCEPT:**

    A. Using the test to predict future behavior

    B. The possibility of results being used improperly

    C. The possibility of the student misinterpreting the test results

    D. The inherent subjectivity of tests administered for counseling purposes

    E. Some students simply do not do well on standardized tests

Answer: A. Using the test to predict future behavior

One of the purposes of testing is to provide a picture of where the student is currently and to anticipate what the student needs to do in order to succeed in the future. The process may include identifying barriers to learning and tools needed to increase access to learning and potentially highlighting a process that would benefit the student. However, tests cannot predict future behavior with any certainty.

(Average) (Skill 4.1)

79. **Informal forms of assessment include all of the following except:**

    A. Behavioral observation

    B. Learning styles inventories

    C. Sentence completion

    D. Interviewing peers

    E. Needs assessments

Answer: D. Interviewing peers

Talking with a student's peers may provide information in a casual context that the school counselor may find useful, but this is not a form of either formal or informal assessment.

(Rigorous) (Skill 4.2)

80. **In the administration of tests, procedures should include all of the following EXCEPT:**

   A. Safeguarding the tests

   B. Informing the students about the nature of the test by giving them questions from the test

   C. Guarding the tests in the exam room when students have access to the room

   D. Guarding the tests by not leaving them where students and unauthorized personnel have access

   E. Following the appropriate procedures for packaging and mailing the completed tests back to the scoring company

Answer: B. Informing the students about the nature of the test by giving them questions from the test

Testing can be one of the tools counselors use to help students recognize their resources, utilize their strengths, and accept their limitations. If students are provided with the test material ahead of time, a true picture of students' abilities and self-concepts will not be identified. There is a distinct difference between counseling and instruction; the counselor's job is not to "teach the test" but to inform students of the objectives and testing parameters prior to the event.

(Rigorous) (Skill 4.3)

81. **The inaccuracy of some test results that is caused by chance is called:**

   A. Standardization

   B. Standard error of measurement

   C. Standard score

   D. Derived score

   E. Standard deviation

Answer: B. Standard error of measurement

Every test has some element of inaccuracy or unreliability due to chance, so this element of the test is taken into consideration when evaluating test results, and an allowance is made for this phenomenon. The degree of error is reported in the standard deviation, a specific band of scores. The formula for obtaining the standard error of measurement is the square root of one minus the reliability coefficient.

(Rigorous) (Skill 4.3)

82. **A statistical concept that measures the relationship between two factors in test validity is:**

   A. Reliability coefficient

   B. Standard deviation

   C. Raw score

   D. Correlation coefficient

   E. Standard error of measurement

Answer: D. Correlation coefficient

The reliability coefficient is a statistical concept that measures how reliable the relationship between two factors in test validity is. The standard deviation is the interval of score differences that indicates levels of achievement. The raw score is the basic score, usually obtained by counting the number of correct answers. It can also be obtained by using the number of wrong answers. The authors of the test can also determine other ways to define a raw score.

(Easy) (Skill 4.4)

83. **If test results need to be interpreted in a group, the counselor should NOT:**

    A. Announce individual test scores

    B. Explain the norm group to which the students have been compared

    C. Provide for private individual interpretation for students

    D. Explain statistics related to the test so students can understand the meaning of their scores

    E. Discuss the possible uses of the test scores

Answer: A. Announce individual test scores

The answers listed in B, C, and D describe appropriate elements of sharing information in a group setting. Providing information about an individual to a group is not only detrimental to the student–counselor relationship, but is also unethical.

(Average) (Skill 4.4)

84. **In interpreting test results, the counselor should NOT:**

    A. Relate the results to the goals that had previously been determined

    B. Provide for individual interpretation

    C. Wait to interpret the test results when the student is scheduling the following year's courses

    D. Give the student input into the interpretation of the test results

    E. Ask for the student's response to the results

Answer: C. Wait to interpret the test results when the student is scheduling the following year's courses

The work of a school counselor is to help the student maximize his or her performance. If a counselor delays providing information to a student, it could contribute to the student's failure instead of success.

(Average) (Skill 4.5)

85. **In interpreting test results to other professionals and parents, the counselor does NOT always have to:**

    A. Be thoroughly familiar with the test

    B. Understand the scoring procedure

    C. Notify the student that the counselor will be sharing the results with his or her parent/guardian(s)

    D. Work with the parents in a counseling relationship to help them understand their child's abilities

    E. Let other staff members see the results of the test

Answer: E. Let other staff members see the results of the test

Sharing test results with other staff members should first be discussed with the student and the student's parents. Depending on the nature of the test, other personnel often do not need to know the results, and it may be best to keep them confidential.

Consulting

(Average) (Skill 5.1)

86. **In interactions with school counselors and other school officials, parents and guardians need respect, information, and:**

    A. Positive feedback on their behavior

    B. Confirmation that they are doing a great job with their child

    C. Validation and support

    D. Detailed descriptions of their child's interactions with peers and teachers

    E. A complete review of their child's grades

Answer: C. Validation and support

Parents and guardians need to be validated and supported in their efforts to help their child. This may or may not include positive feedback, per se, or confirmation that they are doing a great job with their child. It is possible to validate and support their efforts without necessarily giving positive feedback when the situation doesn't warrant it. Certainly, if they are doing a good job, then telling them so might be appropriate. It is generally not helpful for the counselor to give detailed descriptions of their child's

interaction with peers or teachers or to go over the child's grades unless there is an identified problem that needs to be addressed.

(Easy) (Skill 5.1)

87. **In working with parents, a good model to utilize is:**

    A. Collaborative consultation

    B. Mental health consultation

    C. Family counseling

    D. Advising

    E. Medical model consultation

Answer: A. Collaborative consultation

Working with parents and guardians in a collaborative manner where each person brings relevant and important information to the table is useful. In a school setting, the counselor should not serve as a mental health consultant or family counselor, or employ a medical model framework.

(Rigorous) (Skill 5.1)

88. **The consultation process with parents does NOT include:**

    A. Allowing them to vent their frustrations about the school and school officials

    B. Getting to the issue at hand as soon as possible

    C. Inviting the parents' opinion about the issue

    D. Clearly delineating the next steps the parents need to take

    E. Taking care not to make too many suggestions and overwhelm them

Answer: D. Clearly delineating the next steps the parents need to take

Although discussing possible next steps is a significant part of the consultation process with parents, telling them precisely what they need to do is not helpful. This approach conveys an attitude that the "counselor knows best" and discounts the contributions parents and guardians may be able to make in formulating an action plan. It is important to let parents vent their frustrations, because this may be the first time a school official has listened to them. At the same time, getting to the issue at hand quickly is also important.

(Rigorous) (Skill 5.2)

89. **Elements of family dynamics include all of the following EXCEPT:**

    A. Rules and roles within the family

    B. The reinforcement of individual behavior patterns via family interactions

    C. An "identified patient" who serves to divert the family from underlying problems

    D. The parents' childhood backgrounds

    E. The ways in which shared values and conflicts are seen in family interactions

Answer: D. The parents' childhood backgrounds

While a parent's childhood experiences may contribute to who that parent is today and his or her functioning within the family, this background is not fundamentally part of what would be described as "family dynamics." How that parent interacts with his or her partner

and the children and others in the family is considered an element of the family dynamics.

(Average) (Skill 5.3)

90. **The role of consultants in problem-solving processes does not include functioning as:**

    A. An advocate

    B. An expert in a particular area

    C. A school official

    D. A collaborator

    E. A process specialist

Answer: C. A school official

While a school official may be part of the consultation process, he or she may not be trained to provide and facilitate a problem-solving process. This would involve a potential conflict of interest.

(Average) (Skill 5.3)

91. **Procedures in the consultation process include all of the following EXCEPT:**

    A. Relationship building

    B. Monitoring the process of behavior change by a neutral party

    C. Evaluation and summarization

    D. Diagnosis of the problem

    E. Gathering information

Answer: B. Monitoring of the process of behavior change by a neutral party

Consultation is an active, dynamic process. Monitoring is not part of the consultation model.

(Average) (Skill 5.4)

92. **The role the counselor can take in assisting participants in the consultation process does NOT include:**

    A. Demonstrating classroom behavior management techniques

    B. Describing the nature of the problem

    C. Teaching specific skills

    D. Helping devise strategies to change behaviors

    E. Eliciting possible solutions from others

Answer: A. Demonstrating classroom behavior management techniques

The role of the counselor is to observe and provide constructive feedback or to provide direct support in identified areas of need. Classroom behavior management is the educator's responsibility, and areas of weakness should be addressed by the school administration. In this situation, the counselor is present to offer insight to support individual students from a behavioral and social point of view, not to support the classroom educator and his or her class management.

(Average) (Skill 5.4)

93. **In the consultation process, communicating a student's needs to others does NOT include:**

    A. The counselor making a judgment to others regarding what is best for the student

    B. Clarifying the needs of the student with the student

    C. Opening lines of communication between the consultee and the student by having open dialogue

    D. Balancing the needs of the student and the consultee so each can understand the other's position

    E. Asking the consultee to reflect back what he or she has heard

Answer: A. The counselor making a judgment to others regarding what is best for the student

Instead of passing judgment, the counselor's role is to assist stakeholders in the student's success. The counselor's job is to educate them about the student's needs based on information gathered from parents and teachers, to review the student's academic history, and to work with all parties to develop a plan of action.

(Average) (Skill 5.4)

94. **Procedures for successful communication with parents/guardian(s) in the consultation process do NOT include:**

    A. Informing parents frequently about progress on the resolution of the problem

    B. Using parents as a valuable source of information about the student

    C. Involving the parent/guardian(s) in the consultation process from the beginning

    D. Frequent contact to ascertain whether more aid is needed and to check if the student or parent/guardian(s) have additional concerns

    E. Explaining the problem in simple language because parents are probably unaware of all ramifications

Answer: E. Explaining the problem in simple language because parents are probably unaware of all ramifications

It is appropriate for the counselor to take into consideration the parents' primary language and understanding of certain procedures. This can be established by fact finding and consulting with the student before contacting the parent/guardian(s). However, it is inappropriate to make assumptions about parents' abilities and the level of understanding they bring to any process.

(Rigorous) (Skill 5.5)

95. **In the case of abuse by a family or household member, which of the following steps is mandated?**

    A. Reporting the incident to the proper authorities

    B. Maintaining regular contact with outside agencies until the problem is resolved

    C. Including the parent/guardian in the referral process as soon as possible

    D. Getting informed consent of the student and his or her parent/guardian prior to making a referral to an outside agency or practitioner

    E. Waiting 48 hours before reporting the suspected abuse

Answer: A. Reporting the incident to the proper authorities

In the case of abuse by a family or household member, the counselor is mandated to report the incident to the proper authorities. If a parent or guardian is the abuser, it is not prudent to include that person in the referral process. The mandated state organization will approach the parent or guardian.

(Easy) (Skill 5.5)

96. **School counselors may provide information about which of the following resources for families?**

    A. Mental health referrals

    B. Food banks and government aid programs

    C. Local support groups

    D. Community organizations

    E. All of the above

Answer: E. All of the above

School counselors are key to providing families with resources about many topics and needs beyond the obvious ones such as financial aid and vocational training.

(Easy) (Skill 5.6)

97. **All but which of the following are important aspects of crisis intervention?**

    A. Accurate information for those affected by the situation

    B. The latest news reports about the crisis

    C. A school crisis response plan

    D. A systematic way to inform school personnel about the actions to be taken

    E. Debriefing for crisis responders

Answer: B. The latest news reports about the crisis

Although the media may provide some useful information, for the most part, monitoring news reports is not helpful in providing good crisis intervention. Crisis responders need to get information from reliable sources, such as emergency management or law enforcement personnel. Furthermore, the sensationalistic nature of news reports can feed fear and create unnecessary anxiety.

(Rigorous) (Skill 5.7)

98. **An effective advocate does NOT:**

    A. Raise issues that may cause discomfort

    B. Speak up for those who may not have a voice or may not have been heard in the past

    C. Try to facilitate change

    D. Watch for trends that may indicate underserved populations

    E. Share all information gathered about a particular situation

Answer: E. Share all information gathered about a particular situation

During the course of advocacy, people share many personal details with the person helping them. It is not necessary to disclose most of these details in order to effect the needed changes, and in fact it is likely to be viewed as a betrayal of privacy and confidentiality to do so.

Coordinating

(Rigorous) (Skill 6.1)

99. **The goals of the guidance program should NOT include:**

    A. Acquisition of academic skills by the student population commensurate with their abilities

    B. Acquisition of personal insights by students

    C. Learned ability to make intelligent choices

    D. Capacity to cope with life's stressors

    E. Selection of a lifetime career

Answer: E. Selection of a lifetime career

Counselors can and should provide materials and organize events and discussions about careers and occupations with students, teachers, parents, administrators, and members of the surrounding community. A goal of the counseling program should be to facilitate career exploration. In the course of such structured career guidance, a student may feel motivated to pursue a certain career, but this is not a criterion of an effective guidance program.

(Easy) (Skill 6.2)

100. **Components of an orientation program should include each of the following EXCEPT:**

    A. Advance notice by mail

    B. Invitations to the entire community

    C. A tour of the facilities

    D. Introduction of counselors and administrators to students and parents, with a description of their roles

    E. A planned agenda

Answer: B. Invitations to the entire community

Part of advocating for the guidance program and its services is to use a variety of methods to inform and invite parents and students to get to know the program and its staff. It is not an open house for the wider community.

(Rigorous) (Skill 6.3)

101. **The need for specialized programs may be indicated by all of the following EXCEPT:**

    A. Classroom management problems

    B. Targeted grant money

    C. A formal needs assessment

    D. Teachers' or counselors' observations

    E. Identification of underserved students

Answer: B. Targeted grant money

Classroom problems, teachers' or counselors' observations, and formal needs assessments are all reasons to consider developing a specialized program. The availability of grant money for a special program should not dictate program development; such efforts only make sense if there is also a demonstrated need for the program.

(Average) (Skill 6.4)

102. **All of the following are good prevention approaches EXCEPT:**

    A. Informing parent/guardian(s) about their child's behavior in the school setting

    B. Programs on conflict resolution and communication skills

    C. Anger management groups

    D. An open-door policy

    E. Engaging students in community activities

SAMPLE TEST

Answer: A. Informing parent/guardian(s) about their child's behavior in the school setting

Telling parent/guardian(s) about what their child is doing in school may or may not be useful to either the parents or the child. It is not a prevention approach, though at times it may be part of a consultation or problem-solving effort.

(Average) (Skill 6.4)

103. Which of the following is a key prevention concept?

A. Creating a positive school environment

B. Attending to issues of bullying, prejudice, aggression, and violence

C. Teaching communication, self-awareness, and conflict resolution skills

D. Maintaining an open door policy

E. All of the above

Answer: E. All of the above

In addition to providing counseling after a problem has been identified, it is the job of the school counselor to contribute to the school's effort to prevent difficulties before they arise. Central to the notion of prevention is the importance of creating a positive school environment. Further, attending to issues of bullying, prejudice, aggression, and violence in the school setting are key to preventing problems. Teaching communication, self-awareness, and conflict resolution skills to students are effective prevention approaches.

(Average) (Skill 7.2)

104. In evaluating the content of career information, all of the following areas should be included EXCEPT:

A. The impressions of the reader, as indicated by filling out an evaluation form

B. The preparation required for entry-level jobs

C. The work setting and conditions of the career

D. The long-term employment outlook

E. The skills and aptitude needed for a particular career

Answer: A. The impressions of the reader, as indicated by filling out an evaluation form

The phrase "impressions of the reader" denotes subjectivity instead of specific points that can provide the most comprehensive picture of a respective career. The National Career Development Association (NCDA) has compiled guidelines for the preparation and evaluation of career and occupational literature.

(Average) (Skill 7.3)

105. Financial aid specifically earmarked for women and minorities is LEAST likely to be found in:

A. Minority and women's organizations

B. Local organizations committed to higher education for women and minorities

C. General financial aid references

D. The publication "The Higher Education Money Book for Women and Minorities"

E. Local minority houses of worship

Answer: C. General financial aid references

Options A, B, D, and E address the sources for students seeking scholarships specifically for minorities and women.

(Average) (Skill 8.1)

106. **Which of the following best describes qualitative research?**

  A. Applies the scientific method to describing and analyzing the past in order to understand the future

  B. Focuses on the individual and not on the results of group experimentation

  C. Focuses on in-depth interviews, observations, and document analysis

  D. Interprets data using numerical analysis

  E. Involves carefully controlled laboratory experiments

Answer: C. Focuses on in-depth interviews, observations, and document analysis

Qualitative research focuses on in-depth interviews, observations, and document analysis. Methods used include document and content analysis, case studies, and cultural anthropology. This type of research interprets data without the use of numerical analysis.

(Rigorous) (Skill 8.2)

107. **The research evaluation stages of the CIPP model do NOT include:**

  A. Context evaluation

  B. Process evaluation

  C. Input evaluation

  D. Product evaluation

  E. Program evaluation

Answer: E. Program evaluation

The CIPP model has four stages: context evaluation, input evaluation, process evaluation, and product evaluation.

(Rigorous) (Skill 8.2)

108. **Formative evaluation does NOT involve:**

  A. Collection of data in the developmental stage of research

  B. Collection of data in the implementation stage of research

  C. Collection of data prior to the setting of objectives

  D. Collection of data after a program has been in place for a period of time

  E. Collection of data when the research is in the operational stage

Answer: D. Collection of data after a program has been in place for a period of time

This type of evaluation involves the collection of data while a program is in the developmental, implementation, and operational stages.

(Rigorous) (Skill 8.2)

109. The following individuals should be included when conducting a program needs assessment:

A. Students only

B. Administrators only

C. People in the community who have no students in school

D. The community, students, staff, administrators, and parents

E. Anyone who has an opinion about the program

Answer: D. The community, students, staff, administrators, and parents

It is imperative that all members of the school community, including parents, are given the opportunity to provide feedback about guidance counseling services; this is the only way counselors will generate a clear picture of the needs of the community. The integration of all stakeholders is key to the success of any needs assessment.

(Rigorous) (Skill 8.3)

110. Factors that determine the value of a program do NOT include:

A. How well the program fits preconceived ideas of intended outcomes

B. Statistical significance

C. Interpretation of the meaning of the results

D. The practicality of implementing the program for everyday use

E. The value of the program to those benefiting from the program

Answer: A. How well the program fits preconceived ideas of intended outcomes

Evaluative data and the practicality of implementing a program for everyday use should guide the determination of the value of a program. Fitting into preconceived goals is not necessarily useful in assessing a program's value.

(Rigorous) (Skill 8.3)

111. Program objectives are:

A. Created to fit the outcomes of the research

B. Readjusted as the need arises

C. Determined after the program has been operational for a period of time

D. Necessary only when formal research is being conducted

E. Formulated before the research is instituted

Answer: E. Formulated before the research is instituted

An effective guidance program needs to be based on research in order to be sound in its validity.

(Rigorous) (Skill 8.3)

112. **In evaluating a newly created program, the counselor should:**

   A. Ask the guidance staff if they think the program is working

   B. Ask students informally what they think of the program

   C. Conduct an extensive evaluation of all involved that includes surveys, questionnaires, and observations

   D. After three months, evaluate the program and make a recommendation

   E. Consult with parents to see if the program is working

Answer: C. Conduct an extensive evaluation of all involved that includes surveys, questionnaires, and observations

All programs in the guidance curriculum need to be based on clear objectives and evaluated effectively. Using formal and organized methods of assessment provides structure to the information-gathering process and makes it easier to compile statistical information.

(Rigorous) (Skill 8.3)

113. **Before introducing new and innovative programs to the guidance curriculum, the counselor should first:**

   A. Ask the administration for a budget for the program

   B. Conduct a needs assessment survey

   C. Arrange for a pilot program

   D. Contact Board of Education members to get them to agree on the implementation of the program

   E. Determine program objectives

Answer: B. Conduct a needs assessment survey

Just because a program is innovative and has a lot to offer does not mean it will meet the needs of the specific school community. It is critical for school counselors to have a pulse on the needs of the community they serve. It is imperative for the school counselor to develop a program improvement model that clearly outlines action steps for the creation, monitoring, and support of any and all programs that are utilized.

Professional Issues

(Rigorous) (Skill 9.1)

114. **Guidelines for ethical behavior written in the ACA Code of Ethics and Standards of Practice include all of the following areas EXCEPT:**

   A. Client records

   B. Penalties for specific ethical violations

   C. Confidentiality

   D. Resolution of ethical issues

   E. Relationships with other professionals

Answer: B. Penalties for specific ethical violations

The key word to focus on is *guidelines*. There are too many factors involved to discuss penalties for specific violations in this code of ethics.

(Easy) (Skill 9.1)

115. When an ethical issue arises in a counselor's practice, the counselor should:

    A. Refer to the ACA Code of Ethics

    B. Decide what to do immediately so the problem will not linger

    C. Ask the client what to do

    D. Consult with the Board of Education

    E. Consult with an attorney

Answer: A. Refer to the ACA Code of Ethics

The ACA Code of Ethics provides helpful guidelines for counselors facing ethical dilemmas and outlines possible courses of action. Thoughtful consideration of these guidelines can lead the counselor to the next step.

(Rigorous) (Skill 9.2)

116. Parents, guardians, and students have a right to all of the following records EXCEPT:

    A. Copies of all records relating to the student

    B. Copies of all student records containing comparisons of the student with other students

    C. All of the student's records maintained by public institutions

    D. A list of all types of records directly related to the student

    E. The student's complete transcript

Answer: B. Copies of all student records containing comparisons of the student with other students

Parents and eligible students have access to only their specific child's records. It would be a violation of another student's rights to have his or her information viewed by an undesignated person. Confidentiality and parent/student rights are a paramount concern for the school counselor. His or her success and the quality of the program depend on such confidentiality.

(Average) (Skill 9.2)

117. Written permission to release assessment data must be obtained from:

    A. The counselor

    B. The company that scored the test

    C. The student who is over 18 or the student's parent or guardian

    D. The Board of Education

    E. The teacher who generated the assessment data

Answer: C. The student who is over 18 or the student's parent or guardian

Because counseling is a confidential relationship, the counselor should obtain permission from the student to release any information given in confidence. However, if the student is under 18, even if the information is gathered in reference to services provided due to a disability (i.e., IDEA qualifications), written permission needs to be procured from the parent or legal guardian.

(Rigorous) (Skill 9.3)

118. The intent of the Individuals with Disabilities Education Act of 1975 was all of the following EXCEPT:

A. To provide guidelines for assessing disabilities

B. To give children with disabilities a free and appropriate education

C. To provide for the needs of children with disabilities

D. To prevent discrimination against children with disabilities

E. To give children with disabilities special services to make up for past discrimination

Answer: E. To give children with disabilities special services to make up for past discrimination

IDEA is intended to provide students with disabilities equal access to education. No one student should have more access to educational services due to past issues of discrimination.

(Average) (Skill 9.5)

119. School Websites can be helpful to school counselors because they allow the counselor to:

A. Maintain a personal relationship with students

B. Research information about higher education and financial aid

C. Develop presentations for conferences

D. Share information within the school district and the community

E. Assess the value of Web sites used by students and parents/guardians

Answer: D. Share information within the school district and community

Some schools have created interactive Web sites that allow parents, guardians, community members, teachers, and other school personnel to share information.

(Easy) (Skill 9.6)

120. Continuing professional development is important for school counselors for all of the following reasons EXCEPT:

A. To keep abreast of changes in professional practices and standards

B. To utilize all available monies in the budget for staff development

C. To be refreshed and renewed as a professional

D. To further develop counseling skills

E. To learn about new programs and techniques

Answer: B. To utilize all available monies in the budget for staff development

Continuing education and development is geared to support and expand the school counselor's capacity to function well. In many cases, the counselor may spend his or her own money to get appropriate training or learn new skills.

(Rigorous) (Skill 9.3)

118. The intent of the Individuals with Disabilities Education Act of 1975 was all of the following EXCEPT:

   A. To provide guidelines for assessing disabilities

   B. To give children with disabilities a free and appropriate education

   C. To provide for the needs of children with disabilities

   D. To prevent discrimination against children with disabilities

   E. To give children with disabilities special services to make up for past discrimination

Answer: E. To give children with disabilities special services to make up for past discrimination

IDEA is intended to provide students with disabilities equal access to education. No one student should have more access to educational services due to past issues of discrimination.

(Average) (Skill 9.5)

119. School Websites can be helpful to school counselors because they allow the counselor to:

   A. Maintain a personal relationship with students

   B. Research information about higher education and financial aid

   C. Develop presentations for conferences

   D. Share information within the school district and the community

   E. Assess the value of Web sites used by students and parents/guardians

Answer: D. Share information within the school district and community

Some schools have created interactive Web sites that allow parents, guardians, community members, teachers, and other school personnel to share information.

(Easy) (Skill 9.6)

120. Continuing professional development is important for school counselors for all of the following reasons EXCEPT:

   A. To keep abreast of changes in professional practices and standards

   B. To utilize all available monies in the budget for staff development

   C. To be refreshed and renewed as a professional

   D. To further develop counseling skills

   E. To learn about new programs and techniques

Answer: B. To utilize all available monies in the budget for staff development

Continuing education and development is geared to support and expand the school counselor's capacity to function well. In many cases, the counselor may spend his or her own money to get appropriate training or learn new skills.

PRAXIS

XAMonline publishes study guides for the PRAXIS I & II teacher certification examinations.

Titles Include:
- PRAXIS Art Sample Test
- PRAXIS Biology
- PRAXIS Chemistry
- PRAXIS Earth and Space Sciences
- PRAXIS Special Education Knowledge-Based Core Principles
- PRAXIS Special Education Teaching Students with Behavioral Disorders/Emotional Disturbance
- PRAXIS Early Childhood/Education of Young Children
- PRAXIS Educational Leadership
- PRAXIS Elementary Education
- PRAXIS English Language, Literature and Composition
- PRAXIS French Sample Test
- PRAXIS School Guidance and Counseling
- PRAXIS General Science
- PRAXIS Library Media Specialist
- PRAXIS Mathematics
- PRAXIS Middle School English Language Arts
- PRAXIS Middle School Mathematics
- PRAXIS Middle School Science
- PRAXIS Middle School Social Studies
- PRAXIS Physical Education
- PRAXIS Physics
- PRAXIS Para-Professional Assessment
- PRAXIS PPST-I Basic Skills
- PRAXIS Government/Political Science
- PRAXIS Principles of Learning and Teaching
- PRAXIS Reading
- PRAXIS Social Studies
- PRAXIS Spanish

PASS the FIRST TIME with an XAMonline study guide!

Call or visit us online!
1.800.301.4647
www.XAMonline.com

CPSIA information can be obtained at www.ICGtesting.com
Printed in the USA
LVOW031616200412

278500LV00002B/73/P

WITHDRAWAL

9 781607 870678